CW01551233

THE BIRTH TO DEATH BIOGRAPHY OF PROPHET MUHAMMAD(PBUH) BASED ON THE EARLIEST SOURCE

AHMAD AL-MANNAR

Table of content

....
288

THE PROPHETS' LIFE AS
AN OPEN
BOOK

....
289

Conclusion: The Legacy of
Prophet Muhammad - A
Timeless Journey of
Inspiration

....
291

Preface: Exploring the Life of Prophet Muhammad ~ A Journey into Timeless Wisdom

In the tapestry of human history, few individuals have left an indelible mark that spans across cultures, civilizations, and epochs. Among these luminaries, one figure stands as a beacon of divine guidance, compassion, and unwavering faith—Prophet Muhammad. As we embark on a journey to delve into the life of this extraordinary messenger, we find ourselves not only traversing the annals of time but also venturing into the heart of a legacy that continues to illuminate the lives of millions.

"The Life of Prophet Muhammad" is more than a mere historical account—it is an exploration of the life, teachings, and character of a man who shaped the course of human history. Through the pages of this book, we seek to unravel the layers of wisdom embedded in his words, actions, and interactions. We aim to understand the profound impact he had on his contemporaries and the generations that followed, and the timeless relevance of his teachings in today's world.

This journey into the life of Prophet Muhammad is a tapestry woven with threads of spirituality, compassion, resilience, and humility. It is an opportunity to walk alongside him as he navigates the challenges of his time, upholding justice, championing the rights of the marginalized, and embodying the principles of love and mercy. From the early years of his life in the bustling city of Mecca to the heights of his leadership in Medina, we will witness the transformation of a man who carried a message of monotheism, unity, and social reform.

As we delve into the historical context, cultural nuances, and the spiritual depth of Prophet Muhammad's life, we invite readers to approach this journey with an open heart and a quest for understanding. Whether you are well-acquainted with his legacy or encountering it for the first time, our aim is to present a comprehensive and balanced exploration that fosters insight and appreciation.

In the pages that follow, you will find narratives that touch on his kindness to children, his interactions with people of different faiths, his role as a loving family man, and his moments of introspection and divine connection. We will journey through his trials and triumphs, his sacrifices and steadfastness, and ultimately, the legacy he left behind—a legacy that continues to inspire minds and hearts to this day.

With humility and respect, we approach this endeavor, acknowledging that the life of Prophet Muhammad is not only a historical account but a profound spiritual journey. May this exploration offer readers a glimpse into the remarkable life of a man whose example transcends time and invites us to live with purpose, compassion, and devotion.

[Ahmad Al-mannar]

THE LIFE OF PROPHET MUHAMMAD

SEMITES BEFORE THE PROPHET'S (SAW) BIRTH

The Arab Peninsula is located between the massive continents of Asia and Africa. Its residents refer to it as the "Island of the Arabs" since it is cut off from the rest of the world on all sides by natural obstacles. The Red Sea separates it from Africa in the west, the Persian Gulf and the Gulf of Oman separate it from the Asian mainland in the east, the Gulf of Aden and the Indian Ocean surround it in the south, and vast swaths of desert separate it from the north.

The area was green and its mountain peaks were snow-capped in prehistoric times, but as the Ice Age receded, the region became dryer and drier and could no longer maintain all of its inhabitants, so they emigrated from it in waves to more productive climes. Around 4500 BC, the first wave came to Egypt through Bab al-Mandab, where they mixed with the Hamitic people and gave rise to the Ancient Egyptians of history. Around 4000 BC, the second wave traveled to the region between the two rivers, which is now modern Iraq, where they met the Akkadians. They were subject to Akkadian control for a period before forming their own kingdom, Babylon. Hammurabi was a famous Babylonian king who had his laws carved on a stone monument.

The Assyrians were the third wave to come, albeit they were closely related to the Babylonians. They left their imprint on history later than the Babylonians, establishing a militaristic state in which science, medicine, astronomy, and mathematics thrived, as well as art and literature.

The Greeks referred to the Phoenicians as the fourth wave of emigrants. They began approximately 2000 BC and were the ancient world's businessmen and seamen. They constructed large commercial cities like as Sayda, Tyre, and Sidon. These seafarers founded colonies along their trading routes, the most notable of which was the Carthaginian civilization. They were the first to use phonetic writing and brought it with them everywhere they traded in the ancient world. They taught it to the Greeks, who then passed it on to the Romans. Actually, the earliest phonetic writing known to date is a script unearthed in Sinai in the North Arabian language; it is regarded the connection between Ancient Egyptian hieroglyphics and Phoenician writing and dates from 1850 BC.

Other waves of emigration, such as the Aramites, arrived near Babylon and founded the Chaldean civilization circa 2000 BC. In the south, emi- grants settled in Abyssinia and founded the ancient Abyssinian Kingdom, while the Hebrews settled in Palestine.

All of these individuals are known as Semites. The term Semite is derived from Sam (or Shem), Nuh's son. It has no ethnic origins and is a word used to describe a set of languages that share certain traits and are descended from the same mother tongue or proto-language. These languages are classified as northern and southern Semitic. The southern languages are further classified as North Arabian and South Arabian. North Arabian was the language of the Makkans, and it has overtaken other Arabian dialects to become known as Classical Arabic, the language praised by the Qur'an. The language of the southern peninsular civilisations (Yemen and the areas around it) and the Abyssinian civilisation was South Arabian.

We will not chronicle the conflicts, victories, and losses of people who left the peninsula, despite the fact that they were the oldest civilisations in history, since our major focus is with those who stayed. The Arabian Peninsula may be split into two parts: north and south. These two major sections are separated by huge deserts that are impossible to cross. The people of the north have remained nomadic because the harsh terrain of the north discourages stable civilisation and requires the inhabitants to be continuously on the road in search of water and grazing. The inhabitants of the south were able to establish a series of sophisticated civilisations, the remains of which include citadels, dams, monuments, and palaces twenty stories high, testifying to the richness and ability of the people who built them. It was a wholly Arab phenome- nil, with its own laws, codes, constitution, and traditions, and no exterior influences. They have the knowledge and capability to regulate the excessive rains in those areas and store the water in dams, barrages, and reservoirs.

These southern Arabs traded with Syria, Iraq, and Egypt. Their caravans traversed the desert, bringing spices, incense, gum, and myrrh from India and returning with the things produced in these areas. Around 1200 BC, the Mainians established the first significant South Arabian monarchy. It controlled the trade routes and constructed caravanserais along them for their use.

The Mainians were replaced by the Sabaeans, who continued the on-flow of Arab culture and acquired the Mainians' trading routes as well as their civilization. It was one of this kingdom's queens, the Queen of Saba (Sheba), who traveled to see Sulayman (Solomon) Several factors contributed to the Sabaean civilisation's weakening and eventual downfall, including their opulent lifestyle and the maintenance of its dams and barrages after they had become affluent via commerce. Ptolemy the Second developed a navy that could sail the Red Sea, which had previously been regarded unnavigable, in 270 BC. Because they had previously monopolised commerce in the region, this led to their demise. Their barrages had been neglected for some time, and when the Marib Dam burst, the country was inundated and essentially became wasteland, forcing the residents to relocate northward. Some migrated to the north of the peninsula, near Madina, while others traveled all the way up to the borders of Syria and Iraq, establishing new kingdoms.

The Sabaeans worshiped a triad and deified the celestial bodies. The moon, which they named Wudd, was their most powerful deity; the sun was its consort; and a son born of this marriage, probably Venus or Jupiter, was the third. The Sabaeans were the ones who taught the worship of the stars to the Arabs of the north through their trading routes.

During the first century following Christ, Judaism and later Christianity appeared in the area and vied for dominance. The two major nations that ruled the globe at the time, the Roman and Persian Empires, were drawn into this struggle. The Himyarite ruler of Yemen asked the Persian Chosroes for help against his Abyssinian opponents who had seized his realm. As a result, Yemen remained under Persian rule until the establishment of Islam in the nation.

Two Arab nations developed in the north. The first one was Petra, a Nabataean city-state made of solid rock. This civilization lived between 300 BC and 106 CE. when the Jewish revolt prompted the Roman Emperor Titus was tasked with destroying the city and annexing the area to the Romans Empire.

Soon after Petra's destruction, another Arab civilization formed in the Palmyra oasis. It was a great and lucrative commerce center, similar to Petra, and it remained neutral in the conflicts between the Romans and the Persians. It had lush soil and clean, crystalline water. When the Emperor Gallienus was taken by the Parthians who had invaded Syria in 260 CE, it was the Chieftain of Palmyra who freed the Emperor, returned Syria, and pursued the Parthians right up to their capital, Al-Madain.

During the long war between the Persians and the Romans, the Chieftain allied with the Romans and was given the title of Dux Orientalis, or Emperor of the East. He ruled Asia Minor, Egypt, Syria, and North Arabia. Following the death of this Chief, his wife reigned on behalf of her little son. When the Romans saw her generals approach Alexandria and Ankara, they cancelled their alliance with her kingdom, razed the city, and sent the proud Arab queen to Rome in chains. Her narrative is known in Arabic lyric and legend as Al-Zawbae or, in Latin, Zenobia. The Nabataeans rebuilt their civilization after their civilisation was destroyed. were integrated among the northern Arab tribes. The Arabs tended to develop towns farther away from the boundary and from foreign nations' influence.

THE KA'BAH AND MECCA

Makka stood around 80 kilometers from the shore in the eastern mountain range, encircled by mountains on all sides save for three small passages. It was on the tribes' caravan route, but with no water or plant life, it was uninhabited save for the odd passer-by. Ibrahim was told to leave Hajar, his Egyptian wife, and their infant son, Isma'il, in this remote valley where not even a fly could dwell, since Allah desired mankind to travel for the sole purpose of worship and wanted Ibrahim's offspring to go to meet the requirements of the worshipers When the rations Ibrahim had given them ran out, Hajar searched about for a means to get food and water, since her young kid was becoming thirsty. She couldn't locate anything, so she rushed back and forth, searching the horizon, rushing between two promenades named Al-Safa and Al-Marwa to look as far as she could. She walked back and forth seven times, and when she returned to check how her kid was doing, he was kicking the dirt, and water spilled out from beneath his foot.

Hajar stayed in this lonely valley surrounded by mountains with her kid. She started to distribute water to passing tribes in return for anything she need. Banu Jurhum were the first tribe to be drawn to the waters of Zamzam. Hajar agreed to let them camp near her as long as the water remained in her possession. Isma'il married a female from this tribe when he was older. Ibrahim used to see his son on his travels. On one of them, During these encounters, he was told to construct a temple of worship for Allah that would serve as a refuge for the worshippers. As a result, Ibrahim and Isma'il collaborated to build the first house for Allah's worship on Earth. They taught the inhabitants of those areas to worship just one god, Allah. Muslims still worship at the Ancient or Sacred House, also known as the Ka'ba, where Ibrahim taught the people Through commerce, the Makkans became wealthy and powerful throughout the ages. They started to live in luxury, failing to draw enough water from Zamzam (the name of Hajar's spring) to irrigate the land or care for their livestock. They also began to forget Ibrahim and Isma'il's teachings, and when Zamzam began to dry up, they became weaker. Al-Mudad ibn 'Amr of Jurhum, one of their great men, sought to warn them of the repercussions, but they did not listen. He realized that power would soon be taken from them, so he took two gold sculptures in the shape of gazelles and the money from the Ka'ba, lowered them down into the well of Zamzam, and buried them so that no one could find them. Soon after, he fled Makka with Isma'il's descendants.

The Khuza'a tribe, who had competed with Banu Jurhum for the honor of protecting the Sacred House, defeated them and assumed control. They handed on the honorary duties associated with guardianship generation after generation, and it is thought that they were involved in the introduction of idol worship in Makka. The Makkans were also inspired by the Sabaeans, who were star worshipers.

The Khuza'a held power until the reign of Qusayy ibn Kilab, the Prophet Muhammad's great-great-great-great-grandfather. He was well-known among his people for his sound judgment and excellent intelligence, and his business grew as did the number of his sons. The Quraysh tribe, descendants of Isma'il, surrounded him. Khuza'a continued to hold the honorary positions of the Ka'ba. Qusayy had married a girl from this tribe, and when her father died, he had entrusted the keys to her, but since she was a woman, she apologized and delivered them to another guy from her tribe, Abu Ghubshan. Abu Ghubshan was a drinker, and one day, probably while intoxicated, he sold the keys to Qusayy for a chalice of wine. When Khuza'a discovered that the honorary offices of the Ka'ba had slipped into the hands of Qusayy, they resolved to battle him for them, but all the

Makkans, who held Qusayy in high regard, rallied to him and drove Khuza'a out of Makka, making Qusayy their king. Then all the duties of catering to pilgrims, which were regarded as the highest of honors, were Qusayy's by right.

He was the first to declare pilgrim hospitality a responsibility of the Makkans. "People of Quraysh, you are Allah's neighbors and the people of His house and holy precincts. The pilgrims are Allah's guests, the visitors to His house. Of all guests, they are the most worthy of your hospitality, so prepare food and drink for them on the days of pilgrimage until they leave the land," he said to his people.

When there were no hotels and few stores, the tourist had to rely exclusively on the hospitality of the locals. Hospitality to strangers was one of the most important, if not the most important, obligations of Arabs who lived in a world where a man may die from thirst and hunger if aid was not provided. Following Qusayy, the honorary positions of catering to pilgrims were shared among his sons and, later, their descendants. Hashim, the most proficient of his brothers, summoned the Makkans to prepare food and drink for the pilgrims, much like his grandpa, Qusayy. He felt responsible for the people of Makka, and during times of shortage, he would feed and care for the poor. On a journey to Madina (then known as Yathrib), he encountered a beautiful lady who was managing her business and overseeing her dependents. He admired her and requested her hand in marriage. She accepted, knowing his status among his people. Her name was Salma, and she was from the Al-Khazraj clan. This wedding produced a kid named Shayba, whose maternal uncles were Madinans and whose paternal uncles were Makkans.

'ABDU'L MUTTALIB'S

Hashim perished on one of his business travels to Gaza. Al-Muttalib, his brother, became the tribe's leader. He remembered his young nephew living with his mother in Yathrib and decided it was time for him to live with his father's relatives in Makka. So he traveled to Yathrib and returned with the kid to Makka. When they saw him arriving with a small kid riding after him, they assumed it was a new slave he had purchased and dubbed the youngster 'Abdu'l-Muttalib, or Al- Muttalib's slave. When they discovered that he was his nephew, Hashim's son, they kept his first name, referring to him as 'Abdu'l-Muttalib rather than Shayba.

Al-Muttalib intended to give his nephew the money that belonged to his father, Hashim, but another uncle, Nawfal, had taken it and refused to let him have it. When 'Abdu'l-Muttalib got older, he enlisted the help of his Yathribi relatives. Eighty horsemen arrived in Makka to support their young cousin, forcing Nawfal to transfer his father's money to him. 'Abdu'l-Muttalib inherited the roles that his father Hashim had, which included greeting travelers and providing them with water. However, procuring water for the pilgrims was a difficult chore for him since he only had one kid to assist him.

It took several guys to transport the water and bring it from far away regions. All the Makkans remembered Zamzam's water spring with nostalgia, but 'Abdu'l-Muttalib saw it as a treasured fantasy that would make his duty of giving water to the pilgrims much simpler. In his sleep, he would have recurring dreams about this well and someone urging him to re-open it. He continued seeking for it until he was prompted to look among two of the idols near the Ka'ba. He dug there, and water poured forth. He continued excavating until he discovered his ancestor Mudad's two golden gazelles, money, and weapons.

Quraysh begged him to share the riches, but he refused. After some thought, he volunteered to draw lots with them for it. The Makkans used to cast lots by writing their names on arrows and then throwing them into the Ka'ba in a certain location so that the choice was made by their gods. The swords were to be kept by 'Abdu'l- Muttalib, while the sculptures were to be donated to the Ka'ba. 'Abdu'l-Muttalib put the gazelles before the Ka'ba's entryway as an adornment, as well as the swords.

'Abdu'l-Muttalib was the Prophet Muhammad's direct paternal grandfather. Thousands of years ago, Ibrahim prayed to Allah to provide for his descendants who remained in the lonely valley of Makka and to send them a messenger from among themselves to direct them to the correct path. As a result, the Prophet Muhammad used to declare, "I came in response to my grandpa Ibrahim's request."

.

ARABIA DURING THE PROPHET'S SA BIRTH

the Prophet (s.a.w) was born at Mecca. Muhammad (s.a.w), which means "the Praised One," was given to him. To comprehend his life and character, we must first grasp the circumstances that existed in Arabia at the time of his birth.

When he was born, practically all of Arabia followed a polytheistic faith. The Arabs traced their ancestry back to Abrahamas. They were well aware that Abrahamas was a monotheistic teacher. Regardless, they held polytheistic views and engaged in polytheistic behaviors. They defended themselves by claiming that certain people had exceptional touch with God. God accepts their intercession on behalf of others. It is difficult for regular people to approach Him. In order to gain God's pleasure and aid, they must have others plead for them. As a result, they were able to reconcile their admiration for Abraham with their polytheistic views. They said Abrahamas was a saintly guy. He was able to communicate with God without the need for supplication, although regular Meccans could not. As a result, the people of Mecca created idols of pure and virtuous individuals, which they worshiped and sacrificed to in try to appease God via them. This mentality was basic, irrational, and flawed. The Meccans, on the other hand, were unconcerned. They hadn't had a monotheistic teacher in a long time, and once established, polytheism grows and knows no limitations. The number of gods starts to grow. It is reported that during the time of the Prophet's a's birth, claimed there were 360 idols in the Ka'ba alone, the Sacred Mosque of Islam and the sanctuary of worship constructed by Abraham and his son Ishmael. The Meccans seem to have possessed an idol for each day of the lunar year. Other idols may be found in other major cities, indicating that polytheistic religion was prevalent across Arabia. The Arabs were committed to speech culture. They were particularly engaged in the development of their spoken language. Their intellectual objectives, on the other hand, were limited. They know nothing about history, geography, mathematics, and so forth. However, since they were a desert tribe who had to navigate the desert without the aid of landmarks, they had acquired a deep interest in Astronomy. There was not a single school in all of Arabia. It is stated that just a few people in Mecca could read and write.

From a moral standpoint, the Arabs were a paradoxical nation. They had some serious moral flaws, but they also had some outstanding traits. They were prone to binge drinking. For them, being drunk and running wild under the influence of alcohol was a virtue, not a fault. Their idea of a gentleman was someone who would host drinking parties for his friends and neighbors. Every wealthy guy would throw at least five drinking parties every day. Their national sport was gambling. But they'd turned it into a great art. They did not bet to get wealthy. Winners were supposed to amuse their peers. During times of war, monies were raised via gambling. We still have the system of prize bonds to generate funds for wars today. People in Europe and America have resurrected the tradition in our day. But they must understand that they are merely imitating the Arabs. When battle broke out, the Arabian tribes would have a gaming celebration. Whoever prevailed had to face the majority of the war's costs.

The Arabs had little knowledge of the comforts of modern life. Their main business was trading, and they dispatched their caravans to far-flung areas like Abyssinia, Syria, Palestine, and even India. The wealthy among them were huge fans of Indian swords. Yemen and Syria provided the majority of their apparel requirements. The towns served as commerce hubs. Except for Yemen and certain northern areas, the remainder of Arabia was Bedouin. There were no permanent villages or dwellings. The tribes had split the area such that members of one tribe might roam freely in their section of the country. When the water supply in one location was depleted, they would relocate and establish in another. Their capital was made up of sheep, goats, and camels. They fashioned fabric from the wool, and tents from the skins. They sold what was left over on the market. Although gold and silver were not unknown, they were very unusual assets. Cowries and sweet-smelling things were used to make decorations by the impoverished and ordinary people. Melon seeds were washed, dried, and strung together to create necklaces. Various forms of crime and immorality were widespread. Theft was uncommon, but dacoity was frequent. It was considered a birthright to assault and dispossess one another. At the same time, they kept their word better than everyone else.

If a person approached a prominent leader or tribe and asked for protection, that leader or tribe was obligated to protect that person. If this was not done, the tribe's caste would be lost across Arabia. Poets were held in high regard. They received recognition as national leaders. Leaders were supposed to have excellent oratory skills and even to be able to create poems. Hospitality has become a national value. When a lonely wanderer arrives to a tribe's headquarters, he or she is greeted as an honored guest. The finest animals would be butchered for him, with the greatest care. They were unconcerned about the visitor's identity. It was sufficient that a guest had come. The tribe's position and prestige increased as a result of the visit. As a result, it became the tribe's responsibility to honor the guest. It honored itself by honoring him. In this Arab civilization, women had no position and no rights. It was considered honorable among them to execute infant girls. It is, however, a misconception to believe that infanticide was practiced on a national basis. A deadly institution like this could not thrive throughout a nation. That would have meant the race's demise. The fact is that in Arabia—or, for that matter, in India or any other place where infanticide has ever occurred—it was limited to certain households. The Arab households that practiced it either had an inflated sense of their social standing or were otherwise limited. They may have been unable to locate acceptable young men for their daughters to marry, and knowing this, they executed their infant girls. The harm of this institution rests in its savagery and brutality, not in the effects it produces on a nation's inhabitants. Baby girls were killed using a variety of techniques, including burial alive and strangling.

In Arab civilization, only the biological mother was considered a mother. Stepmothers were not considered mothers, and there was no prohibition on a son marrying his stepmother after his father died. Polygamous marriages were prevalent, and a man may have as many women as he wanted. At the same time, more than one sister might be taken to wife by the same guy.

Combatant parties gave each other the harshest treatment throughout battle. They did not hesitate to break the corpses of the injured, pluck out portions, and devour them in cannibal form where hate was intense. They had no qualms about mutilating their opponents' bodies. Cutting off the nose or ears, or plucking out an eye, was a widespread kind of cruelty. Slavery was common. Slaves were taken from weak tribes. The slave had no official standing. Every owner did whatever he pleased with his slaves. A master who mistreated his slave could not be prosecuted. A master might kill his slave without being held accountable. Even if one owner killed another's slave, the punishment was not death. All he had to do was recompense the wronged master appropriately. Slave women were utilized to gratify sexual needs. Children born from such marriages were likewise classified as slaves. Women-slaves who became mothers were still considered slaves. The Arabs were a fairly backward nation in terms of civilization and social advancement. Kindness and regard for others were unheard of. Woman had the lowest possible status. Even yet, the Arabs had certain advantages. Individual courage, for example, might occasionally reach very high levels.

The Holy Prophet (s.a.w) of Islam were born among such people. His father, 'Abdullah, died before he was born. As a result, he and his mother Amina were left in the care of his grandpa, 'Abdul Muttalib. Muhammad (s.a.w) was breastfed by a countrywoman from a village near Ta'if. It was customary in Arabia at the time to hand over children to country women, whose responsibility it was to raise the youngsters, train their speech, and give them a good start in physical health. When the Prophet (s.a.w) was a year old*, his mother died while traveling from Medina to Mecca and had to be buried along the way. A woman-servant carried the infant to Mecca and gave it up to the grandpa. His grandpa died while he was in his seventh year, and Abu Talib, his uncle, became his guardian in accordance with the grandfather's will. The Prophet Sa had two or three chances to leave Arabia. One of them happened when, at the age of twelve, he traveled to Syria with Abu Talib. This tour seems to have taken him solely to the south-eastern cities of

---

* A: According to Imam Baqir in Biharul-Anwar, on the authority of Waqidi, Aminah, the mother of the Holy Prophet (s.a.w), died when he was

four months old, making him an orphan at the age of four months. (BiharulAnwaril-Jami'ati li-Durari Akhbaril-A'immatil-Athar, Babu Mansha'ihi wa Rada'ihi wa ma zahara min I'jazihi 'inda dhalika ila Nubuwwatihi by Sheikh Muhammad Baqir Majlisi, vol.15, p.194; published by

B: However, Hadrat Aminah, the mother of the Holy Prophet (s.a.w), died when he was six years old, according to Ibni Hisham. (Ibni Hisham's Siratun-Nabawiyyah, Babu Wafati Aminata wa Hali Rasulillahi ma'a Jaddihi 'Abdil

Muttalib ba'daha, Darul-Kutubil-'Ilmiyyah Beirut, p.134.

Lebanon, 2001, first edition.)

Syria, since there is no mention of sites like Jerusalem in historical allusions to this voyage. He would stay in Mecca until he reached the age of adulthood. He was taught to contemplate and meditate when he was a toddler. He took no part in the quarrels and rivalries of others, except to put a stop to them. It is stated that weary of endless blood feuds, the tribes of Mecca and the surrounding lands decided to form an organization to assist victims of aggressive and unfair treatment. When the Holy Prophet (s.a.w) learned about it, he eagerly joined in. Members of this organization agreed to the following terms:

As long as the last drop of water remains in the sea, they will assist those who have been oppressed and restore their rights. If they do not do so, they would recompense the victims with their own property (Imam Suhaili's Sirat Ibni Hisham).

No other member of this group seems to have ever been called upon to fulfill the solemn pledge solemnly taken into by members of this association. But opportunity presented itself to the Holy Prophet (s.a.w) once he revealed his Mission. His greatest foe was Abu Jahl, a Mecca leader.

He advocated for a social boycott and public humiliation of Prophet (s.a.w). Around that time, a visitor from the outside world arrived in Mecca. Money was owed to him by Abu Jahl, but he refused to pay. He told others in Mecca about it. Some young males recommended that he approach the Prophet (s.a.w) just for kicks. They expected the Prophet (s.a.w) to refuse to do anything because of fear of the broad resistance to him, notably the opposition of Abu Jahl. He would be considered to have breached his vow to the organization if he refused to assist this individual. If, on the other hand, he did not decline and instead opted to approach Abu Jahl for the repayment of this debt, Abu Jahl was likely to dismiss him with disdain. This guy approached the Prophet (s.a.w) and complained about Abu Jahl. Without hesitation, the Prophet (s.a.w) rose up, followed the guy, and knocked on Abu Jahl's door. When Abu Jahl got out, he noticed that his creditor was with the Prophet (s.a.w). The Prophet (s.a.w) stated the debt and proposed a repayment plan. Abu Jahl was taken aback and paid immediately, offering no excuses. When the other Mecca leaders learned of this, they chastised Abu Jahl, reminding him how weak and inconsistent he had been. He advocated a social boycott of the Prophet (s.a.w), but he personally took instruction from the Prophet (s.a.w) and paid a debt based on his advice. Abu Jahl argued in self-defense that any other individual would have done the same thing. He informed them that as he saw the Prophet (s.a.w) approaching his door, he also noticed two wild camels, one on each side, poised to attack. We have no idea what this event was like. Was it a miraculous sight intended to disturb Abu Jahl, or was it the Prophet (s.a.w)'s awe-inspiring presence that caused this hallucination? A guy despised and mistreated by a whole town had summoned the fortitude to go alone to the town's chief and demand repayment of a debt. Perhaps this sudden sight scared Abu Jahl and made him forget what he had pledged to do against the Prophet (s.a.w), forcing him to do what the Prophet (s.a.w) recommended (Hisham).

MARRIAGE OF THE HOLY PROPHET WITH KHADIJA(ra)

When the Prophet (s.a.w) was around twenty-five years old, his reputation for honesty and neighborliness had spread across the whole community. People would look at him with admiration and remark, "Here was a guy who could be trusted." This reputation reached the ears of a wealthy widow who sought the Prophet's uncle, Abu Talib, and asked him to accompany her trade caravan to Syria. Abu Talib communicated this to the Prophet (s.a.w), who concurred. The mission was a huge success, bringing in unanticipated earnings. KHADIJA(ra), the wealthy widow, was confident that the caravan's success was attributable not just to the market circumstances in Syria, but also to the honesty and effectiveness of its commander. She questioned her slave, Maisara, about the matter, and Maisara agreed with her and warned her that the honesty and compassion with which this young caravan leader had handled her concerns would not be shared by many others. This tale impressed KHADIJA(ra) much. She was forty years old and had been widowed twice. She dispatched a female acquaintance to the Prophet (s.a.w) to see if he might be convinced to marry her. This lady approached the Prophet (s.a.w) and inquired as to why he had not married. The Prophet (s.a.w) responded that he was not wealthy enough to do so. The guest asked whether he would agree if he could find a wealthy and reputable lady to marry. The Prophet (s.a.w) inquired as to who this lady may be, and the visitor said that her name was KHADIJA(ra). The Prophet (s.a.w) apologized, claiming KHADIJA(ra) was too important for him. The guest agreed to deal with any complications that arose. In that scenario, the Prophet (s.a.w) had nothing else to say except to agree. KHADIJA(ra) then spoke with the Prophet's (s.a.w) uncle. The Prophet (s.a.w) and KHADIJA(ra)'s marriage was negotiated and solemnized. A destitute orphaned youngster made his first foray into affluence. He grew wealthy. But how he used his wealth is a lesson for all of humanity. After the marriage, KHADIJA(ra) thought that she was wealthy while he was impoverished, and that this disparity would not lead to happiness. So she offered to the Prophet (s.a.w) that she hands up her possessions and slaves. To ensure KHADIJA(ra)'s sincerity, the Prophet (s.a.w) promised that as soon as he possessed any of Khadija's(ra) slaves, he would set them free. And he did just that. Furthermore, he transferred the majority of the property he inherited from KHADIJA(ra) to the impoverished. Zaid (ra) was one of the slaves Jesus freed in this way. He looked to be smarter and more aware than others. He came from a decent family, had been stolen as a youngster, and had been sold from place to place until he arrived in Mecca.

Young Zaid (ra), freshly emancipated, realized right once that it was preferable to give up freedom for the sake of Prophet (s.a.w) slavery. When the Prophet (s.a.w) liberated the slaves, Zaid (ra) rejected and requested permission to remain with the Prophet (s.a.w). He did so, and his devotion to the Prophet (s.a.w) strengthened over time. But, in the meanwhile, Zaid's(ra) father and uncle were following him and eventually learned that he was in Mecca. They found him at the home of the Prophet (s.a.w) in Mecca. When they arrived to the Prophet (s.a.w), they requested Zaid (ra)'s release and promised to pay whatever ransom demanded by the Prophet (s.a.w). The Prophet (s.a.w) said that Zaid (ra) was free to travel anywhere he pleased. He summoned Zaid (ra) and introduced him to his father and uncle. After the parties had met and wiped their tears, Zaid's(ra) father informed him that he had been released by his compassionate Master and that, since his mother was much distressed by the separation, he should come home. "Father! who does not love his parents? My heart is full of love for you and mother, but I love this man Muhammad (s.a.w) so much that I cannot think of living anywhere else than with him. I have met you, and I am glad, but separation from Muhammad (s.a.w) I cannot endure," Zaid (ra) replied. When the Holy Prophet (s.a.w) saw this, he stated, "Zaid (ra) was already a freedman, but from now he will be my son." Seeing this devotion between Zaid (ra) and the Prophet (s.a.w), Zaid's(ra) father and uncle returned, and Zaid (ra) stayed with the Prophet (s.a.w) (Hisham).

THE PROPHET (s.a.w) HAS HIS FIRST

REVELATION

When the Prophet (s.a.w) was over thirty years old, he became more possessed by his love of God and His worship. He picked a location two or three miles away for his meditations in order to protest the sins, misdeeds, and various vices of the people of Mecca. This was a cave fashioned out of stone on top of a hill. His wife KHADIJA(ra) would prepare food for many days, and he would go for the cave Hira with it. He would worship God in the cave at all hours of the day and night. He had a vision when he was forty years old. It was right here in this cave. He saw someone ordering him to

recite.

In response, the Prophet (s.a.w) said that he did not know what or how to recite. The figure persisted and eventually forced the Prophet (s.a.w) to say the following verses:

Recite in the name of your Lord, who made man from a clot of blood. Recite! And thy Lord is the Most Beneficent, who taught man by writing, teaching him what he did not know (96:2-6).

These verses, the first ever revealed to the Prophet (s.a.w), were included into the Qur'an, along with additional passages revealed afterwards. They have a lot of significance. They tell the Prophet (s.a.w) to rise and be prepared to declare the name of the One God, the One Creator—of the Prophet (s.a.w) and all others—Who created man and planted the seed of His own love and that of fellowmen in his nature. The Prophet (s.a.w) were told to preach the Message of this God and were given His assistance and safety in doing so. The words predicted a day when the world will be taught every sort of knowledge via the pen, even things never previously heard of. The verses are a distillation of the Qur'an. Whatever the Prophet (s.a.w) was to teach in following revelations is present in these passages in embryo. They set the groundwork for a huge and hitherto unknown development in man's spiritual evolution. The meaning and explanation for these passages may be found in their respective sections of this Commentary. We include them here because their revelation was a significant event in the Prophet (s.a.w)'s life. When the Prophet got this revelation, he was terrified of the burden that God had chosen to lay on his shoulders. Any other person in his position would have been thrilled with pride—he would have believed he had achieved greatness. The Prophet (s.a.w) was unique. He might accomplish amazing things yet take little satisfaction in his accomplishments. After this incredible encounter, he returned home upset, his face drawn. On Khadija's(ra)'s inquiry, he recounted the whole incident and summarized his anxieties, adding, "Weak man that I am, how can I handle the duty which God offers to place on my shoulders?" KHADIJA(ra) responded immediately:

God is witness; He did not send you this Word so that you would fail and become worthless, and He would then abandon you. How can God do such a thing when you are nice and sensitive to your family members, support the impoverished and bereaved, and carry their burdens? You are reintroducing qualities that had vanished from our nation. You greet visitors with respect and assist those in need. Can God put you through any test? (Bukhari).

Having stated so, KHADIJA(ra) brought the Prophet (s.a.w) to her Christian relative, Waraqa bin Naufal. When Waraqa heard the story, he said:

"I am confident the angel who descended on Mosesas has fallen on you" (Bukhari).

FIRST TIME CONVERTERS

Waraqa clearly alludes to the prophesy in Deuteronomy 18:18. When Zaid (ra), the Prophet's (s.a.w) emancipated slave, now around thirty years old, and his cousin 'Alira, approximately eleven years old, heard the news, they both reaffirmed their confidence in him. Abu Bakrra, a boyhood buddy, was out of town. As he returned, he started to hear of the Prophet (s.a.w)'s new experience. He was informed that his buddy had gone insane and began to claim that angels sent messages from God to him. Abu Bakrra had entire faith in the Prophet (s.a.w). He had no doubt that the Prophet (s.a.w) was correct—he had known him to be both sane and truthful. He knocked on the Prophet's (s.a.w)'s door and, upon entrance, asked him what had transpired. Fearing that Abu Bakrra might misunderstand, the Prophet (s.a.w) started a lengthy explanation. Abu Bakrra halted the Prophet (s.a.w), insisting that all he needed to know was if an angel had indeed fallen from God and delivered him a Message. The Prophet (s.a.w) sought to explain again, but Abu Bakrra replied he didn't want to hear it. He merely sought an answer to the issue of whether he had received a Message from God. When the Prophet (s.a.w) responded, "Yes," Abu Bakrra immediately announced his faith. He said that if he had not expressed his beliefs, the importance of his faith would have been diminished. He had a long and close relationship with the Prophet (s.a.w). He couldn't disbelieve him, and he didn't need any convincing to believe him. This little group of believers were the first Muslims: a mother of many years, an eleven-year-old son, a liberated slave living among strangers, a young acquaintance, and the Prophet (s.a.w) himself. This was the party that silently resolved to spread God's light across the globe. The people and their leaders laughed and stated that these individuals had gone insane when they heard this. There was nothing to be afraid of or worried about. But, as time passed, the truth started to light, and, as the Prophet Isai (a.s.w.s) (28:13) once remarked, "precept upon precept, precept upon precept; line upon line, line upon line; here a little, and there a little" began to fall upon the Prophet (s.a.w).

THE RIGHTEOUS WERE PERSECUTED

God started speaking to Muhammad (s.a.w) in "another language." The country's young started to wonder. Those seeking the truth got enthralled. From rejection and mockery grew appreciation and admiration. Slaves, young men, and helpless women gathered around Prophet (s.a.w). There was hope for the downtrodden, the sad, and the young in his Message and teaching. Women believed that the moment had come to reclaim their rights. Slaves believed that the day of their release had arrived, and young men believed that doors of opportunity would be opened to them. When ridicule became approbation and indifference became attachment, the leaders of Mecca and the authorities were alarmed. They gathered and conferred. They determined that mockery was not the way to cope with this threat. A more serious solution was required. The new power had to be suppressed by force. It was agreed that persecution and a boycott would be implemented. Practical actions were quickly taken, and Mecca found itself in a major struggle with Islam. The Prophet (s.a.w) and his little following were no longer deemed insane, but rather a burgeoning influence that, if allowed to develop unchecked, would pose a threat to

Mecca's religion, status, customs, and traditions. Islam threatened to demolish and reconstruct Meccan civilization, to establish a new heaven and a new earth, the arrival of which would imply the departure of Arabia's old heaven and heart. Meccans could no longer mock Islam. It was now a matter of life and death for them. Islam was a challenge, and Mecca embraced it, just as opponents of Prophets had always accepted their Prophets' challenges. They chose to wield the sword and put down the hazardous doctrine by force, not to match the Prophet (s.a.w) and his followers' good example, not to respond to nice words in like, but to maltreat the innocent and insult those who spoke pleasantly. Once again, a fight between belief and skepticism erupted throughout the earth; Satan's soldiers began war on the angels. The Faithful, yet a small group, lacked the strength to resist the disbelievers' onslaughts and brutality. A heinous campaign was launched. Women were brutally murdered. Men were massacred. Slaves who had professed trust in the Prophet (s.a.w) were carried through scorching sands and stones. Their skin hardened like that of animals. After a long time, when Islam had spread far and wide, one of these early converts, Khabbab bin Al-Aratra, had his corpse exposed. His buddies saw that his skin had stiffened like that of an animal and questioned him why. Khabbabra laughed and claimed it was nothing more than a recollection from the days when slaves converted to Islam were carried through the streets of Mecca on hard and scorching sands and stones (Musnad, Vol. 5, p. 110).

Slaves who believed came from every community. Suhaib (ra) was a Greek, whereas Bilal (ra) was a black. They were of various religions.Jabr (ra) and Suhaib (ra) were Christians, whereas Bilal (ra) and 'Ammarra worshiped idols. Bilal (ra) was tormented by lying on hot sand filled with stones and having boys dance on his chest, and his master, Umayya bin Khalf, ordered him to forsake Allah and the Prophet (s.a.w) and chant the praises of the Meccan gods, Lat and 'Uzza. Bilal (ra)'s sole words were Ahad, Ahad... (God is One).

Exasperated, Umayya gave Bilal (ra) to street youths, instructing them to tie a string around his neck and pull him through town over jagged stones. Bilal (ra)'s body bled, but he kept chanting, Ahad, Ahad... Later, when Muslims were allowed to live and worship in relative peace in Medina, the Holy Prophet (s.a.w) designated Bilal (ra) a Mu'adhdhin, the official who summons the worshipers to prayer. Bilal (ra), being an African, omitted the (h), in the Arabic Ashhadu (I bear testimony). Medinite followers scoffed at his poor pronunciation, but the Prophet (s.a.w) chastised them and informed them how precious Bilal (ra) was to God for his steadfast faith in the face of Meccan tortures. Abu Bakrra paid the price and freed Bilal (ra) and many other slaves. Suhaib (ra), a successful merchant, was among them, and the Quraish continued to torment him even after his release. Suhaib (ra) wished to accompany the Holy Prophet (s.a.w) as they left Mecca for Medina. But he was stopped by the Meccans. They stated he couldn't take the fortune he'd accumulated in Mecca with him. Suhaib (ra) promised to relinquish all of his possessions and earnings in exchange for his release. The Meccans agreed to the deal. Suhaib (ra) arrived in Medina empty-handed and saw the Prophet (s.a.w), who recognized him and complimented him, saying, "This was the finest deal of your life."

The majority of these slave-converts maintained both outward and interior professions of religion. However, some were feeble. The Holy Prophet (s.a.w) once discovered 'Ammarra moaning in anguish and wiping away his tears. When approached by the Prophet (s.a.w), 'Ammarra claimed to have been assaulted and forced to recant. "But did you believe at heart?" the Prophet (s.a.w) inquired. 'Ammarra replied that he did, and the Prophet (s.a.w) stated that God would forgive him.

weakness.

Disbelievers also harassed 'Ammar's(ra) father, Yasir (ra), and his mother, Samiyyara. The Prophet (s.a.w) happened to pass by on one of these occasions. "Family of Yasir (ra), bear up patiently, because God has prepared for you a Paradise," he murmured, overcome with passion. The prophetic words were shortly realized. Yasirra died as a result of the tortures, and Abu Jahl afterwards stabbed his elderly wife, Samiyyara, with a spear. Zinbirara, a female slave, lost her eyes as a result of the severe treatment of nonbelievers.

Abu Fukaihra, Safwan bin Umayya's slave, was lay on scorching sand with heavy and hot stones placed over his chest, causing his tongue to slip out. Other slaves were mistreated in a similar manner.

These atrocities were unbearable. However, early Christians bore them because God's regular confirmations fortified their hearts. The Qur'an fell on the Prophet (s.a.w), but God's soothing word fell on all believers. The Faithful could not have endured the atrocities they were subjected to if this were not the case. They were abandoned by their peers, friends, and relatives, and they didn't care if they had anybody else. Because of Him, cruelties looked insignificant, insults sounded like pleas, and stones like silk.

The free people who believed were not treated any better. Their elders and leaders tortured them in various ways. 'Uthmanra was an affluent forty-year-old man. When the Quraish decided to persecute Muslims in general, his uncle, Hakam, locked him up and thrashed him. Zubair bin al-

'Awwamra, a valiant young man who went on to become a renowned Muslim commander, was wrapped in a mat by his uncle, smoked from under, and tortured by suffocation. But he refused to apologize. He had discovered Truth and refused to give it up.

up.

Abu Dharrra of the Ghaffar clan heard about the Prophet (s.a.w) and traveled to Mecca to investigate. The Meccans dissuaded him, claiming that they knew Muhammad (s.a.w) well and that his Movement was purely selfish. Abu Dharrra was unimpressed, so he went to the Prophet (s.a.w) and heard the Message of Islam directly from him before being converted. Abu Dharrra inquired if he could keep his religion hidden from his clan. For a few days, the Prophet (s.a.w) stated he could. However, as he walked through the streets of Mecca, he overheard a group of Meccan leaders insulting and attacking the Holy Prophet (s.a.w). He could no longer keep his religion hidden, and he shouted emphatically, "I give testimony that there is no God but Allah, and that there is no one like Allah; that Muhammad (s.a.w) is His Servant and Prophet (s.a.w)." This cry, raised amid an assembly of disbelievers, seemed to them as an affront. They erupted in rage and belaboured him till he collapsed unconscious. The Prophet's (s.a.w) uncle 'Abbasra, who had not yet converted, walked by and started to remonstrate on the victim's behalf. "Your food caravans travel through Abu Dharr'sra tribe," he added, "and his people, enraged at your cruelty, may starve you to death." Abu Dharrra remained at home the next day. But the next day, he returned to the same congregation and found them still assaulting the Holy Prophet (s.a.w). He proceeded to the Ka'ba and discovered others doing the same thing. He couldn't keep himself from standing up and declaring his beliefs loudly. He was treated harshly once again. When this occurred a third time, Abu Dharrra returned to his clan.

The Holy Prophet (s.a.w) were not immune to the brutal punishment meted out to the faithful. He was praying on one occasion. Disbelievers wrapped a robe over his neck and pulled him; his eyes seemed protruded. "You intend to murder him because he says, God is his Master?" said Abu Bakrra. On another time, he fell down in prayer, and they placed the entrails of a camel on his back. He couldn't get up till the weight was lifted. On another time, he was walking down the street when a bunch of street lads followed him. They continued to smack his neck and told the public that he referred to himself as a Prophet (s.a.w). Such was the hostility and malice directed at him, as well as his impotence.

The homes around the Prophet's (s.a.w) house were stoned. Garbage and killed animal carcasses were tossed into his kitchen. On several times, dust was thrown on him while he was praying, forcing him to go to a secure location for his public prayers.

These atrocities, committed against a hapless and vulnerable community and its honest, well-meaning but powerless Leadersa, were not in vain. All of this attracted decent men to Islam. Once upon a time, the Prophet (s.a.w) was resting atop Safa, a hill near the Ka'ba. The Prophet's arch-enemy, Meccan leader Abu Jahl, walked by and started cursing him. The Prophet (s.a.w) remained silent and returned home. This horrific scenario was seen by a woman-slave in his home. The Prophet's (s.a.w) uncle, Hamzara, a valiant man hated by all his townspeople, arrived home after a jungle hunt and entered the house triumphantly, his bow slung over his shoulder. The morning spectacle had not gone unnoticed by the woman-slave. She was appalled to watch

Hamzara go home in such a manner. She mocked him, saying he believed himself courageous because he was armed, but he had no idea what Abu Jahl had done to his innocent nephew in the morning. Hamzara was told about the morning incident. He had nobility of character despite the fact that he was not a believer. He may have been moved by the Prophet's (s.a.w) Message, but not to the point of officially joining. When he learned about Abu's heinous act,

He couldn't help himself, Jahl. His reservations regarding the new Message were vanished. He started to feel that he had been too casual about it so far. He went directly for the Ka'ba, where Mecca's leaders were known to assemble and consult. He drew his bow and aimed it squarely at Abu Jahl. "Count myself as a disciple of Muhammad (s.a.w) as of today," he said. "You assaulted him this morning because he wouldn't say anything; if you're bold, come out and fight me," Abu Jahl was taken aback. His comrades rose to assist, but Abu Jahl stopped them, fearful of Hamzara and his clan, believing that an open conflict would be too costly. He was really to fault for the morning episode (Hisham and Tabari), he said.

THE ISLAMIC MESSAGE

The opposition became stronger. At the same time, the Prophet (s.a.w) and his followers were doing all they could to make the Message of Islam clear to the Meccans. It was a multifaceted message with far-reaching implications not just for Arabs but for the whole globe. It was a divine message. It stated:

The world's Creator is One. Nobody else is worthy of adoration. The Prophets have always considered Him to be One and have instructed their followers to do the same. Meccans must abandon all pictures and idols. Did they not notice that the idols couldn't even get rid of the flies that landed on the sacrifices placed at their feet? They couldn't defend themselves if they were assaulted. They were unable to respond to questions posed to them. They could do nothing if they were requested for assistance. But the One God aided those who sought His assistance, answered those who prayed to Him, conquered His adversaries, and elevated those who prostrated themselves before Him. The light that emanated from Him illuminated His believers. Why, therefore, did the Meccans ignore Him and devote their lives to lifeless representations and idols? Didn't they see that their lack of trust in the One True God had rendered them completely superstitious and inept? They had no concept of what was clean and dirty, of what was good and wrong. They didn't respect their moms. They mistreated their sisters and daughters and denied them their rights. They were not kind to their spouses. They harassed widows, exploited orphans, the destitute and the weak, and attempted to build their wealth on the wreckage of others. They were not embarrassed of lying and cheating, nor of burgling and looting. Their favorite pastimes were gambling and drinking. They didn't care about culture or national advancement. How much longer were they going to disregard the One True God and continue to lose and suffer? Had they not done more to reform? Had they not done better to stop all forms of exploitation, restore rights to those who deserved them, spend their wealth on national needs and improving the lot of the poor and weak, treat orphans as a trust and regard their protection as a duty, support widows, and establish and encourage good works in the entire community, cultivate not just justice and equity, but compassion and grace? Life in this planet should be beneficial. "Leave good works behind," the Message continued, "so that they may grow and bear fruit after you are gone. There is virtue in giving to others, not receiving from them. Learn to surrender so that you may be nearer to your God. Practice self-denial for the sake of your fellowmen, so that you may multiply your credit with God. True, the Muslims are weak, but Truth will triumph. This is the decree of Heaven.

When this Message was conveyed to the people of Mecca, it impacted the well-meaning and contemplative among them. The elders of Mecca took a close look at what was going on. They sent a delegation to the Prophet's uncle, Abu Talib, and addressed him as follows:

You are one of our leaders, and we have so far spared your nephew, Muhammad (s.a.w), for your sake. But the moment has come to put an end to this national catastrophe, this strife in our midst. We request and demand that he refrain from saying anything negative about our heroes. Let him announce that God is One, but let him not criticize our idols. If he agrees to this, our disagreement with him will be resolved. We strongly recommend you to convince him. If you are unable to do so, one of two things must occur. Either you give up your nephew or we, your people, give up on you (Hisham).

Abu Talib was forced to make a difficult decision. It was difficult for him to give up his nephew. It was also difficult for him to be rejected by his people. Arabs lacked financial resources. Their leadership was the source of their renown. They lived for their people, and they lived for their people. Abu Talib was furious. He summoned the Prophet (s.a.w) and conveyed the elders of Mecca's desire. "If you don't agree," he added, his eyes welling up, "then either I have to give you up or my people will give me up," the Prophet (s.a.w) replied, clearly sympathizing with his uncle. Tears welled up in his eyes, and he sobbed:

I implore you not to abandon your people. Please do not stand by me. Instead, you may abandon me and support your people. But the One and Only God is my witness when I declare that even if they put the sun on my right and the moon on my left, I would not stop proclaiming the One God's truth. I must continue to do so till I die. You are free to pursue your own pleasure (Hisham and Zurqani).

Abu Talib's eyes were enlightened by this forceful, direct, and honest response. He was lost in thinking. Though he lacked the guts to believe, he considered himself fortunate to have lived to see such a spectacular display of faith and reverence for responsibility. He then turned to the Prophet (s.a.w).

said:

"Go your way, my nephew. Do your job. Let my people give me up. I am with you" (Hisham).

ABYSSINIAN IMMIGRATION

When oppression reached its apex, the Prophet (s.a.w) gathered his followers and, pointing to the west, informed them about a place beyond the sea where men were not killed for changing their religion, where they may worship God freely, and where there was a righteous monarch. Allow them to go there; maybe the change will offer them relief. In response to this idea, a group of Muslim men, women, and children traveled to Abyssinia. The migration happened on a tiny scale and was quite sad. The Arabs saw themselves as guardian of the Ka'ba, and they were correct. It was a big hardship for them to leave Mecca, and no Arab would consider doing so until life in Mecca had become utterly untenable. Neither were the Meccans willing to allow such a movement. They would not allow their victims to flee and have a chance to live elsewhere. As a result, the group had to keep their preparations for the voyage a well guarded secret and leave without even saying goodbye to their friends and relatives. Their departure, on the other hand, became known to some and impressed them. 'Umarra, who became Islam's Second Khalifah, was nonetheless a disbeliever, a passionate opponent, and a persecutor of Muslims. He met several people of this party by coincidence. Ummi was one of these women.

'Abdullahra. When 'Umarra observed home items packed and placed on animals, he knew it was a group fleeing Mecca to seek sanctuary elsewhere. "Are you going?" he inquired. "Yes, God is our witness," Ummi 'Abdullahra answered. "We are leaving because you are unkind to us here, and we will not return until you change your ways."

Allah pleases to make it simple for us." 'Umarra was impressed and replied, "God be with you," his voice full of passion. This hushed situation had irritated him. When the Meccans learned about it, they sent a group to pursue it. This group got as far as the sea, but the Muslims had already left. They agreed to send a mission to Abyssinia to incite the monarch against the refugees and encourage him to deliver them up to Meccans again after failing to seize them. 'Amr bin al-'Asra, one of the delegates, subsequently converted to Islam and conquered Egypt. The party traveled to Abyssinia, where they met the monarch and were fascinated with his court. But the king stood fast, and despite the pressure from the Meccan delegation and his own courtiers, he refused to hand over the Muslim refugees to their persecutors. The party returned disheartened, but they quickly devised another plot in Mecca to compel the return of Muslims from Abyssinia. They spread the rumor that all of Mecca had joined Islam among the caravans heading to Abyssinia. When the rumor reached Abyssinia, many Muslim exiles rejoiced and returned to Mecca, only to discover that the story had been fabricated. Some Muslims returned to Abyssinia, while others chose to remain. Among them was 'Uthman bin Maz'unra, son of a powerful Meccan lord. 'Uthmanra started to live in peace after receiving protection from a friend of his father, Walid bin Mughira. But he witnessed that other Muslims were still being brutally persecuted. It irritated him greatly. He went to Walid and asked for his protection back. He believed he shouldn't have such security when other Muslims suffered. Walid informed the Meccans of this.

Labid, Arabia's poet-laureate, sat among the leaders of Mecca one day, reading his poem. He read a passage that said that all graces must eventually expire. 'Uthmanra boldly contradicted him, saying, "The graces of Paradise will be everlasting." Labid, who was not used to such contradictions, became enraged and exclaimed, "Quraish, your guests have never been insulted like this before; whence has this fashion begun?" To appease Labid, a man from the audience rose and said, "Go on and take no notice of this fool." 'Uthman bin Maz'unra insisted that he had said nothing foolish, which enraged the Quraishite, who sprang upon 'Uthmanra and gave him a sharp blow, knocking out an eye. Walid was present at the scene. He could not endure such treatment of his deceased friend's son, but 'Uthmanra was no longer under his formal protection, and Arab custom now forbade him to take sides.

protection. You should be grateful to yourself."

'Uthman ra responded,'

"I've yearned for this. I don't mourn the loss of one eye since the other is on its way to the same destiny. Remember, we seek no peace while the Prophet (s.a.w) suffers" (Halbiyya, Vol. 1, P. 348).

'UMARra ACCEPTED ISLAM'

Another significant event occurred around this time. 'Umarra, who later became the Second Khalifah of Islam, was still one of Islam's fiercest and most feared enemies. He felt that no effective steps had yet been taken against the new Movement and decided to end the Prophet's (s.a.w) life. He took his sword and set out. A friend was puzzled to see him going and asked where he was going and with what intent. "To kill Muhammad (s.a.w)," said 'Umarra.

"But will you be secure from his people now?" And how well do you know how things are going? Do you know your sister and her spouse have converted to Islam?"

It came like a bolt from the blue and greatly upset 'Umarra. He decided to go and have done with his sister and her husband first. As he reached their house he heard a recitation going on inside. The voice was that of Khabbabra who was teaching them the Holy Book. 'Umarra entered the house swiftly. Khabbabra, alarmed by the hurried steps, had already hid himself. 'Umar'sra sister, Fatimara, put away the leaves of the Qur'an. Confronting her and her husband,

'Umarra said, "I hear you have renounced your own faith," and, saying this, he raised his hand to strike her husband, who was incidentally his own cousin. Fatimara threw herself between 'Umarra and her husband; so 'Umar'sra hand fell on Fatima'sra face and struck her on the nose, from which blood flowed freely. The blow made Fatimara all the braver. She said, "Yes, we are Muslims now and shall remain so; do what you may." 'Umarra was a brave man, though rough. His sister's face, dyed red by his own hand, filled him with remorse. Soon he was a changed man. He asked to be shown those leaves of the Qur'an they were reading from. Fatimara refused lest he should tear them up and throw them away. 'Umarra promised not to do so. But, said Fatimara, he was not clean. 'Umarra offered to have a bath. Clean and cooled, he took the leaves of the Qur'an in his hand. They contained a portion of the Chapter Ta Ha. And he came upon the verses:

"I am Allah, and there is no other God save Me." So serve Me and remember Me via prayer. Surely, the Hour is approaching, and I will make it known, so that every soul may be repaid for its efforts" (20:15, 16).

The firm assertion of God's existence, the clear promise that Islam would soon establish genuine worship in place of the customary one in Mecca—these and a slew of other related ideas had to have moved 'Umarra. Faith welled up in his heart, and he exclaimed, "How wonderful, how inspiring!"" Khabbabra emerged from his hiding place and said, "God is my testimony, just yesterday I heard the Prophet (s.a.w) plead for 'Umarra's conversion."

'Amr ibn Hisham,' he says. 'Umar'sra mind was made up. He asked where the Prophet (s.a.w) was and made straight for him at Dari Arqam, his bare sword still in hand. As he knocked at the door, the Prophet (s.a.w) Companions could see 'Umarra through the crevices. They feared lest he should have some evil design. But the Prophet (s.a.w) said, "Let him come in." 'Umarra entered, sword in hand."Prophet (s.a.w) of God," said 'Umarra, "I am here to become a Muslim." Allahu Akbar, cried the Prophet (s.a.w). Allahu Akbar, cried the Companions. The hills around Mecca echoed the cries. News of the conversion spread like wildfire, and from then on, 'Umarra, the much-feared persecutor of Islam, himself began to be persecuted along with other Muslims.

PERSECUTION INCREASES

Persecution became more and more serious and more unbearable. Many Muslims had already left Mecca. Those who stayed behind had to suffer more than ever before. But Muslims swerved not a bit from the path they had chosen. Their hearts were as stout as ever, their faith as steadfast. Their devotion to the One God was on the increase and so was their hatred for the national idols of Mecca. The conflict had become more serious than ever. The Meccans convened another big meeting. At this they resolved on an all-out boycott of the Muslims: The Meccans were to have no normal dealings with Muslims. They were neither to buy from them, nor to sell them anything. The Prophet (s.a.w), his family and a number of relations who, though not Muslims, still stood by him, were compelled to take shelter in a lonely place, a possession of Abu Talib. Without money, without means and without reserves, the Prophet's (s.a.w) family and relations suffered untold hardships under this blockade. For three years there was no slackening of it. Then at last, five decent members of the enemy revolted against these conditions. They went to the blockaded family, offered to annul the boycott, and asked the family to come out. Abu Talib came out and reproved his people. The revolt of the five became known all over Mecca, but good feeling asserted itself again, and Meccans decided they must cancel the savage boycott. The boycott was over, but not its consequences. In a few days the Prophet's (s.a.w) faithful wife, KHADIJA(ra), met her death, and a month later his uncle, Abu Talib.

The Holy Prophet (s.a.w) had now lost the companionship and support of KHADIJA(ra), and he and the Muslims had lost the good offices of Abu Talib. Their passing away naturally also resulted in the loss of some general sympathy. Abu Lahab, another uncle of the Prophet (s.a.w), seemed ready at first to side with the Prophet (s.a.w). The shock of his brother's death and regard for his dying wish were still fresh in his mind. But the Meccans soon succeeded in antagonizing him. They made use of the usual appeals. The Prophet (s.a.w) taught that disbelief in the Oneness of God was an offence, punishable in the Hereafter; his teaching contradicted everything they had learnt from their forefathers, and so on. Abu Lahab decided to oppose the Prophet (s.a.w) more than ever. Relations between Muslims and Meccans had become strained. A three-year boycott and blockade had enlarged the gulf between them. Meeting and preaching seemed impossible. The Prophet (s.a.w) did not mind the illtreatment and the persecution; these were nothing so long as he had the chance to meet and address people. But now it seemed that he had no such chance in Mecca. General antagonism apart, the Prophet (s.a.w) now found it impossible to appear in any street or public place. If he did, they threw dust at him and sent him back to his house. Once he returned home, his head covered with dust. A daughter wept as she removed the dust. The Prophet (s.a.w) told her not to weep for God was with him. Ill-treatment did not upset the Prophet (s.a.w). He even welcomed it as evidence of interest in his Message. One day, for instance, the Meccans by a general intrigue said nothing to him nor did they ill-treat him in any way. The Prophet (s.a.w) retired home disappointed, until the reassuring voice of God made him go to his people

again.

THE PROPHET SA VISITS TA'IF

It seemed that in Mecca now nobody would listen to him and this made him sad. He felt he was stagnating. So he decided to turn elsewhere for the preaching of his Message, and he chose Ta'if, a small town about sixty miles to the south-east of Mecca and famed for its fruit and its agriculture. The Prophet's (s.a.w) decision was in keeping with the traditions of all Prophet (s.a.w)s. Mosesas turned now to the Pharaoh, now to Israel, and now to Midian. Jesusas, similarly, turned now to Galilee, now to places across the Jordan, and now to Jerusalem. So the Holy Prophet (s.a.w) of Islam, finding that Meccans would illtreat but not listen, turned to Ta'if. In polytheistic beliefs and practices Ta'if was not behind Mecca. The idols to be found in the Ka'ba were not the only, nor the only important, idols in Arabia. One important idol, al-Lat, was to be found in Ta'if; because of it Ta'if also was a centre of pilgrimage. The inhabitants of Ta'if were connected with those of Mecca by ties of blood; and many green spots between Ta'if and Mecca were owned by Meccans. On arrival at Ta'if, the Prophet (s.a.w) had visits from its chiefs but none seemed willing to accept the Message. The rank and file obeyed their leaders and dismissed the teaching with contempt. This was not unusual. People immersed in worldly affairs always regard such a Message as something of an interference and even an offence. Because the Message is without visible support—such as numbers or arms—they also feel they can dismiss it with contempt. The Prophet (s.a.w) was no exception. Reports of him had already reached Ta'if, and here he now was, without arms or following, a lone individual with only one companion, Zaid (ra). The towns folk thought him a nuisance which should be ended, if only to please their chiefs. They set vagabonds of the town and street boys at him who pelted him with stones and drove him out of the town. Zaid (ra) was wounded and the Prophet (s.a.w) began to bleed profusely. But the pursuit continued until this defenceless party of two was several miles out of Ta'if. The Prophet (s.a.w) was sorely grieved and dejected when an angel descended upon him and asked if he would like his persecutors to be destroyed. "No," said the Prophet (s.a.w). "I hope that of these very tormentors would be born those who would worship the One True God." (Bukhari, Kitab Bad'ul-

Khalq.)

Exhausted and dejected, he stopped at a vineyard owned by two Meccans who happened to be present. They were among his persecutors at Mecca, but on this occasion they became sympathetic. Was it because a Meccan had been ill-treated by the people of Ta'if, or was it because a spark of human kindness suddenly glowed in their hearts? They sent to the Prophet (s.a.w) a tray full of grapes with a Christian slave, 'Addasra by name and belonging to Nineveh. 'Addasra presented the tray to the Prophet (s.a.w) and his companion.

While he looked wistfully at them, he became more curious than ever when he heard the Prophet (s.a.w) say, "In the name of Allah, the Gracious, the Merciful." His Christian background was enlivened and he felt he was in the presence of a Hebrew Prophetas. The Prophet (s.a.w) asked him where he belonged and 'Addasra said Nineveh, upon which the Prophet (s.a.w) said, "Jonahas, son of Amittai, who belonged to Nineveh, was a holy man, a Prophet like me." The Prophet (s.a.w) also told 'Addasra of his own Message. 'Addasra felt charmed and believed at once. He embraced the Prophet (s.a.w) with tears in his eyes and started kissing his head, hands and feet. The meeting over, the Prophet (s.a.w) turned again to Allah and said:

Allah, I submit my complaint to Thee. I am weak and without means. My people look down on me. Thou art Lord of the poor and the weak, and Thou art my Lord. To whom wilt Thou abandon me—to strangers who push me around or to the enemy who oppresses me in my own town? If Thou art not angered at me, I care not for my enemy. Thy mercy be with me. I seek refuge in the light of Thy face.

Having said this prayer, he set back for Mecca. He stopped en route at Nakhla for a few days and set out again. According to Meccan tradition he was no longer a citizen of Mecca. He had left it because he thought it hostile and could not return to it except with the permission of the Meccans. Accordingly, he sent word to Mut'im bin 'Adi—a Meccan chief, to ask if Meccans would permit him to come back. Mut'im, though as bitter an enemy as any other, possessed nobility of heart. He collected his sons and relatives. Arming themselves, they went to the Ka'ba. Standing in the courtyard he announced he was permitting the Prophet (s.a.w) to return. The Prophet (s.a.w) then returned, and made a circuit of the Ka'ba. Mut'im, his sons and relatives, with swords unsheathed, then escorted the Prophet (s.a.w) to his house. It was not protection in the customary Arabian sense which had been extended to the Prophet (s.a.w). The Prophet (s.a.w) continued to suffer and Mut'im did not shield him. Mut'im's act amounted to a declaration of formal permission for the Prophet (s.a.w) to

return.

Even the adversaries of Islam have praised the Prophet's (s.a.w) voyage to Ta'if, as Sir William Muir says in his history of the Prophet (s.a.w) (referring to the travel to Ta'if):

There is something lofty and heroic about Muhammad (s.a.w)'s journey to At-Ta'if; a solitary man, despised and rejected by his own people, going boldly forth in the name of God, like Jonah to Nineveh, and summoning an idolatrous city to repent and support his mission; it sheds a strong light on his intensity of belief in the divine origin of his calling (Life of Muhammad (s.a.w) by Sir W. Muir, 1923 edition, pp.

The Prophet's (s.a.w) home town became hell for him again, but he persisted in telling people of his Message. The formula, "God is One," began to be heard here and there. With love and regard, and a sense of fellow-feeling, the Prophet (s.a.w) persisted in the exposition of his Message. People turned away, but he addressed them again and again. He made his proclamation, whether the people cared or not, and persistence seemed to pay.

Meanwhile, revelations received by the Prophet (s.a.w) began to hint at the near possibility of migration from Mecca. Some idea of where they were to migrate to was also given to him. It was a town of wells and dategroves. He thought of Yamama, but quickly dismissed the thought. He then waited in the assurance that whatever place they were destined to go to would undoubtedly become the cradle of Islam.

ISLAM EXTENDS TO THE MEDINA

The annual Hajj drew near, and from all parts of Arabia pilgrims began to arrive in Mecca. The Prophet (s.a.w) went wherever he found a group of people, expounded to them the idea of One God and told them to give up excesses of all kinds and prepare for the Kingdom of God. Some listened and became interested. Some wished to listen but were sent away by the Meccans. Some who had already made up their minds, stopped to ridicule. The Prophet (s.a.w) was in the valley of Mina when he saw a group of six or seven people. He found that they belonged to the Khazraj tribe, one in alliance with the Jews. He asked them if they would listen to what he had to say. They had heard of him and were interested; so they agreed. The Prophet (s.a.w) spent some time telling them that the Kingdom of God was at hand, that idols were going to disappear, that the idea of One God was due to triumph, and piety and purity were once again going to rule. Would they not, in Medina, welcome the Message? The group became much impressed. They accepted the Message and promised, on their return to Medina, to confer with others and report next year whether Medina would be willing to receive Muslim refugees from Mecca. They returned and conferred with their friends and relations. There were, at the time, two Arab and three Jewish tribes at Medina. The Arab tribes were the Aus and the Khazraj and the Jewish tribes the Banu Quraiza, the Banu Nadir, and the Banu Qainuqa'. The Aus and the Khazraj were at war. The Quraiza and the Nadir were in alliance with the Aus and the Qainuqa' with the Khazraj. Tired of unending warfare, they were inclined to peace. At last they agreed to acknowledge the Khazraj Chief, 'Abdullah bin Ubayy bin Salul, as King of Medina. From the Jews, the Aus and the Khazraj had heard of prophecies in the Bible. They had heard Jewish tales of the lost glory of Israel and of the advent of a Prophet (s.a.w) "like unto Mosesas." This advent was near at hand, the Jews used to say. It was to mark the return to power of Israel and the destruction of their enemies. When the people of Medina heard of the Prophet (s.a.w), they became impressed and began to ask if this Meccan Prophet (s.a.w) was not the Prophet (s.a.w) they had heard of from the Jews. Many young men readily believed. At the next Hajj twelve men from Medina came to Mecca to join the Prophet (s.a.w). Ten of these belonged to the Khazraj and two to the Aus tribe. They met the Prophet (s.a.w) in the valley of Mina and, holding the Prophet's (s.a.w) hand, solemnly declared their belief in the Oneness of God and their resolve to abstain from all common evils, from infanticide, and from making false accusations against one another. They also resolved to obey the Prophet (s.a.w) in all good things. When they returned to Medina, they started telling others of their New Faith. Zeal increased. Idols were taken out of their niches and thrown on the streets. Those who used to bow before images began to hold their heads high. They resolved to bow to none except the One God. The Jews wondered. Centuries of friendship, exposition and debate had failed to produce the change which this Meccan Teacher had produced in a few days. The people of Medina would go to the few Muslims in their midst and make inquiries about Islam. But the few Muslims could not cope with the large numbers of inquiries, nor did they know enough. They decided, therefore, to address a request to the Prophet (s.a.w) to send them some one to teach Islam. The Prophet (s.a.w) agreed to send Mus'abra, one of the Muslims who had been in Abyssinia. Mus'abra was the first missionary of Islam to go out of Mecca. At about this time, the Prophet (s.a.w) had a grand promise from God. He had a vision in which he saw that he was in Jerusalem and Prophets had joined behind him in congregational worship. Jerusalem only meant Medina, which was going to become the centre of the worship of the One God. Other Prophets congregating behind the Prophet (s.a.w) of Islam meant that men following different Prophets would join Islam, and Islam would thus become a universal religion.

Conditions in Mecca had deteriorated to the point that persecution had taken on its most heinous form. Meccans scoffed at this vision, dismissing it as wishful thinking, unaware that the foundations of the New Jerusalem had been constructed.

Nations of the East and West were agog, wanting to hear God's Last Great Message. In those days, the Kaiser and the Chosroes of Iran went to war. Chosroes was victorious. Syria and Palestine were overrun by Iranian armies. Jerusalem was destroyed. Egypt and Asia Minor were mastered. Iranian Generals were able to pitch their tents at the mouth of the Bosphorus, only ten miles from Constantinople.

revelation:

The Romans have been defeated in nearby territory, and they will be victorious in a few years—Allah's command before and after that—and on that day will the believers rejoice with Allah's help. He helps whom He pleases; and He is the Mighty, the Merciful. Allah has made this promise. Allah does not break His promise, but most men do not know (30: 3-7).

The prophecy was fulfilled in a few years, when the Romans defeated the Iranians and reclaimed the territories they had lost to them. The part of the prophecy that said, "On that day the believers shall rejoice with the help of God," was also fulfilled, and Islam began to advance. The Meccans believed they had put an end to it by convincing people not to listen to Muslims, but to show active hostility instead.

"Why doesn't he bring us a Sign from his Lord?" they ask."Has not the clear evidence come to them in what is contained in the previous books? And if We had destroyed them before it, they would have surely said, "Our Lord, why didst Thou not send to us a Messenger that we might have followed Thy commandments before we were humbled and disgraced?""Say, "Everyone is waiting; so, wait, and you will know who is on the straight road and who follows real direction" (20: 134-136).

The Meccans complained about a lack of Signs, and they were told that the prophecies about Islam and the Prophet (s.a.w) recorded in earlier books should suffice. Had the Meccans been destroyed before the Message of Islam could be explained to them, they would have complained about a lack of opportunity to consider the Signs.

Every day, revelations promising victory for believers and defeat for unbelievers were received. When the Meccans saw their own power and prosperity and the powerlessness and poverty of Muslims, and then heard of the Prophet's (s.a.w) daily revelations promising divine help and Muslim victories, they wondered and wondered. Were they insane, or was the Prophet (s.a.w) ?

And it is not the word of a poet; little is it that you believe; nor is it the utterance of a soothsayer; little is it that you heed. It is a revelation from the Lord of the worlds. And if he had forged any sayings in Our name, We would surely have seized him by the right hand, and then surely would We have severed his life-artery, and not one oath.

The Prophet (s.a.w) was not a poet, a soothsayer, or a pretender. The Qur'an was a reading for the pious. True, it had its detractors, but it also had its secret admirers, those who were jealous of its teaching and truths. The promises and prophecies contained in it would all be fulfilled. The Prophet (s.a.w) was asked to ignore all opposition and continue celebrating his Mighty God.

The third Hajj arrived, and among the pilgrims from Medina was a large party of Muslims. Due to Meccan opposition, these Muslims from Medina wished to see the Prophet (s.a.w) in private. The Prophet's (s.a.w) own thoughts were turning more and more to Medina, as a likely place for migration. He mentioned this to his closest relatives, but they tried to dissuade him from all thoughts of this kind.

AQABA'S FIRST PLEDGE

After midnight, the Prophet (s.a.w) met the Muslims from Medina in the valley of 'Aqaba for the second time. His uncle 'Abbasra accompanied him. Seventy-three Muslims from Medina were present, sixty-two of them belonged to the Khazraj tribe and eleven to the Aus. Ummi 'Ammarara of the Banu Najjar was one among the ladies in the party. Mus'abra had taught them Islam, and they were full of faith and resolve. They all proven to be Islamic pillars. Ummi 'Ammarara is one such case. She instilled in her children an unwavering devotion to Islam. In an encounter after the Prophet's (s.a.w) death, one of her sons, Habibra, was taken prisoner by Musailima, the Pretender. Musailima attempted to shake Habib'sra faith. "Do you think Muhammad (s.a.w) is a God-sent Messenger?" he inquired. "Yes," was the response. "Do you think I am a Messenger of God?" Musailima inquired. "No," Habibra answered. Musailima then ordered that one of his limbs be severed. After then, he questioned Habibra again, "Do you think Muhammad (s.a.w) is a Messenger of God?" "Yes," Habibra responded. "Do you think I am a Messenger of God?" Musailima demanded that another limb be severed from Habib'sra's corpse. Habib'sra's corpse was reduced to several parts as limb after limb was severed in this manner. He died in a harsh way, but he left an indelible example of personal courage and sacrifice for religious faith (Halbiyya, Vol. 2, p. 17).

Ummi 'Ammarara fought with the Prophet (s.a.w) in various conflicts.

In summary, these group of Medina Muslims achieved significant reputation for their commitment and religion. They traveled to Mecca not for riches, but for faith, and they found it in abundance.

'Abbasra addressed the guests, moved by familial connections and feeling genuinely responsible for the Prophet (s.a.w)'s safety:

This my connection is regarded here by his people, O Khazraj. Despite the fact that they are not all Muslims, they defend him. But he has decided to leave us and come to you. Do you know what will happen, Khazraj? Arabia as a whole will be against you. If you understand the hazards involved in your invitation, take him away; if you do not, abandon your objective and let him remain.

Al-Bara'ra, the party's head, responded confidently:

We did hear you. Our resolve is unwavering. God's Prophet (s.a.w) have control over our life. We have made our choice and are merely waiting for his decision (Halbiyya, Vol. 2, p. 18).

The Prophet (s.a.w) provided a more detailed explanation of Islam and its teachings. He explained this by telling the group that he would travel to Medina if they would value Islam as much as they valued their wives and children. He hadn't finished when this group of seventy-three followers yelled, 'Yes,' 'Yes,' in unison. They overlooked that they may be overheard in their haste. 'Abbasra warned them to keep their voices down. However, the celebration was full of hope. Death has become insignificant in their eyes. When 'Abbasra warned the group, one of them said, "We are not scared, O Prophet of Godsa; permit us, and we may deal with the Meccans right now and punish the wrongs they have done you," but the Prophet (s.a.w) responded he had not yet been instructed to battle.

The conference was then adjourned after the party took the oath of fidelity.

The Meccans were made aware of this meeting. They proceeded to the Medina encampment to report to their leaders about these guests. 'Abdullah bin Ubbayy bin Salul, the Chief of Chiefs, had no idea what had transpired. He told the Meccans that it had to be a rumor they had heard. Medina's followers had embraced him as their leader and could not act without his knowledge and approval. He had no idea that the people of Medina had rejected Satan's reign in favor of God's government.

THE HIJRA FORMULA

The group returned to Medina, and the Prophet (s.a.w) and his supporters began to plan their exodus. Family after family started to vanish. Muslims were full of bravery because they believed the Kingdom of God was close. During the course of a night, a whole lane may be empty. When Meccans saw the doors sealed in the morning, they realized the people had moved to Medina. They were astounded by Islam's rising impact.

Except for a few slave converts and the Prophet (s.a.w), Abu Bakrra, and 'Alira, not a single Muslim remained in Mecca. The Meccans were aware that their victim was preparing to flee. The chiefs gathered again and resolved to slay the Prophet (s.a.w). It seems that the day they set for executing the Prophet (s.a.w) was also set for his escape by a particular divine purpose. The Prophet (s.a.w) was moving away in the middle of the night as the Meccan group gathered in front of the Prophetssa's home with the aim to murder. The Prophet (s.a.w) must have been terrified of the Meccans' evil plan. They moved slowly, and when the Prophet (s.a.w) himself went by, they mistook him for someone else and retreated to avoid being spotted. Abu Bakrra, the Prophet's (s.a.w) closest companion, had been notified of the Prophet's (s.a.w) intention the day before. He dutifully joined, and they both left Mecca for a cave called Thaur, approximately three or four miles away across a hill. When the Meccans learned of the Prophet's (s.a.w)'s escape, they gathered and sent an army to pursue him. They arrived in Thaur, led by a tracker. The tracker, who was standing at the entrance of the cave where the Prophet (s.a.w) and Abu Bakrra were hiding, said that Muhammad (s.a.w) was either in the cave or had gone to heaven. When Abu Bakrra heard this, his heart sunk. "The enemy is almost on us," he said quietly. "Fear not, God is with us," the Prophet (s.a.w) said. "I worry not for myself, but for you," Abu Bakrra said, "because if I die, I am just an ordinary mortal; but if you die, it will mean the loss of religion and soul" (Zurqani). "Even so, worry not," the Prophet (s.a.w) comforted them, "we are not two in this cave; there is a third—God." (Bukhari).

Meccan despotism was doomed to fail. Islam was to be given an opportunity to develop. The pursuers had been duped. They mocked the tracker's decision. They stated it was too open a cave for anybody to seek refuge in, since it was infested with snakes and vipers. They could have seen the two if they had only bowed their heads slightly. But they didn't, and after dismissing the tracker, they went back to work. Mecca.

The Prophet (s.a.w) and Abu Bakrra waited in the cave for two days. According to the plan, two fleet camels were brought to the cave on the third night, one for the Prophet (s.a.w) and the guide, and the other for Abu Bakrra and his servant, 'Amir bin Fuhairara.

SURAQA GOES AFTER THE PROPHET

Before leaving, the Prophet (s.a.w) returned their gaze to Mecca. His heart was filled with emotions. His birthplace was Mecca. He had lived there as a kid and a man, and there he had received the Divine Call. It was where his ancestors had lived and thrived since the time of Ishmael. With these thoughts, he took one last long look at it and said, "Mecca, thou art dearer to me than any other place in the world, but thy people would not let me live here." Abu Bakrra responded, "The place hath turned out its Prophet (s.a.w). It only awaiteth its destruction." A hundred camels would be awarded to whomever seized and returned to the Meccans the Prophet (s.a.w) or Abu Bakrra, dead or alive. The news was made to the tribes in the vicinity of Mecca. Suraqa bin Malikra, a Bedouin leader, set off in pursuit of the company, eventually seeing them on the route to Medina. He noticed two riding camels and urged his horse, certain they were carrying the Prophet (s.a.w) and Abu Bakrra. Suraqara fell with the horse as it reared and fell before it had gone very far. Suraqa'sra's version of events is intriguing. He states:

After falling off the horse, I consulted my luck in the superstitious manner typical among Arabs by throwing arrows. The arrows predicted bad luck. However, the lure of the prize was strong. I remounted and began my chase, almost overtaking the group. The Prophet (s.a.w) rode proudly and without looking behind. Abu Bakrra, on the other hand, kept looking back (obviously out of concern for the Prophet (s.a.w)'s safety). My horse reared again as I approached them, and I tumbled off. I checked the arrows again, and they again predicted bad luck. My horse's hooves dug into the sand. It felt tough to mount again and resume the chase. The celebration was then under heavenly protection, I realized. I yelled at them and begged them to stop. When I got close enough, I informed them about my bad aim and my change of heart. I informed them that I was abandoning the chase and going home. The Prophet (s.a.w) let me leave but made me pledge not to tell anybody about their location. I grew sure that the Prophet (s.a.w) was the genuine article, doomed to success. I asked the Prophet (s.a.w) to write me a peace promise to serve me when he became ruler. The Prophet (s.a.w) requested that 'Amir bin Fuhairara write me a guarantee, which he did. As I prepared to return with it, the Prophet (s.a.w) received a vision of the future and said, "Suraqara, how wilt thou feel with the gold bangles of the Chosroes on thy wrists?" Astounded by the prophecy, I asked, "Which Chosroes? Chosroes bin Hormizd, the Emperor of Iran?"

The prophesy was literally fulfilled sixteen or seventeen years later. Suraqara converted to Islam and traveled to Medina. After the Propheta died, first Abu Bakrra and later 'Umarra became the Khalifahs of Islam. The increasing popularity of Islam made the Iranians envious, leading them to attack the Muslims, but instead of subjugating the Muslims, they were enslaved by them. The Muslims conquered Iran's capital, capturing its wealth, notably the gold bangles worn by the Chosroes during State events. Suraqara used to recount his pursuit of the Prophet (s.a.w) and his party after his conversion, as well as what happened between him and the Prophet (s.a.w). When the trophies of battle from the fight with Iran were laid in front of 'Umarra, he saw the gold bangles and recalled what the Prophet (s.a.w) had instructed Suraqara. It was a big forecast made in the midst of complete hopelessness. 'Umarra resolved to put on a public display of the prophecy's fulfillment. As a result, he summoned Suraqara and instructed him to put on the gold bangles. Suraqara objected, claiming that Islam forbade males from wearing gold. 'Umarra said that this was correct, but that this was an exception. The Prophet (s.a.w) had predicted Chosroes' gold bangles on his wrists, therefore he had to wear them now, even if it meant facing punishment. Suraqara was opposing out of regard to the Prophet's (s.a.w) teaching; otherwise, he was just as anxious as everyone else to bring visual confirmation of the big prophecy's fulfillment. He put on the bangles, and Muslims saw the fulfillment of the prophesy (Usud al-Ghaba). Prophet (s.a.w), the fugitive, had become king. He was no longer a part of this planet. Those who succeeded him, on the other hand, could see his words and dreams come true.

THE PROPHET (S.A.W) LANDS IN MEDINA

To return to our Hijra tale. After dismissing Suraqara, the Prophet (s.a.w) resumed his trip to Medina unmolested. When the Prophet (s.a.w) arrived at Medina, he found the people excitedly waiting for him. A more fortuitous day could not have arrived. The sun, which had risen for Mecca, had instead arrived to light on Medina.

They had heard that the Prophet (s.a.w) had left Mecca and were anticipating his arrival. They searched for him for kilometers outside of Medina. They went in the morning and returned in the evening dejected. When the Prophet (s.a.w) finally arrived at Medina, he opted to rest for a time in Quba, a neighboring town. When a Jew saw the two camels, he assumed they were conveying the Prophet (s.a.w) and his Companions. Everyone in Medina who heard this call hastened to Quba, while the inhabitants of Quba, pleased at the appearance of the Prophet (s.a.w) in their midst, sung songs in his honor.

An occurrence that occurred at this period in Quba exemplifies the Prophet (s.a.w)'s complete simplicity. The Prophet (s.a.w) had never been seen by the majority of the people in Medina.

Many of them mistook Abu Bakrra for the Prophet (s.a.w) when they spotted his entourage seated beneath a tree. Although younger, Abu Bakrra had a greyer beard and was better clothed than the Prophet (s.a.w). So they turned to him and sat in front of him, after giving him the Prophet (s.a.w)'s obeisance. When Abu Bakrra realized he was being misidentified as the Prophet (s.a.w), he rose, got his cloak, and hung it against the sun, saying, "Prophet (s.a.w) of God, you are in the sun; I create this shade for you" (Bukhari). He explained their mistake to tourists from Medina with tact and civility. The Prophet (s.a.w) halted in Quba for 10 days before being taken to Medina by the people of Medina. When he arrived in town, he saw that everyone, men, women, and children, had gathered to greet him. Among the songs they performed were:

The fourteenth night's moon has risen on us from behind al-Wida'. It is required upon us to praise God as long as we have someone in our midst who invites us to God. We submit our entire obedience to you, whom God has given to us (Halbiyya).

The Prophet (s.a.w) did not approach Medina from the east. When the people of Medina referred to him as a "moon of the fourteenth night," they were referring to the fact that they had been living in the dark until the Prophet (s.a.w) arrived to shine his light on them. The Prophet (s.a.w) arrived at Medina on a Monday. It was a Monday when he left the cave Thaur, and, strangely enough, it was a Monday when he took Mecca 10 years later.

AS PROPHET'S (S.A.W) HOST, ABU AYYUB ANSARIʀᴀ

Everyone wanted to be the Prophet (s.a.w)'s host in Medina while he was there. Families would form a queue to greet him as his camel went through a lane. "Here we are with our homes, our property, and our lives to receive you and to offer you our protection; come and live with us," they would say in unison. Politely, the Prophet (s.a.w) would reject, saying, "Leave my camel alone; she is under God's order; she will stop where God wants her to stop." Eventually, it came to a rest at a Banu Najjar tribal orphanage. The Prophet (s.a.w) dismounted and inquired, "It seems that here is where God wants us to halt." A trustee for the orphans stepped forward and gave the Prophet (s.a.w) the location. The Prophet (s.a.w) said that he would not accept the offer until he could pay for it. A price was agreed upon, and the Prophet (s.a.w) decided to construct a mosque and some dwellings on it. After then, the Prophet (s.a.w) inquired as to who resided closest to the place. Abu Ayyub Ansarira stood up and claimed that his home was the closest and that the Prophet's (s.a.w) might utilize his services. The Prophet (s.a.w) requested that he create a place for him in his home. The residence of Abu Ayyub was two-story. He donated the top level to the Prophet (s.a.w). However, the Prophet (s.a.w) favored the lowest story for the comfort of his guests.

The loyalty of the people of Medina to the Prophet (s.a.w) shown itself once again. Abu Ayyubra consented to allow the Prophet (s.a.w) take the bottom story, but refused to sleep on the floor where the Prophet (s.a.w) dwelt. It was considered impolite by him and his wife. A pitcher of water was shattered by mistake, and water spilled on the floor. Fearing that some water might leak into the Prophet (s.a.w)'s chamber, Abu Ayyubra grabbed his blanket and dried up the water before it could leak through. In the morning, he summoned the Prophet (s.a.w) and recounted the events of the previous night, after which the Prophet (s.a.w) decided to inhabit the top floor. Abu Ayyubra cooked and delivered meals. The Prophet (s.a.w) ate whatever he pleased, and Abu Ayyubra ate whatever was left. Others requested a portion of the Prophet (s.a.w)'s entertainment after a few days. Until the Prophet (s.a.w) moved into his own home and established his own arrangements, he was entertained in turn by the people of Medina. Anasra, a widow's sole kid, was around eight or nine years old. She took the kid to the Prophet (s.a.w) and presented him as a personal service to the Prophetssa. This Anasra was commemorated throughout

Islamic history. He became a highly knowledgeable and wealthy guy. He lived to be over a hundred years old and was well regarded by everybody throughout the Khalifah period. According to Anasra, despite the fact that he joined the Prophet (s.a.w)'s service as a youngster and stayed with him until the Prophet (s.a.w) died, the Prophet (s.a.w) never spoke unkindly to him, never admonished him, and never assigned him a task that was too difficult for him to do. Only Anasra accompanied the Prophet (s.a.w) throughout his stay in Medina. Thus, Anasra's account depicts the Prophet's (s.a.w) character as it grew throughout his expanding influence and riches in Medina.

Later, the Prophet (s.a.w) sent Zaid (ra), his freedman, to Mecca to retrieve his family and relatives. The abrupt and well-planned departure of the Prophet (s.a.w) and his entourage had stunned the Meccans. For a while, they did nothing to irritate him. When the Prophet's family and Abu Bakrra's family departed Mecca, they made no fuss. The two families arrived in Medina unharmed. Meanwhile, the Prophet (s.a.w) built the foundations of a mosque on land he had purchased for the purpose. He then constructed dwellings for himself and his companions. They took around seven months to complete.

LIFE IN MEDINA IS RISKY

The pagan tribes of Medina grew interested in Islam within a few days after the Prophet's arrival, and the bulk of them converted. Many others who were not convinced joined as well. In this manner, a group of people who were not Muslims in heart entered the fold of Islam. Its members had a very evil role in later history. Some of them converted to Islam. Others remained dishonest and appealing against Islam and Muslims. Some people refused to participate at all. They couldn't abide the New Faith's rising power, so they moved from Medina to Mecca. Medina was converted into a Muslim city. The worship of the One God was founded in it. There was no other town in the world that could make this claim at the time. It brought the Prophet (s.a.w) and his companions great satisfaction when, after a few days of their migration, a whole village opted to abandon idol worship in favor of worshiping the One Invisible God. But there was still no peace for Muslims. In Medina, a group of Arabs had only nominally converted to Islam. They were the Prophet (s.a.w)'s sworn foes on the inside. Then there were the Jews, who were always plotting against him. The Prophet (s.a.w) was well aware of these threats. He stayed vigilant and warned his friends and fans to be on the lookout. He often stayed up all night (Bari, Vol. 6, p. 60). Tired by his nightly watch, he once voiced a wish for assistance. He soon heard the sound of armor. "What is this?" he inquired. "It is Sa'd bin Waqqasra, O Prophet (s.a.w), who has arrived to serve as your guard" (Bukhari and Muslim). Medinans were aware of their enormous duty. They had asked the Prophet (s.a.w) to live among them, and it was now their responsibility to safeguard him. The tribes conferred and determined that each tribe would defend the Prophet's (s.a.w) residence in turn.

There was no difference between the Prophet's (s.a.w) life in Mecca and his life in Medina in terms of his personal safety and the lack of tranquility for his followers. The only distinction was that Muslims in Medina could pray in public in the mosque they had constructed in God's honor. They were able to gather for this purpose five times throughout the day without interruption.

It had been two or three months. The inhabitants of Mecca recovered from their confusion and began devising plans to annoy Muslims. They quickly discovered that just causing difficulty for Muslims in and around Mecca would not serve their aim. It was essential to assault the Prophet (s.a.w) and his followers in Medina and drive them from their new home. As a result, they wrote a letter to 'Abdullah bin Ubayy ibn Salul, a Medina leader who had been recognized as Medina's monarch by all parties before to the Prophet's arrival. They said in their letter that they were astonished by the Prophet's (s.a.w) appearance in Medina and that it was inappropriate for the people of Medina to provide him with sanctuary. Finally, they stated:

Now that you have accepted our adversary into your midst, we vow by God and announce that we, the people of Mecca, shall join an assault on Medina unless you, the people of Medina, agree to drive him out or battle him together. We shall slaughter all able-bodied males and enslave all women when we assault Medina (Abu Dawud, Kitab al-Kharaj).

'Abdullah bin Ubayy ibn Salul saw this letter as a miracle. He contacted other hypocrites in Medina and convinced them that allowing the Prophet (s.a.w) to live in peace among them would attract Mecca's anger. It was consequently incumbent upon them to wage war against the Prophet (s.a.w), if only to pacify the Meccans. The Prophet (s.a.w) became aware of this. He went to 'Abdullah bin Ubayy ibn Salul and attempted to persuade him that such an action would be suicidal. Many individuals in Medina had become Muslims and were willing to die for Islam. If 'Abdullah waged war against Muslims, the majority of Medinans would fight with them. A conflict like this would cost him dearly and lead to his own demise. This suggestion convinced 'Abdullah to abandon his ambitions.

The Prophet (s.a.w) made another significant advance at this period. He gathered the Muslims and proposed that every two Muslims be tied together like two brothers. The concept was well-received. Medinite was taken.

Meccan serves as his brother. The Muslims of Medina promised to share their possessions and goods with the Muslims of Mecca under this new brotherhood. One Medinite Muslim promised to divorce one of his two wives and marry her to his Meccan brother instead. Out of consideration for the needs of the Muslims of Medina, the Meccan Muslims refused to accept their proposals. However, the Muslims of Medina were adamant, and the matter had to be taken to the Prophet (s.a.w). The Muslims of Medina argued that since the Meccan Muslims were their brothers, they should share their possessions with them. The Meccan Muslims had little knowledge of land management. They could, however, share the land's output if not the property itself. The Meccan Muslims politely refused this very substantial offer, preferring to pursue their own commerce. Many Meccan Muslims recovered their fortunes. But Medina's Muslims never forgot their pledge to share their property with Meccan Muslims. There have been several occasions where a Medinite

When Muslim died, his sons split their estate with their Meccan brethren. For many years, the practice persisted until the Qur'an outlawed it via its instruction on inheritance partition (Bukhari and Muslim).

PACT BETWEEN VARIOUS MEDINA TRIBES

In addition to unifying Meccan and Medinite Muslims in brotherhood, the Holy Prophet (s.a.w) established a covenant between all Medinites. Arabs and Jews were unified into a shared citizenship with Muslims as a result of this covenant. The Prophet (s.a.w) stated to both Arabs and Jews that before the Muslims appeared as a group in Medina, there were only two groups, but now there were three. It was only natural for them to reach an agreement that would link them all and provide some sense of peace for all of them. Eventually, a deal was reached. The contract said:

Between the Prophet (s.a.w) of God and the Faithful on the one side, and all those who freely consent to enter on the other. If one of the Meccan Muslims is slain, the Meccan Muslims will be held accountable. They will also have responsibility for ensuring the release of their detainees. Similarly, the Muslim tribes of Medina will be held accountable for their own lives and those of their captives. Anyone who rebels or fosters hostility and chaos will be seen as a common enemy. It will be the responsibility of everyone else to fight him, even if he is a son or a close relative. If a believer kills a disbeliever in combat, his Muslim relatives will not seek vengeance. They will also not support nonbelievers against believers. Muslims will assist Jews who sign this vow. The Jews will not face any difficulties. Their adversaries will not be assisted in their fight against them. No disbeliever will give anybody from Mecca any quarter. He will not serve as a trustee for Meccan property. He will not fight in a conflict between Muslims and nonbelievers. If a believer is mistreated without justification, Muslims have the right to combat those who mistreat. If a shared adversary attacks Medina, the Jews will join with the Muslims and split the combat costs. The Jewish tribes, in agreement with the other tribes of Medina, shall enjoy privileges comparable to Muslims. The Jews will maintain their religion, and the Muslims will maintain theirs. The privileges enjoyed by Jews will be shared by their followers as well. The residents of Medina will not be able to declare war without the Prophet (s.a.w)'s permission. However, this does not exclude any person from avenging an individual injustice. The Jews will pay the costs of their own organization, as Muslims will shoulder the costs of their own. In the event of conflict, however, they will act as one. Those who join the pact will view Medina as precious and untouchable. Strangers who come under its citizens' protection shall be considered as citizens. However, the people of Medina will not admit a lady to citizenship without the approval of her relatives. All disagreements will be decided by God and the Prophet (s.a.w). The covenant's signatories will not be able to engage into any agreements with the Meccans or their allies. This is because the covenant's signatories have agreed to oppose their shared foes. In peace as well as in conflict, the parties will stay unified. No party will make a separate peace. However, no side will be forced to participate in a conflict. A party who goes overboard, on the other hand, will face a penalty. God is unquestionably the defender of the upright and the faithful, and Muhammad (s.a.w) is His Prophet (s.a.w).

(Hisham).

In summary, this is the covenant. It was created using bits discovered in historical sources. It underscores unequivocally that the guiding principles in resolving conflicts and disagreements between the parties at Medina were to be honesty, truth, and justice. Those that committed excesses were to be held accountable for their actions. The agreement makes it obvious that the Prophet (s.a.w) of Islam were committed to treat the other people of Medina with decency and compassion, and to consider and deal with them as brothers. If further disagreements and conflicts emerged, it was the duty of the

Jews.

As previously said, two or three months elapsed before Meccans could restart their premeditated animosity against Islam. Sa'd bin Mu'adhra, leader of the Aus tribe of Medina, gave an opportunity when he came in Mecca for the tour of the Ka'ba. "After giving protection to this apostate Muhammad (s.a.w), do you expect you can come to Mecca and circuit the Ka'ba in peace? Do you think you can protect and save him? I swear by God, you could not have returned safe to your family if it hadn't been for Abu Sufyanra."

"Take it from me, if you Meccans block us from going and circumnavigating the Ka'ba, you will have no peace on your way to Syria," Sa'd bin Mu'adhra said. Walid bin Mughira, a Meccan ruler, got critically sick about the same time. He realized his time had arrived. The other Mecca leaders were gathered. Walid couldn't stop himself from crying. The Meccan leaders were perplexed and inquired as to why he was sobbing. "Do you think I am scared of death? No, what I dread is that the Faith of Muhammad (s.a.w) will expand and even Mecca will fall under him." Abu Sufyanra told Walid that as long as they lived, they would combat the spread of this Faith with their life (Khamis, Vol. I).

MECCANS GETTING READY TO ATTACK MEDINA

This account of events clearly shows that the break in Meccan enmity was only short. Mecca's authorities were planning a fresh assault against Islam. Dying chiefs swore pledges of animosity against the Prophet (s.a.w) and stirred their survivors to battle against him and his supporters. The residents of Medina were asked to take up arms against the Muslims, and if they refused, the Meccans and their allied tribes would assault Medina, murder their males, and enslave their women. If the Prophet (s.a.w) had remained silent and done nothing to defend Medina, he would have had a grave responsibility. As a result, the Prophet (s.a.w) established a reconnaissance system. He sent men to the areas around Mecca to report on evidence of war preparations. There were occasional incidents—scuffles and fights—between these groups and Meccans. According to European sources, the Prophet (s.a.w) started these episodes, and as a result, he was the aggressor in the battles that followed. But we have thirteen years of Meccan oppression, their plots to turn the people of Medina against the Muslims, and the fear of an assault on Medina itself. Nobody who recalls all of this can hold the Prophet (s.a.w) responsible for starting these tragedies. If he sent out groups of Muslims for reconnaissance, it was for self-defense. Thirteen years of oppression were sufficient reason for Muslims to prepare for self-defense. If hostilities sprang out between them and their Meccan adversary, Muslims were not to blame. The shaky foundations on which Christian countries currently make war on one other are widely recognized. If the Meccans did half of what they did to Muslims now, they would feel justified in going to war. Does it not grant the victims the right to declare war when the people of one nation arrange the slaughter of another on a vast scale, or when one people forces another to flee their homes? After Muslims arrived in Medina, there was no need for them to launch war on the Meccans. However, the Prophet (s.a.w) proclaimed no war. He was patient and limited his defense actions to reconnaissance. The Meccans, on the other hand, continued to annoy and harass the Muslims. They infuriated the residents of Medina and interfered with their freedom to pilgrimage. They altered their usual caravan routes and began passing through tribal territories near Medina in order to incite the tribes against the Muslims. The peace of Medina was jeopardized, hence it was the clear duty of Muslims to accept the Meccans' fourteen-year-old challenge to battle. Nobody could doubt Muslims' right to accept this challenge under the circumstances.

While the Prophet (s.a.w) was busy reconnoitring, he did not forget his followers' routine and spiritual requirements in Medina. The vast majority of the people in Medina had become Muslims, both outwardly and inwardly. Some had merely joined by profession. As a result, the Prophet (s.a.w) began imposing the Islamic system of governance in his limited followers. Arabs used to resolve their conflicts with the sword and individual violence. The Prophet (s.a.w) instituted legal processes. Judges were chosen to resolve disputes filed by people or parties against one another. A claim was not allowed unless a court deemed it to be fair and truthful. In the past, intellectual pursuits were regarded with disdain. The Prophet (s.a.w) promoted literacy and a love of study. Those who could read and write were required to teach the same skills to others. Injustice and brutality were put a stop to. Women's rights were created. The wealthy were to pay for the poor's necessities and to improve Medina's social facilities. Workers were protected from exploitation. Arrangements were created for the appointment of trustees for weak and incapable heirs. Loan transactions started to be documented in writing. The significance of completing all tasks started to dawn on me. Excessive treatment of slaves was prohibited. Public cleanliness and hygiene started to get emphasis. A population census was conducted. Lanes and roadways were enlarged, and measures were made to maintain them clean. In summary, rules were enacted to promote an ideal family and social life. For the first time in their history, the wild Arabs were taught to the standards of courtesy and civilized living.

BADR'S BATTLE

While the Prophet (s.a.w) prepared for the practical establishment of rules that would benefit not just his own generation of Arabs, but all humanity for all time, the people of Mecca plotted for war. The Prophet (s.a.w) prepared a law that would provide peace, honor, and advancement to his own people and all others; his Meccan adversary plotted to destroy that law. The Meccan intentions culminated in the Battle of Badr. It was the eighth month after the Hijra. Abu Sufyanra was leading a merchant caravan returning from Syria. The Meccans formed a big army to defend the caravan and decided to carry it to Medina. These arrangements were made known to the Holy Prophet (s.a.w). He also received visions from God that the time had come to repay the adversary in his own currency. He left Medina with a large group of disciples. Nobody knew whether this Muslim group would have to battle the caravan from Syria or the army from Mecca at the moment. The group comprised about 300 people. A business caravan back then didn't only comprise of camels laden with goods. It also featured armed men who guarded and guided the caravan during its route. Since there had been tension between the Meccans and the Muslims of Medina, the Meccan commanders had began to take extra care in equipping the guard. Two further caravans came along this path not long before, according to history. Two hundred armed men were supplied as guard and escort in one of them, and three hundred in the other. It is incorrect to claim, as some Christian sources do, that the Prophet (s.a.w) led three hundred followers to an undefended commerce convoy. The suggestion is sly and false. The caravan presently leaving Syria was huge, and given its size and the armed escort supplied for earlier caravans, it appears plausible to assume that four to five hundred armed guards were provided to act as its escort. To imply that the Prophet (s.a.w) led a Muslim band of three hundred unarmed men to assault such a well-armed caravan with the goal of plundering it is unfair in the extreme. Such a view can only be prompted by blatant prejudice and persistent hostility against Islam. If the Muslim party's mission had been to confront only this caravan, their adventure could have been described as a war adventure, albeit one of self-defense, because the Muslim party from Medina was small and unarmed, while the Meccan caravan was large and well-armed, and they had been carrying on a campaign of hostility against the Muslims of Medina for a long time.

In truth, the circumstances under which this tiny group of Muslims left Medina were significantly more dire. As previously said, they had no idea whether they would face the caravan from Syria or the army from Mecca. The Qur'an alluded to the ambiguity under which Muslims labored. But the Muslims were ready for either. The hesitation with which the Muslims departed Medina reflects their faith and remarkable earnestness. After they had traveled some distance from Medina, the Prophet (s.a.w) informed them that they would have to face the vast Meccan army rather than the tiny Syrian caravan.

Muslims had heard rumors about the magnitude of the Meccan army. The most reasonable of these estimates put the number at 1,000, with all of them being seasoned warriors trained in the art of combat. The Prophet (s.a.w) were accompanied by just 313 men, many of whom were untrained and inexperienced, and the majority were ill-armed. The vast bulk of them traveled on foot or on camel. There were just two horses in the whole group. This team, which was as ill-equipped with weaponry as it was inexperienced, had to face a force three times its size, primarily made up of veteran warriors. It was clearly the most risky act ever attempted in history. The Holy Prophet (s.a.w) was intelligent enough to guarantee that no one participated in it without proper information and without his will and heart. He made it apparent to his group that they were no longer facing the caravan, but the army of Mecca. He requested the party's counsel. His Meccan adherents stepped up one after the other, assuring the Prophet (s.a.w) of their allegiance and fervor, as well as their commitment to combat the Meccan adversary who had come to assault the Muslims of Medina in their houses. When the Prophet (s.a.w) heard a Meccan Muslim, he sought additional guidance and advice. Medina's Muslims had remained mute. The aggressors were from Mecca and had blood ties to several of the Muslims who had gone to Medina with the Prophet (s.a.w) and were now members of this tiny group. The Muslims of Medina were frightened that their enthusiasm to combat the Meccan adversary might hurt their Meccan brethren's sentiments. When the Prophet (s.a.w) pressed on more and more advice, one of the Medinite Muslims rose up and said, "Prophet (s.a.w) of God, you have all the counsel you desire, yet you continue to seek for more; maybe you refer to us, the Muslims of Medina," to which the Prophet (s.a.w) replied, "Yes."

"You ask for our counsel," he said, "because you think that when you came to us, we agreed to fight on your side only in case you and your fellow emigrants from Mecca were attacked in Medina. But now we seem to have come out of Medina, and you feel that our agreement does not cover the conditions under which we find ourselves today. But O Prophet (s.a.w) of God, when we entered into that agreement we did not know you as well as we do now. We know now what high spiritual station you hold. We care not for what we agreed to. We now stand by you, whatever you ask us to do. We will not behave like the followers of Mosesas who said, 'Go you and your God and fight the enemy, we remain here behind.' If we must fight, we will and we will fight to the right of you, to the left of you, in front of you and behind you. True, the enemy wants to get at you. But we assure you that he will not do so, without stepping over our dead bodies. Prophet (s.a.w) of God, you invite us to fight. We are prepared to do more. Not far from here is the sea. If you command us to jump into it, we will hesitate not." (Bukhari, Kitab al-Maghazi, and Hisham).

This was the attitude of commitment and sacrifice demonstrated by the early Muslims, which is unparalleled in global history. The example of Mosesas' disciples has already been mentioned. We know that Jesus' followers abandoned him at a key juncture. One of them sold him for a pittance. Another cursed him, and the other ten fled. The Muslims who joined the Prophet (s.a.w) from Medina had only been with him for a year and a half. But they had become so strong in their faith that if the Prophet (s.a.w) had not commanded it, they would have thrown themselves into the water without hesitation. The Prophet (s.a.w) sought advice. But he had no doubts about the dedication of his followers. He sought advice in order to weed out the weaklings and send them away. However, he saw that the Meccan and Medinite Muslims competed in their demonstration of devotion. Both were certain that they would not abandon the enemy, despite the fact that the adversary was three times their number and significantly more prepared, armed, and experienced. They would rather place their confidence in God's promises, respect Islam, and lay down their lives in its defense.

The Prophet (s.a.w) proceeded after being assured of this commitment by both Meccan and Medinite Muslims. When he arrived at Badr, he took the advice of one of his disciples and directed his army to dwell along the Badr creek. The Muslims acquired hold of this supply of water, but the terrain on which they established their positions was mostly sand and so unsuited for combat movements. The Prophet (s.a.w)'s disciples were understandably concerned about this disadvantage. The Prophet (s.a.w) felt his followers' worry and spent the whole night praying. He repeated himself:

My God, there are just these three hundred persons on the whole face of the globe right now who are committed to Thee and resolved to build Thy religion. My God, who will be left to exalt Thy name if these three hundred soldiers perish tonight at the hands of their adversary in this battle? (Tabari).

God answered the prayers of His Prophet (s.a.w). Rain fell overnight. The sandy area of the field held by the Muslims became moist and firm. The enemy's dry half of the field turned muddy and treacherous. Perhaps the Meccan enemies picked one portion of the field and left the other for the Muslims because their experienced eye favored dry terrain for their troops and cavalry to march on. But a timely act of God turned the tables on them. The rain that fell overnight rendered the sandy section of the field that the Muslims controlled hard and the hard area where the Meccans had tented slick. During the night, the Prophet (s.a.w) received a strong indication from God that key members of the enemy would be killed. Individual identities were even disclosed to him. The locations where they were gonna die were also given. They died as predicted and were buried where it had been predicted.

This little group of Muslims demonstrated incredible bravery and dedication throughout the struggle. This is shown by one event. 'Abdur Rahman bin 'Aufra, one of Mecca's leaders and an accomplished soldier in his own right, was one of the Muslim force's few generals. When the combat started, he turned to his right and left to see who was supporting him. To his surprise, he discovered that he only had two Medina guys on his flanks. "Every General needs assistance on his flanks, especially on this day," 'Abdur Rahman bin 'Aufra adds, "but I only have two raw guys. What can I do with them?" 'Abdur Rahman bin 'Aufra claims he had just finished thinking this to himself when one of the boys touched his side with his elbow. As he bent over to hear the boy, he said, "Uncle, we have heard of one Abu Jahl, who used to harass and torment the Prophet (s.a.w). Uncle, I want to fight him; tell me where he is." 'Abdur Rahman bin 'Aufra had not yet responded to this youthful inquiry when his attention was drawn by the boy on the other side, who asked him the same question. 'Abdur Rahmanra was astounded by these two lads' bravery and commitment. He, a seasoned soldier, did not believe he would choose the enemy leader for an individual confrontation. 'Abdur Rahmanra pointed to Abu Jahl, who was armed to the teeth and stood behind the lines, guarded by two senior Generals with drawn swords. 'Abdur Rahmanra hadn't even lowered his finger when the two youngsters raced through the opposing lines like eagles, heading straight for their objective. The assault came out of nowhere. The troops and guards were taken aback. They assaulted the lads. One of the lads had his arm amputated. They remained rattled and undefeated, though. They assaulted Abu Jahl with such ferocity that the great leader was gravely wounded and fell to the ground. The zealous resolve of these two boys demonstrates how strongly the Prophet (s.a.w)'s followers, both old and young, had been moved by the brutal persecution to which they and the Prophet (s.a.w) had been subjected. We only know about them through history, yet we are strongly moved by them. Eyewitnesses told the people of Medina about these atrocities. The emotions they must have had are easily imagined. They had heard about Meccan cruelty on the one hand, and the Prophet (s.a.w)'s patience on the other. No surprise they were so determined to revenge the wrongs done to the Prophet (s.a.w) and the Muslims of Mecca. They were merely looking for a chance to inform the Meccan oppressors that if the Muslims did not react, it was not because they were impotent, but because God had not given them permission to do so. Another event demonstrates how determined this tiny Muslim troop was to die fighting. When Abu Jahl despatched a Bedouin leader to the Muslim side to report on their numbers, the battle had not yet begun. This leader returned and stated that there were three hundred or more Muslims. Abu Jahl and his supporters rejoiced. They considered Muslims to be easy victims. "But," the Bedouin leader said, "don't fight these guys; every one of them appears prepared to die! I have seen not men but death riding on camels" (Tabari and Hisham). The Bedouin leader was correct: people who are willing to die do not die easy.

A GREAT PROPHECY WAS MET

The fight was approaching. The Prophet (s.a.w) emerged from the little cabin where he had been worshiping and declared:

"The hosts will undoubtedly be routed and exposed."

These were the words revealed to the Prophet (s.a.w) in Mecca some time ago. They obviously had a connection to this conflict. When Meccan brutality had reached its apex and Muslims were fleeing to safer havens, the Propheta had the following scriptures revealed to him by God:

Warners undoubtedly came to the people of Pharaoh. They all disregarded Our Signs. So We grabbed them in the manner of One Mighty and Omnipotent. Are your skeptics superior than those? Or do you have a biblical exemption? The hosts will very definitely be routed and exposed. The Hour, on the other hand, is their assigned hour, and the Hour will be most disastrous and painful. The culprits will undoubtedly be in a state of perplexity and blazing inferno. On the day they will be taken into the Fire on their faces and told, "Taste the touch of burning" (54:42-49).

These verses are from Surah Al-Qamar, which was revealed at Mecca, according to all accounts. Muslim scholars locate its revelation between the fifth and tenth years of the Prophet's (s.a.w) Call, or at least three years before the Hijra (the Prophet's (s.a.w) departure from Mecca to Medina). It was most likely exposed eight years before. European authorities have the same opinion. The whole of this Chapter, according to Noldeke, was revealed after the fifth year of the Prophet's (s.a.w) Call. Wherry believes that this date is a bit early. He dates the Chapter to the sixth or seventh year before Hijra, or after the Prophet's (s.a.w) Call. In summary, Muslim and non-Muslim authority both agree on this.

Years before the Prophet (s.a.w) and his followers moved from Mecca to Medina, this chapter was revealed. The prophetic significance of the Meccan words is undeniable. These lines provide a strong indication of what was to come for the Meccans on the battlefield of Badr. It is apparent that their destiny was predetermined. When the Prophet (s.a.w) emerged from his hut, he repeated the prophetic account from the Meccan Chapter. During his prayers in the hut, he must have been reminded of the Meccan passages. He reminded his followers that the Hour foretold in the Meccan revelation had arrived by repeating one of the lines.

And the Hour has arrived. The prophet Isai(a.s.w.s) (21:13-17) predicted this exact hour. The war started despite the fact that Muslims were unprepared for it and non-Muslims were instructed not to participate. Three hundred and thirteen Muslims, the most of whom were untrained and unfamiliar with battle, and virtually all of whom were unarmed, faced a force three times their size, all of whom were seasoned warriors. Many prominent Mecca leaders were killed in a matter of hours. The splendour of Kedar vanished, just as the Prophet Isai(a.s.w.s) predicted. The Meccan army retreated in haste, leaving behind their dead and some captives. Among the detainees was the Prophet's (s.a.w) uncle, 'Abbasra, who had typically supported the Prophet (s.a.w) throughout his time in Mecca. 'Abbasra was forced to join the Meccans and battle the Prophet (s.a.w). Another prisoner was Abu'l 'Asra, the Prophet (s.a.w)'s son-in-law. Among the slain was Abu Jahl, commander-in-chief of the Meccan army and, by all accounts, Islam's arch-enemy.

Victory arrived, but it left the Prophet (s.a.w) with mixed emotions. He was overjoyed at the fulfillment of heavenly promises that had been repeated throughout the previous fourteen years, promises that had also been documented in some of the oldest religious books. At the same time, he lamented the fate of the Meccans. What a pitiful end they had met! He would have leaped with pleasure if this win had come to someone else in his stead. The sight of the captives in front of him, tied and chained, brought tears to the Prophet (s.a.w) and his devoted companion Abu Bakrra's eyes. 'Umarra, the Second Khalifah of Islam who followed Abu Bakrra, observed something but couldn't comprehend it. Why should the Prophet (s.a.w) and Abu Bakrra cry after a win? 'Umarra was perplexed. So he dared to ask the Prophet (s.a.w), "Prophet (s.a.w) of God, explain me why you grieve since God has given you such a great victory; if we must weep, I will weep with you, or at the very least put on a tearful face." The Prophet (s.a.w) pointed to the horrible state of the Meccan captives. This was the result of God's disobedience.

The Prophet Isai(a.s.w.s) talked again of the justice of this Prophet (s.a.w), who had triumphed in a bloody war. On this day, there was a large protest. On his route back to Medina, the Prophet (s.a.w) stopped for the night. The ardent followers who were watching him saw that he was turning from side to side and couldn't sleep. They quickly deduced that it was due to his hearing his uncle, 'Abbasra, who lay nearby, shackled tight as a prisoner of war. They unhooked the cable.

'Abbasra.' Abbasra's moaning came to a halt. The Prophet (s.a.w) fell asleep, no longer troubled by his moans. He awoke a little while later, puzzled as to why he was no longer hearing 'Abbasra moan. He assumed 'Abbasra had gone into a trance. However, the Companions guarding 'Abbasra informed him that they had loosened the chain on 'Abbasra to allow him (the Prophet (s.a.w)) to sleep peacefully. "No, no," the Prophet (s.a.w) said, "there must be no injustice; if 'Abbasra is related to me, other prisoners are related to others; loosen the cords on all of them or tie the cord tight on 'Abbasra as well." When the Companions heard this admonition, they decided to loosen the cords on all of the prisoners and take responsibility for their safe custody. Those captives who were literate were offered release provided they agreed to educate 10 Meccan lads as their payment for liberation. Those who had no one to pay a ransom for them were granted their freedom for the asking. Those who could afford to pay the ransom were released after it was paid. By releasing the captives in this manner, the Prophet (s.a.w) put a stop to the barbaric practice of transforming prisoners of battle into slaves.

THE BATTLE OF UHUD

When the Meccan army escaped from Badr, they declared that they would return to Medina and exact vengeance on the Muslims for what the Meccans had endured in the fight; and just a year later, they did so in full force. The Meccan leaders prevented surviving relatives from weeping over those who had fallen in the fight because they were ashamed and disgraced by their loss. They also stipulated that proceeds from trade caravans would go towards a military fund. With proper preparations, an army of three thousand men led by Abu Sufyanra invaded Medina. The Prophet (s.a.w) convened a council and asked his people whether they would face the enemy in Medina or elsewhere. He personally preferred the first option. He preferred that the Muslims remain in Medina and have the enemies assault them in their houses. This, he reasoned, would shift the blame for hostility and assault on the adversary. But there were many Muslims in the council who had missed out on taking part in the Battle of Badr and now yearned to battle for God. They insisted on a direct and open combat and the opportunity to die fighting. The Prophet (s.a.w) heeded the general counsel (Tabaqat).

During the argument, the Prophet (s.a.w) recounted a vision of his. "I had a vision. I saw a cow, and I also saw my sword with its point broken. I saw the cow being killed, and that I had placed my hand inside a suit of armour. I also saw myself riding a ram," he said to the Companions.

"The butchering of the cow indicates that some of my Companions will be killed in battle; the broken point of my sword indicates that some important one among my relations will meet his death; or perhaps, I myself will suffer pain or injury of some kind; putting my hand in a coat of armour appears to indicate that it is better for us if we stay in Medina; and the fact that I have seen myself riding a ram indicates that we will overpower the commander of the disbeli

This vision and its interpretation made it obvious that Muslims should remain in Medina. The Prophet (s.a.w), on the other hand, did not insist on it since his interpretation of the vision was his personal and not part of given truth. He followed the majority's opinion and chose to leave Medina to confront the enemy. As he moved off, a more fanatical part of His followers approached the Prophet (s.a.w) and said, "Prophet (s.a.w) of God, the route you suggested sounds preferable; we should remain in Medina and confront the enemy in our streets."

"Not now," the Prophet (s.a.w) replied. "Now the Prophet (s.a.w) of God have put on their armour; come what may, now we will move forth; and if you show steadfastness and perseverance, God will support you" (Bukhari and Tabaqat). So saying, he marched forth with a thousand men. They camped for the night a little distance from Medina. It was the Prophet's (s.a.w) tradition to give his battle troops some time to relax before confronting the enemy. He went around during the morning prayers. He discovered that other Jews had also joined the Muslims. They professed to have alliance contracts with the Medina tribes. Because the Prophet (s.a.w) was aware of Jewish machinations, he sent the Jews. 'Abdullah bin Ubayy ibn Salul, commander of the hypocrites, left with his three hundred adherents as soon as he did so. He said that the Muslim army was no longer a match for the adversary. Participating in the conflict meant definite death. The Prophet (s.a.w) had erred in dispatching his own comrades. As a consequence of this last-minute defection, just 700 Muslims remained under the Prophet's leadership. The seven hundred faced an army more than four times their size and many times more equipped. There were 700 armoured soldiers in the Meccan army, but only one hundred in the Muslim army. The Meccans had a mounted army of 200 horses, whereas the Muslims had just two. The Prophet (s.a.w) arrived at Uhud. Over a tiny uphill route there, he stationed a garrison of fifty men, tasked with resisting any enemy assault or effort to seize it. The Prophet (s.a.w) plainly stated their mission. It was to stand where they had been put and not move until ordered to do so, regardless of what happened to the Muslims. The Prophet (s.a.w) proceeded to combat with the last 650 soldiers against an army five times their size. But, with God's aid, the six hundred and fifty Muslims drove away three thousand trained Meccan troops in a short period of time. The Muslims pursued him. The mountainous pass where fifty Muslims had been stationed was in the distance. "The enemy is defeated; it is time we take part in the combat and gained our honors in the next world," the guard stated to the commander. The commander halted them, reminding them of the Prophet (s.a.w)'s unambiguous commands. The guys, however, stressed that the Prophet's (s.a.w) command was to be followed in spirit rather than text. It made little sense to continue guarding the pass when the adversary was fleeing for his life.

DEFEAT INSTEAD OF VICTORY

They argued their way out of the pass and into the combat. Khalid bin Walidra, a prominent Muslim commander, was among the fleeing Meccan army. His acute eye was drawn to the unprotected pass. It was now guarded by just a few guys. Khalidra summoned another Meccan commander, 'Amr bin al-'Asra, and requested him to inspect the pass behind him. 'Amrra did so, thinking it was the best opportunity of his life. Both generals halted their troops and mounted the hill. They slaughtered the few Muslims who were left defending the route and launched an assault on the Muslims from the eminence. Hearing their war cries, the beaten Meccan army regrouped and returned to the battlefield. The onslaught on Muslims came out of nowhere. They had spread over the whole field in pursuit of the Meccan force. There was no Muslim opposition to this fresh invasion. Only a few Muslim fighters were observed fighting the enemy. Many of these people died in battle. Others retreated. A few formed a circle around the Prophet (s.a.w). They couldn't have numbered more than twenty in all. The Meccan army launched a furious assault on this ring. The Muslims in the ring were slaughtered one by one by Meccan swordsmen. The archers launched volleys of arrows from the hill. Talhara, a Quraish and Muhajirin (Meccan Muslims who had taken sanctuary in Medina at the time), saw that the enemy arrows were all aimed towards the Prophet (s.a.w)'s face. He extended his hand and placed it to the Prophet's (s.a.w)'s face. Arrow after arrow hit Talha'sra's hand, yet it did not fall, despite being riddled through with each shot. It was eventually utterly mutilated. Talhara lost his hand and had to go about with a stump for the rest of his life. During the reign of the Fourth Khalifah of Islam, when internal strife erupted, an opponent mockingly referred to Talhara as the handless Talhara. "Handless, yes, but do you know where he lost his hand? At the Battle of Uhud, when he lifted his hand to cover the Prophet's (s.a.w) face from the enemy's arrows," Talhara's buddy said.

Long after the Battle of Uhud, Talhara's friends asked him, "Did not your hand smart under the arrow shots, and the pain almost make you cry?" Talhara replied, "It made me smart, and it almost made me cry, but I resisted both because I knew that if my hand shook even slightly, it would expose the Prophet's (s.a.w) face to the volley of enemy arrows." An hostile party rushed forward and forced them back. The Prophet (s.a.w) then remained alone, like a wall, until a stone hit his forehead, causing a large wound. Another punch pushed the helmet rings into his cheeks. When the arrows began to rain thick and fast and the Prophet (s.a.w) was wounded, he begged to God, "My God, pardon my people, because they know not what they are doing" (Muslim). The Prophet (s.a.w) fell on the dead, on those who had died in his defense. Other Muslims stepped up to protect the Prophet (s.a.w) from further assaults. They died as well. Among these dead corpses lay the Prophet (s.a.w), who was unconscious. When the enemies saw this, they assumed he was dead. In the assurance of triumph, they retreated and lined up again.

'Umarra was one of the Muslims who had been defending the Prophet (s.a.w) while being forced back by an onslaught of hostile soldiers. The battleground had now been cleansed. When 'Umarra saw this, he was certain that the Prophet (s.a.w) had died. 'Umarra was a courageous guy. He demonstrated it again and again, most notably while battling the mighty Empires of Rome and Iran at the same time. He was never known to blench under pressure. This 'Umarra sat on a stone, wailing like a child, with drooping spirits. Meanwhile, another Muslim, Anas bin Nadrra, came strolling along, certain that the Muslims had prevailed. He'd witnessed them overcome the enemy, but having had nothing to eat since the night before, he'd retreated from the battlefield, clutching some dates. He was startled when he observed 'Umarra sobbing and inquired, "'Umarra, what is wrong with you that instead of celebrating over a beautiful victory achieved by the Muslims, you are crying?"

"Anasra, you do not know what has happened. You only saw the first part of the battle. You do not know that the enemy captured the strategic point on the hill and attacked us fiercely. The Muslims had dispersed, believing they had won. There was no resistance to the enemy's attack. Only the Prophet (s.a.w) with a handful of guards stood against the entire enemy and all of them fell down fighting," 'Umarra replied.

"If this is true," Anasra remarked, "what is the use of remaining here and crying? Where our dear Master has gone, we must follow."

Anasra was holding the final date. He was about to put it in his mouth when he flung it aside, exclaiming, "O date, except thee, is there anything between Anasra and Paradise?"

He unsheathed his sword and charged towards the opposing army, one against three thousand. He couldn't accomplish much, yet one believing soul triumphs over many. Anasra was injured after fighting heroically, yet he continued to battle. The opposing rabble pounced barbarously upon him as a result. When the conflict was done and the dead were recognized, Anas'sra's corpse was declared to be unidentified. It was divided into seventy parts. Finally, Anasra's sister, recognizing it by a mangled finger, stated, "This is my brother's body" (Bukhari).

Those Muslims who formed a ring around the Prophet (s.a.w) but were forced back raced forward as soon as they saw the enemy retreat. They exhumed the Prophet's (s.a.w) corpse from the dead. Abu 'Ubaida bin al-Jarrahra grasped the rings that had sunk into the Prophet's (s.a.w) cheeks between his teeth and yanked them out, losing two teeth in the process.

The Prophet (s.a.w) regained consciousness after a little while. The guards who encircled him sent messages to summon Muslims to reassemble. A fragmented force started to form. They led Prophet (s.a.w) to the bottom of the hill. When the enemy commander saw the Muslim remnants, he boasted, "We have killed Muhammad (s.a.w)." The Prophet (s.a.w) heard the boastful cry but forbade the Muslims from responding, lest the enemy learn the truth and attack again, leaving the exhausted and badly-wounded Muslims to fight this savage horde. After getting no response from the Muslims, Abu Sufyanra concluded that the Prophet (s.a.w) was no longer alive. He followed his initial scream with a second, saying, "We have also slain Abu Bakrra," and the Prophet (s.a.w) prohibited Abu Bakrra from responding. "We have also slain 'Umarra," Abu Sufyaran stated, and the Prophet (s.a.w) prohibited 'Umarra from responding. Abu Sufyanra shouted out that they had slain all three. "We are all alive and, with God's grace, ready to fight you and break your heads," Abu Sufyanra cried, "Glory to Hubal. Glory to Hubal. For Hubal has put an end to Islam." (Hubal was the Meccans' national idol.) The Prophet (s.a.w) could not bear this boast against the One and Only God, Allah, for Whom he and the Muslims were willing to sacrifice everything. He had refused to retract a statement about his own death. For strategic considerations, he had declined to alter a proclamation of Abu Bakrra's and 'Umarra's deaths. Only the remains of his little army remained. The opposing troops were many and powerful. However, the adversary had now offended Allah. Such an insult could not be tolerated by the Prophet (s.a.w). His soul was ablaze. "Why stay mute and offer no response to this insult to Allah, the Only God?" he raged at the Muslims who surrounding him.

"What should we say, O Muslims?" they wondered.

"Say, 'Allah alone is Great and Mighty. Allah alone is Great and Mighty. He alone is High and Honoured.'"

The Muslims responded in kind. The opponent was stunned by this yell. They were dismayed to learn that the Prophet (s.a.w) had not died after all. A group of injured and tired Muslims stood before them. It was simple enough to complete them. They did not, however, dare to assault again. They returned with great joy, content with the kind of triumph they had achieved.

In the Battle of Uhud, Muslim triumph was transformed into loss. Nonetheless, the combat provides proof of the Prophet (s.a.w)'s accuracy. Because the prophesies uttered by the Prophet (s.a.w) before going into war were fulfilled in this conflict. Muslims were initially triumphant. Hamzara, the Prophet's loving uncle, was killed in battle. The enemy commander was killed early in the action. The Prophet Sa was injured, and many Muslims were killed. All of this occurred exactly as predicted in the Prophet's (s.a.w) vision.

Aside from the fulfillment of the previously mentioned incidents, this battle provided numerous proofs of Muslims' sincerity and devotion. Their behavior was so exemplary that history has failed to provide a parallel. We've already discussed some examples of this. One more seems worthwhile to mention. It demonstrates the Prophet's (s.a.w) Companions' certainty of conviction and devotion. When the Propheta retired to the foot of the hill with a small group of Muslims, he dispatched some of his Companions to tend to the wounded on the field. After a long search, a Companion discovered a wounded Muslim from Medina. He was on the verge of death. The Companion bent over him and said, "Peace be with you." The wounded Muslim raised a trembling hand and said, "I was waiting for someone to come."

"You're in a critical condition," the visitor told the soldier. "Do you have anything to say to your relatives?"

"Yes, yes," the dying Muslim said. "Say peace to my relatives and tell them that as I die here, I leave behind a priceless trust to be taken care of by them. That trust is the Prophet of Godsa. I hope my relations would preserve his person with their life and remember this my solitary dying request" (Mu'atta and Zurqani).

final folks have much to say to their families, but these early Muslims, even in their final moments, thought not of their relations, sons, daughters or spouses, nor of their possessions, but only of the Prophet (s.a.w). They faced death in the confidence that the Prophet (s.a.w) was the saviour of the world. Their offspring if they lived, would accomplish very little. If they died defending the Prophet's (s.a.w) person, they would have served both God and man. They felt that in sacrificing their family they benefited humanity and they served their God. In inviting death for them they ensured life forever for humanity at large.

The Prophet (s.a.w) gathered the injured and the dead. The injured were given first-aid and the deceased were buried. The Prophet (s.a.w) then discovered that the enemy had handled the Muslims most cruelly, that they had mangled the corpses of the deceased Muslims and chopped off a nose here and an ear there. One among the mangled corpses was that of Hamzara, the Prophet's (s.a.w) uncle. The Prophet (s.a.w) was affected, and stated, "The deeds of disbelievers now justify the treatment which we so far considered was wrong." As he said this, he was told by God to allow the disbelievers alone and to continue to show them compassion.

RUMOUR OF PROPHET'S (S.A.W) DEATH REACHES MEDINA

The word of the Prophet's (s.a.w) death and the news of the dispersion of the Muslim army reached Medina, before the remains of the Muslim military could return to the town. Women and children bolted towards Uhud. Many of them returned after learning the truth from returning troops. One lady from the Banu Dinar clan continued till she arrived at Uhud. In the war, this widow had lost her husband, father, and brother. She had also lost a son, according to some narrators. When a returning soldier approached her, he informed her that her father had perished. "I don't care about my father; tell me about the Prophet (s.a.w)," she said. Because the soldier knew the Prophet (s.a.w) was alive, he did not respond immediately, but instead went on to tell her about her brother and husband, both of whom had perished. She remained unfazed by each story, repeatedly asking, "What has the Prophet (s.a.w) of God done?" It was an odd term to use, but when we consider it was a woman who uttered it, it no longer appears so unusual. A woman's emotions are powerful. She often addresses a deceased person as if he were living. If she is connected to him, she would usually protest and question why he is abandoning her and leaving her behind uncared for and unlooked after. It is usual for women to grieve the death of loved ones in this manner. As a result, the term employed by this lady is suitable for a woman mourning the Prophet's (s.a.w) death. This lady loved the Prophet (s.a.w) and refused to accept he was dead, even after being told he was. At the same time, she did not dispute the news, but instead proceeded to cry, in typical womanly sadness, "What has the Prophet (s.a.w) of God done?" By saying this, she assumed the Prophet (s.a.w) was still alive and grieved that a devoted leader like him had decided to cause them all the agony of separation.

When the returning soldier saw that this lady was unconcerned with the deaths of her father, brother, and husband, he realized the intensity of her devotion to the Prophet (s.a.w) and informed her, "As for the Prophet (s.a.w), he is as you desire, completely alive." He indicated one area of the field. "My father and mother be sacrificed to thee, O Prophet of Godsa, if thou livest, I care not who else dies," the lady murmured (Hisham), holding his robe in her hand and kissing it.

As a result, we can witness what courage and dedication Muslims—both men and women—displayed in this war. Christian authors proudly portray the account of Mary Magdalene and her companions, praising their dedication and fortitude. It is believed that they snuck through the Jews in the early hours of the morning and made their way to Jesus' tomb. But how does this compare to the devotion of this Muslim lady from the Dinar tribe?

Another example may be found in history. When the Prophet (s.a.w) returned to Medina after the dead had been buried, he noticed women and children who had come out of Medina to greet him. Sa'd bin Mu'adhra, a Medina leader, clutched the dromedary's string. Sa'dra was proudly guiding the dromedary. He appeared to declare to the world that Muslims had succeeded in bringing the Prophet (s.a.w) back to Medina in good health. As he moved forward, he saw his own elderly mother moving forward to welcome the returning group of Muslims. This elderly lady was legally blind. Sa'dra noticed her and remarked to the Prophet (s.a.w), "This is my mother, O Prophet (s.a.w)." "Let her come forward," the Prophet (s.a.w) said. The lady stepped closer, searching for the Prophet's (s.a.w)'s face with a blank expression. She felt relieved when she finally saw it. When the Prophet (s.a.w) saw her, he exclaimed, "Woman, I mourn the death of thy son." "But," the loyal lady said, "when I saw you alive, I have eaten all my troubles," using the Arabic idiom "I have cooked my misfortune and swallowed it" (Halbiyya, Vol. 2, p. 210). What level of emotion is shown by this expression? Grief normally consumes a person, and here was an elderly widow who had lost her son, a staff for her old age. But she said that instead of allowing her sadness to consume her, she had consumed her grief. Her son's sacrifice for the Prophet (s.a.w) would sustain her for the rest of her life.

The Prophet (s.a.w) arrived at Medina. Many Muslims were killed and injured in this conflict. Nonetheless, Muslims cannot be considered to have lost the struggle. The instances described above demonstrate the opposite. They demonstrate that Uhud was as significant a victory for

Muslims as any other. Muslims who read about their forefathers might get nourishment and motivation from Uhud.

The Prophet (s.a.w) resumed his ministry at Medina. He began training and educating his people once again. But, like previously, his effort was not continuous. After Uhud, the Jews grew more audacious, and the hypocrites raised their heads once again. They came to believe that eradicating Islam was within their capabilities and ability. They only needed to make a concerted effort. As a result, the Jews used new techniques of vexation. They would print vile invective in poem, thereby insulting the Prophet (s.a.w) and his family. When the Prophet (s.a.w) was summoned to settle a disagreement, he was required to go to a Jewish castle. The Jews intended to kill him by dropping a stone slab on him. God forewarned the Prophet (s.a.w) about this. It was his habit to get such timely warnings. The Prophet (s.a.w) stood up and walked away without saying anything. The Jews subsequently acknowledged to their heinous plot. In the streets, Muslim women were insulted. In one such event, a Muslim was killed. On another instance, Jews stoned a Muslim girl, who died in agony. The Jews' behavior damaged their ties with Muslims, forcing them to battle against the Jews. However, Muslims simply drove them out of Medina. One of the two Jewish tribes made their way to Syria. Others moved to Syria, while others settled in Khaibar, a well-fortified Jewish bastion to the north of Medina.

The world saw an exceptional example of Islam's effect on its believers during the period of calm between Uhud and the following conflict. We're talking about the alcohol ban. We said that Arabs were certified drunkards while discussing the situation of Arab civilization prior to Islam. Drinking five times a day was fashionable in every Arab household. Losing oneself under the influence of alcohol was a frequent behavior, and the Arabs were not embarrassed of it. Rather, they saw it as a virtue. When a visitor came, it was the housewife's responsibility to provide refreshments. Weaning such a population off this lethal habit was no simple task. However, in the fourth year after the Hijra, the Prophet (s.a.w) received the order that drinking was prohibited. Drinking was prohibited in Muslim culture after this edict was issued. When the revelation declaring alcohol prohibited was revealed, the Prophet (s.a.w) went for a Companion and commanded him to broadcast the new decree throughout Medina's streets. A drinking party was taking place at the home of an Ansari (a Muslim from Medina). A large number of people had been invited, and glasses of wine were being served. One enormous pot had been consumed, and a second was about to be consumed. Many people had lost their wits, and many more were on their way. In this state, they heard someone say that drinking had been outlawed by the Prophet (s.a.w) by a divine order. One of the party stood up and said, "It appears to be a proclamation against drinking; let us find out if this is so." Another stood up, struck the earthen pot full of wine with his staff, broke it to pieces, and said, "First obey, then inquire. It is not meet that we should continue drinking while we make inquiries. It is rather our duty to let the wine flow in the street and then inquire about the proclamation" (Bukhari). This Muslim was correct. For, if drinking had been prohibited, they would have been guilty of an offense had they continued to drink; on the other hand, if drinking had not been prohibited, they would not have lost anything if they let the wine in their pots pour into the streets for once. Following this pronouncement, drinking was prohibited in all Muslim societies. This fundamental shift did not need any particular effort or promotion.

Muslims who heard this instruction and saw the quick reaction to it lived for up to seventy or eighty years. There is no documented example of a Muslim who, having heard of this restriction, shown the weakness of offending against it. If there was such an instance, it has to be of someone who did not have the opportunity to be directly influenced by the Prophet (s.a.w). Compare this to the prohibition campaign in America and the attempts to encourage temperance that have been undertaken in Europe for many years. In one example, a brief declaration by the Prophet (s.a.w) was sufficient to eradicate a societal evil deeply embedded in Arab civilization. In the other, prohibition was imposed by special legislation. Police and the army, customs officials and excise inspectors all worked together to combat the evil of alcohol, but they failed and had to admit their failure. The drunkards prevailed, and the drink evil was unbeatable. Ours is regarded to be a socially progressive era. But, when we compare our era to that of early Islam, we ask which merits this designation more: ours or the one in which Islam brought about this immense social change.

What transpired in Uhud would not be readily forgotten. The Meccans considered Uhud to be their first triumph against Islam. They disseminated the story across Arabia in order to incite Arab tribes against Islam and convince them that Muslims were not invincible. If they continued to thrive, it was not due to their own power, but to the weakness of Arab orthodoxy. It was because of the frailty of the Arab idolaters. Overpowering the Muslims was not a tough task provided the Arab idolaters worked together. As a consequence of this advertising, anti-Muslim sentiment started to become stronger. Other Arab tribes came to outnumber the Meccans in their harassment of Muslims. Some started openly attacking them. Some started to inflict losses on them covertly. Two Arab tribes, the 'Adl and the Qara, sent delegations to the Holy Prophet (s.a.w) in the fourth year after the Hijra to report that many of their men were leaning towards Islam. They asked the Prophet (s.a.w) to send them some Muslims who were well-versed in Islamic doctrine to live among them and teach them the New Religion. Actually, this was a plot devised by the Banu Lihyan, Islam's arch-enemy. They sent these emissaries to the Prophet (s.a.w) with the promise of a large prize. The Prophet (s.a.w), unknowingly, accepted the request and sent 10 Muslims to educate the tribes the doctrines and values of Islam. When this group arrived in the region of the Banu Lihyan, their guards informed the tribesmen and encouraged them to arrest or execute the party. On the basis of this heinous idea, two hundred armed Banu Lihyan men started off in pursuit of the Muslim company, eventually overtaking them at Raji'. A battle took occurred between 10 Muslims and two hundred enemies. The Muslims were filled with hope. The opponent lacked any. The 10 Muslims ascended an altitude and confronted the two hundred. The enemies used nasty intrigue to try to overwhelm the Muslims. They promised to save them if they would only come down. However, the party's leader responded that they had had enough of disbelievers' promises. As a result, they turned to God and prayed. God was fully aware of their situation. Was it not proper for Him to tell their Prophet (s.a.w) of this? When the disbelievers discovered the tiny group of Muslims to be steadfast, they started their attack. The party battled without regard for defeat. Seven of the 10 died in battle. The disbelievers reaffirmed their vow to spare the lives of the three who remained on the condition that they come down from the height. These three succumbed after believing the skeptics. The disbelievers bound them up as soon as they did so. "This is the first violation of your plighted oath; God alone knows what you will do next," one of the three replied, refusing to accompany them. The skeptics began to torment the sufferer and pull him down the path. They were so taken aback by this one man's defiance and drive that they assassinated him on the spot. They kidnapped the other two and sold them as slaves to the Quraish of Mecca. Khubaibra was one of the two, and Zaid (ra) was the other. The buyer of Khubaibra intended to murder him in order to revenge the death of his own father, who was murdered at Badr. Khubaibra once requested a razor to finish his toilet. Khubaibra was holding the razor when a curious member of the family approached him. Khubaibra picked up the infant and placed him on his knee. When the mother of the kid saw this, she felt horrified. Her mind was racing with guilt, and here was a guy they were about to kill holding a razor perilously close to their kid. She was certain Khubaibra would kill the kid. "Do you think I'm going to kill your child? Do not believe so for a second. I cannot do such a vile thing. Muslims do not play false," Khubaibra responded, seeing the woman's concern.

Khubaibra's honest and direct manner and behavior impressed the lady. She recalled this for the rest of her life and used to remark she'd never seen a prisoner like Khubaibra. Finally, the Meccans brought Khubaibra to an open field to publicly celebrate his murder. When the prescribed time arrived, Khubaibra requested permission to pray two rak'ats. The Quraish consented, and Khubaibra made his last petitions to God in this world in full view. He stated he wanted to continue praying after he finished, but he didn't because he was frightened of dying. He then casually handed up his neck to the executioner. He hummed the lines as he walked:

While I die a Muslim, I don't care whether my decapitated corpse falls to the right or the left. What's the point? My death is in God's hands; if He so desires, He might bless every component of my dismembered corpse (Bukhari).

When the executioner's blade descended on Khubaibra's neck and his head slumped to one side, he had just completed reciting these lyrics. Among those there to commemorate this public murder was one Sa'id bin 'Amirra, who eventually converted to Islam. Sa'id'sra is reported to have had a fit whenever the murder of Khubaibra was mentioned in his presence (Hisham). Zaid (ra), the second prisoner, was likewise carried out to be slain. Among those there was Mecca's leader, Abu Sufyanra. "Wouldn't you rather have Muhammad (s.a.w) in your place?" Abu Sufyanra questioned Zaid (ra).

Wouldn't you rather be secure at home while Muhammad (s.a.w) was in our care?"

"What, Abu Sufyanra? What do you say? By God, I would sooner die than that the Prophet (s.a.w) might foot on a thorn in a Medina street," Zaid (ra) said proudly. Abu Sufyanra couldn't help but be amazed by such dedication. "God is my witness, I have not known any one love another as much as the Companions of Muhammad (s.a.w) love Muhammad (s.a.w)," he asserted unequivocally, but in measured tones (Hisham, Vol. 2).

Around this time, several Najd residents approached the Prophet (s.a.w), asking Muslims to teach them Islam. The Prophet (s.a.w) did not have faith in them. However, Abu Bara', leader of the 'Amir tribe, was in Medina at the time. He volunteered to serve as a guarantor for the tribe, assuring the Prophet (s.a.w) that they would not cause any trouble. The Prophet (s.a.w) chose seventy Muslims who were well-versed in the Qur'an. When this delegation arrived in Bi'r Ma'una, Haram bin Malhanra proceeded to the leader of the 'Amir tribe (a nephew of Bara') to deliver the word of Islam to him. Haramra was apparently favourably accepted by the tribesmen. But, while he was speaking to the chief, a guy came up behind him and hit Haramra with a lance. Haramra was killed on the scene. "God is magnificent, the Lord of the Ka'ba is my witness, I have accomplished my purpose," Haram'sra was heard saying as the lance struck his neck (Bukhari). After murdering Haramra in this heinous way, the tribal elders incited the tribe to attack the remainder of this group of Muslim instructors. "But," the tribesmen continued, "our leader, Abu Bara', volunteered to serve as guarantor; we cannot attack this group." The tribal chiefs then assaulted the Muslim party, aided by the two tribes that had gone to the Prophet (s.a.w) to request Muslim instructors and several other tribes. "We have come to preach and educate, not to fight," was the straightforward message. They began slaughtering the guests. Except for three, all of the seventy were slain. One of the survivors was crippled and had climbed a hill prior to the meeting. Two others had gone to feed their camels in the woods. When they returned from the woods, they discovered sixty-six of their friends dead on the field. The two counseled each other. "We should go and report this to the authorities," one said. Prophet (s.a.w), Holy Prophet (s.a.w)."

"I cannot leave a site where the head of our group, whom our Prophet (s.a.w) selected as our commander, has been assassinated," said the other, and he charged the disbelievers alone and perished fighting. The other was imprisoned but eventually freed in fulfillment of a commitment made by the tribe head. Among those killed was 'Amir bin Fuhairara, an Abu Bakrra freedman. Jabbarra, his assassin, eventually converted to Islam. Jabbarra linked his conversion to the Muslim genocide.

"When I started murdering 'Amirra," Jabbarra says, "I heard 'Amirra say, 'By God, I have met my goal.' I asked someone why a Muslim said this sort of thing when he was meeting his death, and that person explained that Muslims regarded death in the path of God as a blessing and a victory." Jabbarra was so impressed by this reply that he began a systematic study of Islam, and eventually became Ghaba).

The news of the two tragic tragedies, in which around eighty Muslims were killed as a consequence of a malicious plot, arrived at Medina at the same time. These were not ordinary folks who were assassinated. They were the Qur'an's carriers. They had done no crime and had caused no damage to anybody. They weren't fighting anything. A deception perpetrated in the name of God and religion had decoyed them into enemy hands. These findings demonstrated unequivocally that Islam was reviled and despised. On the other hand, Muslims' devotion to Islam was as fervent and sincere.

MEET WITH BANU MUSTALIQ

Mecca had a terrible famine after the Battle of Uhud. Despite the Meccans' animosity against him, and despite their efforts to foment disaffection against him across the land, the Prophet (s.a.w) established a fund to assist the impoverished of Mecca in their time of need. Even with this gesture of goodwill, the Meccans were unimpressed. Their animosity persisted unabated. In fact, things became worse. Tribes that had previously been friendly to Muslims became hostile. Banu Mustaliq was one such tribe. They got along well with Muslims. They had, however, begun to plan an assault against Medina. When the Prophet (s.a.w) learned of their plans, he sent men to discover the truth. The guys came back and validated the reports. The Prophet (s.a.w) made the decision to go confront this new onslaught. As a result, he assembled a troop and marched it to Banu Mustaliq land. When the Muslim troop encountered the enemy, the Prophet (s.a.w) attempted to urge the enemy to leave without fighting. They declined. The battle was joined, and the enemy was crushed in a matter of hours.

Because the Meccan disbelievers were set on mischief and friendly tribes were becoming hostile, hypocrites among Muslims had also risked to fight on the Muslim side on this occasion. They undoubtedly assumed they'd have an opportunity to cause trouble. Banu Mustaliq's interaction lasted just a few hours. As a result, the hypocrites had little opportunity to cause trouble during the combat. The Holy Prophet (s.a.w), on the other hand, chose to spend a few days at the settlement of Banu Mustaliq. During his visit, a dispute erupted between a Meccan and a Medinite Muslim over the use of a well. The Meccan had previously been a slave. He hit the Medinite, who raised an alert and called out for other Medinites, known as the Ansar, or Helpers. The Meccan also sounded the warning and pleaded for other Meccans, known as Muhajirin or Refugees. Excitement was in the air. Nobody questioned as to what had occurred. Both sides' young men pulled their swords. 'Abdullah bin Ubayy ibn Salul considered it a blessing. He made the decision to pour gasoline to the fire. "You have gone too far in your indulgence to the Refugees; your excellent treatment of them has turned their heads, and now they are attempting to control you in every manner." The speech may have had the intended effect. The argument may have gotten out of hand. But it didn't work. 'Abdullah miscalculated the impact of his devious remarks. He went so far as to imply, however, that he believed the Ansar were being persuaded:

Let us go back to Medina. The most esteemed among its inhabitants would thereafter become the most reviled (Bukhari).

He meant himself as the most respected citizen, and the Prophets as the most hated. As soon as he stated this, devout Muslims could see through the ruse. They said that they had not heard an innocent discourse, but rather the words of Satan, who had come to lead them astray. A young guy rose and reported to the Prophet (s.a.w) through his uncle. The Prophet (s.a.w) summoned 'Abdullah bin Ubayy ibn Salul and his companions and inquired as to what had occurred. 'Abdullah and his pals denied any involvement in the event that had been reported to them. The Prophet (s.a.w) remained silent. However, word of the truth started to spread. Over time, 'Abdullah bin Ubayy ibn Salul's own son, 'Abdullahra, became aware of it. "O Prophet (s.a.w), my father has insulted you. Death is his punishment. If you decide so, I would rather have you command me to kill my father. If you command someone else, and my father dies at his hands, I may be led to avenge my father by killing that man. Perhaps I incur God's displeasure in this way."

"But," the Prophet (s.a.w) said, "I have no such intention; I will treat your father with compassion and consideration." When young 'Abdullahra compared his father's disloyalty and discourtesy to the Prophet (s.a.w)'s compassion and kindness, he set out for Medina full of suppressed anger toward his father. He stopped his father on the way to Medina and told him he wouldn't allow him go any farther unless he apologized for his insults against the Prophet (s.a.w). "The lips that said, 'The Prophet (s.a.w) is despised and you are honoured,' must now say, 'The Prophet (s.a.w) is honoured and you are despised.' Until you say this, I will not let you go." 'Abdullah bin Ubayy ibn Salul was stunned and terrified and said, "I agree, my son, that Muhammad (s.a.w) is honoured and that I am despised."

We already described two Jewish tribes that had to be expelled from Medina due to their devious schemes and homicidal plots. Banu Nadir, one of the two, relocated partially to Syria and partly to a village named Khaibar on Medina's northwestern outskirts. In Arabia, Khaibar was a well-defended Jewish center. Jews who had moved there started to incite Arabs against Muslims. The Meccans had already declared war on Islam. There was no need for a new provocation to incite the Meccans' hatred of Muslims. Similarly, the Ghatafan of Najd were hostile to Muslims due of their cordial connections with the Meccans. The Jews of

Khaibar had already established contacts with the Quraish of Mecca and the Ghatafan of Najd. They also intended to convert Banu Sulaim and Banu Asad against Islam. They also encouraged Banu Sa'd, a Jewish-allied tribe, to join the Meccans in an anti-Islam coalition. After much deliberation, a confederacy of Arab tribes was formed to oppose the Muslims. This comprised the Meccans, tribes from the lands around Mecca, tribes from Najd, and tribes from the territories north of Medina.

THE DITCH BATTLE

In the sixth year of the Hijra, a massive army was assembled. Historians estimate the army's size to be between ten and twenty-four thousand soldiers. However, a confederated army formed from the various tribes of Arabia could not be ten thousand strong. Twenty-four thousand seems more accurate. It may easily have been 18 or 20 thousand. The town of Medina that this army wanted to invade was a little one, incapable of withstanding a coordinated onslaught by all of Arabia. It had a population of little over three thousand males (including elderly men, young men, and children) at the time. The adversary had created an army of twenty to twenty-four thousand able-bodied men, skilled in battle, and (having been collected from various regions of the nation) a well-selected personnel against this population. The population of Medina, on the other hand, contained men of all ages who might be called upon to repel this massive force. One can evaluate the odds that the Muslim inhabitants of Medina had to face. It was a completely uneven match. The enemy was twenty to twenty-four thousand strong, while the Muslims were only around three thousand, including, as previously said, all of the town's men, young and old. When the Prophet (s.a.w) learned of the massive enemy preparations, he convened a council and sought guidance. Salmanra the Persian, the first Muslim convert from Persia, was among those consulted. The Prophet (s.a.w) inquired of Salmanra what they did in Persia when faced with defending a town against a massive army. "If a town is unfortified and the home army is tiny," Salmanra said, "the norm in our land is to construct a trench around the town and defend from inside." The Prophet (s.a.w) agreed. Medina is surrounded by hills on one side. On that side, they offered natural protection. Another side with a lot of roadways had a dense population. The town could not be assaulted from this side. The third side featured residences and palm trees, as well as the castles of the Jewish tribe, Banu Quraiza, which could be seen from a distance. The Banu Quraiza had made a peace treaty with the Muslims. As a result, this side was likewise thought to be secure from hostile assault. The fourth side was an open plain, and the enemy onslaught was most likely and feared to come from here. As a result, the Prophet (s.a.w) decided to build a trench on this open side to keep the enemy from striking unexpectedly. The labor was divided among Muslims, with 10 men digging ten yards of ditch. A mile-long ditch with adequate breadth and depth had to be dug.

During the digging, they came upon a rock that Muslim sappers found difficult to move. A report was conveyed to the Prophet (s.a.w), who rushed to the location. He whacked the rock with a pickaxe. Sparks flew, and the Prophet (s.a.w) exclaimed, "Allahu Akbar!" He hit once more. Again, a light appeared, and the Prophet (s.a.w) screamed out, "Allahu Akbar!" He struck for the third time. The light returned, the

Prophet (s.a.w) cried, "Allahu Akbar," and the rock was shattered. The Companions enquired of the Prophet (s.a.w) about all of this. Why did he keep saying "Allahu Akbar"?

"Three times I struck this rock with this pickaxe, and three times I saw scenes of the future glory of Islam revealed to me. The first time, I saw the Syrian palaces of the Roman Empire, and I was given the keys to those palaces. The second time, I saw the illumined palaces of Persia at Mada'in, and I was given the keys to the Persian Empire. The third time, I saw the gates of San'a, and I was given the keys to the

With their limited manpower, the trench that the Muslims were able to construct could not have been flawless in terms of military strategy, but it did seem to protect the town from an unexpected attack by the enemy. The battle's following circumstances plainly demonstrated that it was

not insurmountable. There was no other way for the enemy to assault the town.

As a result, the vast army of Arabian tribesmen started to approach Medina from the other side of the ditch. When the Prophet (s.a.w) learned of this, he came out with twelve hundred soldiers to protect it, having sent other men to guard other areas of town.

Historians disagree on how many people guarded the ditch. Some estimate it to be three thousand, others twelve to thirteen hundred, and yet others seven hundred. These estimations seem to be quite difficult to reconcile. However, after analyzing the facts, we have concluded that all three estimates of the Muslim numbers involved in the ditch defense are accurate. They correspond to various phases of the war.

FIGHT AGAINST STRONG ODDS

We've previously agreed that once the hypocrites fled Uhud, there were just seven hundred Muslims remained in the field. Only two years after the Battle of Uhud, the Battle of the Ditch took place. There are no big conversions to Islam documented in history during these two years. It seems unlikely that the number of combatant Muslims would rise from 700 to 3,000 throughout this period. At the same time, it does not make sense that there was no increase in the number of combatant Muslims between Uhud and the Ditch. Between the Battle of Uhud and the Battle of the Ditch, Islam's population continued to grow, and we might anticipate a rise. Based on these two arguments, it seems that the estimate of one thousand two hundred Muslim warriors in the Battle of the Ditch is accurate. The only mystery is why some authorities put the figure at three thousand and others at seven hundred. Our explanation is that the two figures represent two separate phases of the war. The Ditch Battle was fought in three parts. We had the first stage before the enemy arrived in Medina, and Muslims started building the trench. During this period, we may reasonably presume that children and, to a lesser degree, women assisted in carrying the excavated soil. As a result, we may infer that three thousand people were engaged on the Muslim side in the trench digging. Children and women were among those counted. Children were able to assist in hauling the soil, and women, who had always competed with males in aiding all Muslim battles, must have been beneficial in numerous auxiliary activities associated with the digging. This premise is supported by evidence. When the digging began, even youngsters were invited. The digging included almost the whole population. However, as soon as the enemy came and the combat started, the Prophet (s.a.w) ordered all boys under the age of fifteen to leave the battlefield. Those beyond the age of fifteen were permitted to participate if they so desired (Halbiyya, Vol. 2). According to this, Muslim numbers were substantially higher during the time of digging than when the conflict started. The extremely young guys had all retreated at the time of the conflict. Estimates of three thousand Muslims in the war refer primarily to the digging, whereas estimates of one thousand two hundred pertain to the actual conflict, in which only mature men participated. The only estimate we haven't taken into consideration is the one that puts the total at 700. This estimate, too, is accurate in our opinion. It has been suggested by a credible source such as Ibn Ishaq, who is backed up in this estimation by none other than Ibn Hazm. This estimate is tough to call into doubt. Fortunately, when we look at the other aspects of the conflict, we find that even this estimate is right. There is evidence that when the Banu Quraiza joined the enemy and prepared to assault Medina from behind, the Holy Prophet (s.a.w), having been informed of their wicked purpose, chose to deploy guards in the portion of town vulnerable to the Banu Quraiza attack. Because the Banu Quraiza were in partnership with Muslims, this portion of Medina was first left undefended. And it was expected that the enemy would not assault the town from their side. When the defection of the Banu Quraiza was reported to the Prophet (s.a.w) and it became clear that Muslim women, who had been considered safe in this part of town due to the alliance, were no longer safe, the Prophet (s.a.w) decided to send two forces, each of two and three hundred men, to guard two different parts of the now exposed town. The Prophet (s.a.w) instructed them to yell "Allahu Akbar" on occasion so that the main Muslim soldiers would know the Muslim ladies were secure. Ibn Ishaq's estimate, which puts the number of participants in the Battle of the Ditch at 700, is therefore right. Only seven hundred soldiers could survive if five hundred men out of one thousand two hundred were deployed to protect the town's rear. As a result, all three estimates of the size of the Muslim army at the Battle of the Ditch are true.

The Holy Prophet (s.a.w) had just seven hundred warriors to defend the ditch. The trench had really been dug. But facing and repelling an army the size of the enemy's appeared almost impossible, even with the aid of the ditch. But, as always, Muslims believed God and depended on His assistance. While the ladies and children were transferred to two presumably secure corners of town, their little army waited for the enemy host. When the enemy reached the ditch, they were taken aback since this strategy had never been utilized in an Arab war before. So they decided to camp on their side of the ditch and plan their assault and entry into Medina. The ditch sheltered one side. Hills provided natural shelter on the other side. A third side included stone buildings and forest groves. It was hard for the enemy to launch an unexpected assault on any portion of town. The enemy leaders conferred and determined that it was vital to attempt to wean the Banu Quraiza, the last Jewish tribe in Medina, from their allegiance with the Muslims and persuade them to join the Arab confederates in this crucial offensive on Medina. Only the Banu Quraiza knew how to get them to town. Finally, Abu Sufyanra instructed Huyai bin Akhtab, head of the exiled tribe of Banu Nadir and primary motivator of Arab tribes against Medina, to negotiate with the Banu Quraiza for permission to assault the town from the rear. Huyai bin Akhtab went to the Jewish castle to visit the Banu Quraiza chief. They first refused to see him. But when he emphasized that this was an excellent opportunity to destroy the Muslims, he won over one of the Quraizites, Ka'b. He claimed that the whole Arab world has come out to fight and kill the Muslims. The army on the opposite side of the ditch was not an army, but an ocean of able-bodied men against whom the Muslims had no chance. It was eventually determined that as soon as the army of disbelievers succeeded in pushing the ditch, the Banu Quraiza would assault the area of Medina where the Holy Prophet (s.a.w) had sent all the women and children for protection. This strategy, it was thought, would crush the Muslim opposition and turn their whole population—men, women, and children—into a death trap. If this strategy had been even partially successful, it would have cost the Muslims a lot of money and made life extremely difficult for them.

They would have had no way out of this death trap.

BANU QURAIZA'S TRAINER

As previously stated, the Banu Quraiza allied with the Muslims. Even if they did not enter the combat on the Muslim side, it was anticipated that they would block the enemy's path on their side. As a result, the Prophet (s.a.w) had left that portion of town completely unattended. The Banu Quraiza were aware that the Muslims had confidence in them. So, when they chose to join the Arabs, it was agreed that they would not do so publicly, should the Muslims grow alarmed and take efforts to protect the section of town on the Banu Quraiza's side. It was a very risky scheme.

When it was decided that Muslims would be attacked from both sides, the Arab army began attacking the ditch. However, nothing occurred for a few days. Then they had the bright notion of stationing their archers atop an elevation and commanding them to strike Muslim defense groups protecting the ditch. These stood on the rim, separated by small distances. When the Muslim defense began to fray, the disbelievers attempted to cross the ditch with the assistance of their top-notch horsemen. They hoped that if similar raids were repeated, they would gain control of a location on the Muslim side of the ditch from which they could land soldiers for a full-fledged attack on the town. As a result, assault after attack was launched. Muslim defenders had to battle nonstop. One day, they were so preoccupied with resisting these assaults that they missed portions of the regular prayers. The Prophet (s.a.w) was unhappy and shouted, "God punish the unbelievers, they have disrupted our prayers." This episode demonstrates the ferocity of the enemy onslaught. However, it also demonstrates that the Prophet's (s.a.w) first and foremost concern was God's worship. Medina has been attacked from all sides. Women and children, in addition to males, faced certain death. The whole community was in a state of panic. However, the Prophet (s.a.w) considered conducting the daily prayers at their assigned times. Muslims, unlike Christians and Hindus, do not worship God just once a week. Muslims must pray five times every day. Even having one public prayer during a fight is tough, much alone five prayers a day in congregation. However, the

Even throughout war, Prophet (s.a.w) held the five daily prayers. It hurt him if one of these prayers was disrupted by an enemy strike.

Returning to the combat, the enemy was assaulting from the front, while the Banu Quraiza planned to strike from the rear, but not in such a manner that the Muslim people would be alarmed. They intended to infiltrate the town from behind and murder the women and children who were sheltering there. The Banu Quraiza dispatched a spy one day to see whether guards had been deployed to safeguard women and children, and if so, how strong they were. The adversary considered a particular enclosure for families to be their special objective. The spy arrived and started to linger about this cage, looking around suspiciously. While he was doing so, Safiyyara, the Prophet (s.a.w)'s aunt, saw him. Only one male adult was on guard duty at the time, and even he was sick. Safiyyara told him what she had observed and advised him to apprehend this spy before he could notify the enemy about how vulnerable the ladies and children were in that section of town. When the ill Muslim refused to do anything, Safiyyara took up a staff and started fighting this unwanted guest. She was able to overpower and murder him with the aid of other ladies. It was later revealed that this individual was a Banu Quraiza agent. Muslims felt concerned and started to suspect further assaults from this side, which they had previously assumed to be secure. However, the frontal assault was so powerful that the whole Muslim army was required to repel it. Nonetheless, the Prophet (s.a.w) agreed to reserve a portion of the army to safeguard women and children. As we discussed in our study of the Muslim numbers in this fight, the Prophet (s.a.w) despatched five hundred men out of a total of twelve hundred to guard the ladies in the town. Only seven hundred soldiers were left to defend the ditch against an army of between eighteen and twenty thousand. Many Muslims were alarmed by the odds they had to confront. They went to the Prophet (s.a.w) and told him how dire the situation was and how difficult it seemed to be to rescue the village. They asked the Prophet (s.a.w) to pray for them. They also asked him to teach them a unique prayer for the occasion. "Have no fear; just pray to God to protect you from your shortcomings, strengthen your hearts, and ease your anxieties," the Prophet (s.a.w) responded.

words:

God, You have given the Qur'an to me. You are not waiting to bring anybody to account. Give the hordes who have come to assault us defeat. I entreat thee once again, God: Defeat them, make us rule over them, and frustrate all their wicked intents (Bukhari).

And one more:

God, You hear those who cry out to You in their anguish and suffering. Thou respondest to those who are distressed. Please relieve my pain, worry, and dread. You know the chances against me and my companions (Zurqani).

The hypocrites got more anxious than the rest of the Muslim army. All care for their side's honor and the protection of their community, their women and children, had vanished from their hearts. But they didn't want to be humiliated in front of their own people. As a result, they started to abandon the Muslims one by one on flimsy grounds. This is mentioned in the Qur'an in 33: 14.

And some of them even sought the Prophet (s.a.w) for permission, saying, 'Our dwellings are exposed and defenseless.' They were not exposed. They merely wanted to get away.

The following verses in the Qur'an describe the current state of combat and the situation in which the Muslims stood at the time:

When they arrived from above and below you, and your eyes grew preoccupied, and your hearts reached your necks, and you imagined many ideas about Allah. The believers were then severely tested, and they were violently rattled. 'Allah and His Messenger offered us nothing but deception,' murmured the hypocrites and those with a cancer in their hearts. And when one of them said, 'O people of Yathrib, you may not be able to stand against the enemy; therefore, turn back' (33: 11-14), the rest of them agreed.

Muslims are reminded here of how they were assaulted from the front by a confederacy of Arab tribes and from the back by Jews. They are reminded of how unhappy they were at the time. Their hearts were in their lips as their eyes flinched. They even started to have questions about God. The followers were subsequently put on trial. They were all given a jolt. 'We have all been duped by false promises offered to us by God and His Prophet (s.a.w)!' started the hypocrites and spiritually ill.' A portion of them even started to unnerve the Muslim army stating, 'There is no fighting today. There is nothing else to do except return.'

The Qur'an also describes how sincere believers acted on this occasion:

When the believers saw the confederates, they exclaimed, 'This is what Allah and His Messengersa promised us, and Allah and His Messengerra told the truth.' This further strengthened their faith and obedience. Men who have kept the commitment they made with Allah are among the faithful. Some have fulfilled their commitment, while others are still waiting, and their circumstances have not altered (33: 23, 24).

The sincere believers, in contrast to the hypocrites and the weak. When they saw the overwhelming numbers of the enemy, they were reminded of what God and His Prophet (s.a.w) had previously taught them. This coordinated onslaught by Arabian tribes was confirmation solely of the reality of God and the Prophet (s.a.w). True believers were unmoved. Rather, they grew in the spirit of obedience and the zeal of faith. True believers stuck to their agreement with God. Some of them had already accomplished the aim of their life by dying. Some were merely waiting to die in God's way and achieve their aim.

The enemy launched an all-out assault on the ditch. He was sometimes successful in clearing it. One day, prominent generals from the enemy were able to pass. But the Muslims assaulted them so valiantly that they had to retreat. Naufal, a prominent leader of the disbelievers, was killed in this confrontation. This leader was so powerful that the detractors believed they would be unable to bear any disrespect to his dead corpse. They thus sent news to the Prophet (s.a.w) that if he returned this chief's corpse, they would pay ten thousand dirhams. It was a steep price to pay for the body's return. The offer was made as a result of guilt. The disbelievers had disfigured the dead Muslim at Uhud and feared that Muslims would do the similar. But Islam's doctrine was different. The mutilation of the dead was explicitly forbidden in Islam. When the Prophet (s.a.w) heard the message and the offer, he answered, "What use have we for this body? We want nothing in exchange for this; take away the body if it pleases you" (Zurqani, Vol. 2, p. 114).

A passage in Muir's Life of Mohammad (London, 1878, p.322) portrays the ferocity of the onslaught against Muslims beautifully. We make no apologies for using it here:

The next morning, Mahomed discovered the whole Ally army arrayed against him. To impede the enemy's maneuvers, he needed to be very active and vigilant at all times. Now they would threaten a general assault; then, breaking up into divisions, they would attack various posts in rapid and distracting succession; and finally, watching their opportunity, they would mass their troops on the least protected point and attempt to force the trench under cover of a sustained and galling arrow discharge. Such illustrious commanders as Khalidra and 'Amrra staged valiant raids against the city and Mahomedsa's tent, only to be repulsed by repeated counter-marches and unrelenting archery. This lasted throughout the day, and since Mahomedsa's force was only large enough to protect the lengthy line, there could be no relieve. Even at night, Khalidra kept the alarm going with a large company of horsemen, endangering the line of defense and necessitating outposts at regular intervals. However, all of the enemy's efforts proved futile. The trench had not been spanned.

The fight had lasted two days. There had been no hand-to-hand combat or major carnage. After twenty-four hours of warfare, just three people had died on the opposing side and five on the Muslim side. Sa'd bin Mu'adhra, the Aus tribe's leader and a follower of the Prophet (s.a.w), was injured. strikes on the ditch, on the other hand, caused some damage, making subsequent strikes simpler. Great acts of bravery and devotion were observed. It had been a frigid night, maybe the coldest in Arabia. We have it on good word from 'A'ishara, the Prophet's (s.a.w) holy spouse, that the Prophet (s.a.w) awoke often from his slumber to monitor the damaged section of the trench. He was fatigued. He went back to bed, but after warming up a bit, he went back to patrol the ditch. He was so weary one day that he seemed to be unable to move. Then he expressed his desire for a devout Muslim to come and relieve him of the physical labor of guarding the ditch in the dead of night. He soon heard a voice. Sa'd bin Waqqasra it was.

The Prophet (s.a.w) inquired as to why he had come.

"To protect your person," Sa'dra said.

"There is no need to watch my person," the Prophet (s.a.w) responded. "A section of the ditch has been broken; go and monitor it so that Muslims may be secure." Sa'dra left, and the Prophet (s.a.w) was able to sleep. (There was some irony in this, for when the Prophet (s.a.w) came in Medina and the risk to his person was considerable, it was Sa'dra who volunteered himself as a guard.) On another occasion during these difficult days, the Prophet (s.a.w) heard the sound of guns. "Who is it?" inquired Prophet (s.a.w). "'Ibad bin Bishrra," was the response.

"Do you have anybody else with you?" the Prophet (s.a.w) inquired. "Yes," 'Ibadra said, "a team of Companions, and we will protect your tent."

"Leave my tent alone; disbelievers are attempting to cross the ditch; attack them" (Halbiyya, Vol. 2).

As previously stated, the Jews attempted to sneak into town. In the process, a Jewish spy was killed. When they discovered that their plot had been exposed, they started to publicly assist the Arab confederates. A coordinated assault in the rear, on the other hand, was not attempted since the field on this side was small and a large-scale attack had become difficult with the deployment of the Muslim guards. However, a few days later, the Jews and their pagan allies planned to launch a surprise assault on the Muslims.

THE CONFEDERATES ARE DISPERSING

This hazardous scheme, however, was miraculously halted by God. This is how it occurred'. One Nu'aimra, a member of the Ghatafan tribe, grew interested in Islam. He had arrived with the pagan army but was looking for a way to support the Muslims. He couldn't accomplish much on his own. But when he realized that Jews had joined forces with the Arabs and Muslims seemed to be doomed to death and ruin, Nu'aimra resolved to do all in his power to rescue the Muslims. He visited the Banu Quraiza and spoke with their leaders. What did they anticipate Muslims to do if the Arab troops fled? Shouldn't the Jews, who have made an agreement with the Muslims, be prepared to face retribution for those who break the agreement? The Jewish leaders were terrified by the questioning. They inquired as to what they should do. Nu'aimra instructed them to request 70 pagans as hostages. If the pagans were truthful about a coordinated assault, they would not decline the request. They should explain that these seventy would protect their key sites while they assaulted the Muslims from behind. He went to the heathen chiefs after his meetings with the Jews. He asked them what they would do if the Jews broke their agreement; if, in order to appease the Muslims, they demanded heathen captives and then gave them over to the Muslims. Wasn't it vital for them to put the Jews to the test by asking them to join the common onslaught right away? This counsel pleased the pagan leaders. Acting on it, they sent word to the Jews, asking if they would not assault the town from behind now that they (the confederates) were prepared for the intended onslaught. The Jews responded that the next day was their Sabbath, and they could not fight. Second, they claimed that they belonged to Medina and that the Arab confederates were all strangers. What were the Jews planning to do if the Arabs fled the battle? As a result, the Arabs should provide seventy men as hostages. The Jews would be ready to carry out their portion of the assault at that point. Suspicion was already in the air. The

Arabs turned down the Jewish plea. If the Jews were sincere in their agreement with the Arabs, the kind of proposition they had made had no significance. Suspicion being a subversive of bravery, the Arab troops lost their enthusiasm and went to sleep laden with uncertainties and troubles when night fell. In a sad attitude, both commanders and soldiers returned to their tents. Then a miracle occurred, with aid from above appearing to the Muslims. A strong breeze started to blow. The tent walls were washed away. Cooking pans fell on flames. Some flames were put out. The pagans believed in keeping a fire going all night. A roaring campfire was a positive omen, but a smoldering one was a terrible omen. When a fire in front of a tent was doused, the inhabitants would retreat from the combat for the day, only to rejoin later. The pagan leaders were already filled with apprehension. When some campers packed out, others assumed the Muslims had launched a nocturnal attack. The idea quickly spread. They all began packing and leaving the field. Abu Sufyanra was supposed to be sleeping in his tent. His ears were alerted to the unexpected retreat of the pagan divisions. He stood up, irritated, and rode a tethered camel. He pushed the animal, but it refused to move. His comrades pointed out what he was doing, untied the animal, and Abu Sufyanra was allowed to depart the area with his buddies.

It was two-thirds of the way through the night. The battlefield had already been cleansed. An army of twenty to twenty-five thousand troops and supporters vanished, leaving a total wilderness in its wake. Just then, the Prophet (s.a.w) had a revelation that the enemy had departed as a consequence of a divine act. To learn out what had transpired, Prophet (s.a.w) planned to dispatch one of his disciples to scan the battlefield and report back. It was really chilly outside. It's no surprise that the ill-dressed Muslims were chilly. When the Prophet's (s.a.w) shouted out in the middle of the night, some people heard him. They wanted to respond but were unable to. The cold felt oppressive. "Yes, Prophet (s.a.w) of God, what do you want us to do?" only Hudhaifara could utter loudly.

The Prophet (s.a.w) yelled once more. Because of the cold, no one could respond. Only Hudhaifara responded once more. The Prophet (s.a.w) sent Hudhaifara to assess the battleground since God had told him that the enemies had retreated. Hudhaifara approached near the ditch and noticed that the enemy had left the field. There were no troops or guys present. Hudhaifara went back to the Prophet (s.a.w), chanted the Kalima, and announced that the enemies had departed. On the next day, Muslims unpegged their tents and began packing for the city. A twenty-day long harsh trial had come to an end.

BANU QURAIZA HAS BEEN PUNISHED

Muslims were allowed to breathe freely once again. But they still had to deal with the Banu Quraiza. The Banu Quraiza had broken their contract with the Muslims, which could not be overlooked. The Prophet (s.a.w) gathered his tired forces and informed them that there would be no respite for them. They had to attack the Banu Quraiza's defences before the sun set. Then he sent 'Alira to the Banu Quraiza to inquire as to why they had broken their sacred promise. The Banu Quraiza expressed no remorse or desire for pardon. Instead, they insulted 'Alira and the other Muslim representatives and began shouting filthy insults at the Prophet (s.a.w) and his family's ladies. They said they did not like Muhammad (s.a.w) and had never made an agreement with him. When 'Alira returned to report the Jews' response, he saw the Prophet (s.a.w) and Companions moving on the Jewish walls. The Jews had been mistreating the Prophet (s.a.w), as well as his wife and daughters. Fearing for the Prophet (s.a.w), 'Alira advised that there was no need for the Prophet (s.a.w) to participate since the Muslims could deal with the Jews on their own. "You want me not to hear their insults, 'Alira?" the Prophet (s.a.w) comprehended.

"Exactly," 'Alira responded.

"But why?" asked Prophet (s.a.w). "Mosesas was of their family, but they inflicted more anguish on him than they have on me," the Prophet (s.a.w) said. The Jews erected defenses and began fighting. Their wives joined them as well. Some Muslims sat at the base of a wall. When a Jewish lady saw this, she threw a stone at them, killing one called Khalladra. The siege lasted many days. The Jews believed they would not be able to hold out for long at the conclusion of this time. Then their rulers requested that the Prophet (s.a.w) send Abu Lubabara, an Ansari chief of the Aus, a friendly tribe to the Jews. They wanted to talk to him about a potential settlement. The Prophet (s.a.w) sent Abu Lubabara to the Jews, who asked him whether they should lay down their guns and accept the Prophet (s.a.w)'s prize. They should, according to Abu Lubabara. At the same moment, he made the death sign with his finger over his neck. Nobody had heard anything from the Prophet (s.a.w) about this. But, feeling that the Jews' guilt deserved nothing but death, Abu Lubabara accidentally made this gesture, which proved catastrophic for the Jews. The latter refused to accept the Prophet's (s.a.w) honor after rejecting Abu Lubaba'sra's advise. If they had accepted it, the most severe penalty would have been exile from Medina. However, as fate would have it, they declined to accept the Prophet's (s.a.w) honor. They declared they would take the prize of Sa'd bin Mu'adhra, leader of their friends, the Aus, instead of the Prophet's (s.a.w). They would accept whatever penalty he offered. A disagreement emerged among the Jews as well. Some of them started to claim that their people had broken their promise to the Muslims. Muslims' behavior, on the other hand, demonstrated that they were truthful and honest, and that their religion was likewise true. Those who believed in this manner converted to Islam. One of the Jewish rulers, 'Amr bin Ma'dira, rebuked his people, saying, "You have committed a breach of trust and gone back on your plighted word; the only path now available to you is to embrace Islam or offer jizya."

"We will neither embrace Islam nor offer jizya, since dying is preferable than providing jizya," they responded. 'Amr replied that in that case, he stood absolved, and with that, he departed the fort.

Muhammad bin Maslamara, commander of a Muslim column, saw him and asked him who he was. When he discovered his identity, he encouraged him to go in peace and prayed aloud:

"God, grant me the ability to filter the faults of the decent forever."

He meant that this Jew had expressed guilt and sadness for the actions of his people. As a result, Muslims had a moral obligation to forgive persons like him. He had done the right thing by letting him go, and he begged to God to give him the opportunity to do so again and again. When the Prophet (s.a.w) learned of Muhammad bin Maslamara's actions, he did not condemn him for releasing this Jewish leader. He, on the other hand, approved of what had been done.

Individual Jews have declared their willingness to make peace and receive the Prophet (s.a.w)'s honor. They stayed steadfast and refused to accept the prize of the Prophet (s.a.w), instead requesting the honor of Sa'dra bin Mu'adh (Bukhari, Tabari, and Khamis). The Prophet (s.a.w) agreed to their petition and summoned Sa'dra, who was laying injured, to come and deliver his verdict on the Jewish violation of trust. As soon as the decision of the Prophet's (s.a.w) was revealed, the Ausites, who had long been supporters of the Banu Quraiza, went to Sa'dra and started to persuade him to deliver his prize to the Banu Quraiza. They said that the Khazraj had always attempted to preserve Jewish allies. It was up to Sa'dra to rescue the Jews who had joined forces with his people. Sa'dra rode his horse to the Banu Quraiza. Men from his clan accompanied him on both sides, pleading with him not to punish the Banu Quraiza. Sa'dra's only response was that the person who had to make an award possessed a trust. He had to fulfill the trust with honesty. "I will therefore make my award, taking everything into account, and without fear or favor," he stated. When Sa'dra arrived to the Jewish fortification, he noticed the Banu Quraiza waiting for him against the fort's wall. Muslims were on the opposite side. When Sa'dra approached them, he said, "Will you accept my award?" They replied, "Yes."

SA'D'Sra AWARD IN CONNECTION WITH THE BIBLE

He addressed the same question to the Banu Quraiza, and they agreed. Then, sheepishly, he pointed to the side where the Prophet (s.a.w) was seated and asked whether the people on that side consented to follow his reward as well. When the Prophet (s.a.w) heard this, he said, "Yes" (Tabari and Hisham). Then Sa'dra presented his reward in line with the following Bible requirement. According to the Bible:

When thou approachest a city to battle against it, profess peace to it. And it shall be, if it gives thee an answer of peace and opens to thee, that all the people found therein shall be tributaries to thee, and they shall serve thee. And if it will make no peace with thee, but will make war against thee, then thou shalt besiege it: And when the Lord thy God hath delivered it into thine hands, thou shalt smite every male thereof with the edge of the sword: But the women, and the little ones, and the cattle, and all that is in the city, even all the spoil thereof, shalt thou take unto thyself; and thou shalt eat the spoil of thine enemies, which the Lord thy God hath given thee. Thus shalt thou do unto all the cities which the Lord thy God giveth thee for an inheritance; thou shalt utterly destroy them; namely, the Hittites, and the Amoiites, the Canaanites, and the Perizzites, the Hivites, and the Jebusites; as the Lord thy God hath commanded thee: That they teach you not to do after all their abominations, which they have done un

According to biblical doctrine, if the Jews had prevailed and the Prophet (s.a.w) had lost, all Muslims—men, women, and children—would have been executed. We know from history that this was the Jews' objective. The least the Jews might have done was execute the males, enslave the women and children, and steal the Muslims' goods, as is prescribed in Deuteronomy for enemies residing in remote areas of the earth. The Banu Quraiza were friendly to Sa'dra. His tribe had formed an alliance with theirs. When he realized that the Jews had refused to accept the Prophet (s.a.w)'s prize, and therefore the milder penalty required for such an offense in Islam, he chose to punish the Jews with the punishment that Mosesas had set down. This prize is not the fault of the Prophet (s.a.w) or the Muslims, but of Mosesas and his doctrine, as well as of the Jews who had treated the Muslims so harshly. They were given what would have been considered a sympathetic reward. Instead of accepting this, they insisted on a Sa'dra prize. Sa'dra determined to punish the Jews in line with Mosesas' Law. Despite this, Christians continue to malign the Prophet (s.a.w) of Islam and claim that he was harsh to the Jews. If the Prophet (s.a.w) was violent to Jews, why wasn't he cruel to others or on other occasions? On several instances, the Prophet's opponents flung themselves at his mercy, and they never asked for his pardon in vain. On this case, the adversary insisted on the award being made by someone other than the Prophet (s.a.w). This Jewish candidate, acting as an arbiter between them and the Muslims, publicly asked the Prophet (s.a.w) and the Jews whether they would accept his honor. He only announced it after the parties had reached an agreement. And what was his prize? It was nothing more than the application of Moses' Law to the Jewish offense. So why shouldn't they have embraced it? Did they not consider themselves Mosesas' followers? If there was any brutality, it was committed by Jews against Jews. The Jews refused to accept the Prophet's (s.a.w) reward, instead inviting their own religious law to be applied to their offense. If there was any cruelty, it was committed by Mosesas, who established this sentence for a besieged enemy and recorded it in his book at God's order. Christian authors should not unleash their rage on the Prophet (s.a.w) of Islam. They should punish Moses, who imposed this horrible sentence, as well as Moses' God, who instructed him to do so.

After the Battle of the Ditch, the Prophet (s.a.w) proclaimed that from then on, pagans would not fight Muslims; rather, Muslims would attack pagans. The tide was about to change. Muslims were ready to go on the offensive against tribes and groups who had previously attacked and harassed them. The Prophet (s.a.w)'s words were not hollow threats. The Arab confederates had suffered no significant casualties in the Battle of the Ditch. They had only lost a few guys. They might have assaulted Medina again in less than a year, with even superior preparations. Instead of a twenty-thousand-man army, they might have formed a forty- or even fifty-thousand-man army for a fresh offensive. An army of a hundred or a hundred and fifty thousand men was not beyond their capabilities. But, over the last twenty-one years, Islam's opponents had done all they could to eradicate Islam and Muslims. Their confidence had been undermined by their schemes' continued failure. They had began to fear that what the Prophet (s.a.w) taught was real, and that their national idols and gods were untrue, that the Creator was the One Invisible God taught by the Prophet (s.a.w), and that the Creator was the One Invisible God taught by the Prophet (s.a.w). The dread that the Prophet (s.a.w) was correct and they were not had began to seep in. However, there was no visible evidence of this concern. Physically, the disbelievers went about their business as usual. They went to their idols and prayed to them, as was customary. But their spirit had been shattered. They lived outwardly as pagans and disbelievers, yet their hearts appeared to echo the Muslim cry, 'There is no God but Allah.'

As previously stated, after the Battle of the Ditch, the Prophet (s.a.w) proclaimed that from then on, disbelievers would not fight Muslims, but that Muslims would attack disbelievers. The endurance of Muslims had reached its limit. The tide was turning (Bukhari, Kitabal Maghazi).

DO THE PROPHET (S.A.W) WISH TO CONTINUE WAR?

In previous conflicts, Muslims had either stayed in Medina or traveled some distance outside of it to combat disbelievers' attacks. Muslims did not initiate these meetings and showed no desire to prolong them once they began. Normally, hostilities may only be stopped in two ways: an agreed-upon peace or the subordination of one side to the other. So yet, there has been no sign of reconciliation between Muslims and nonbelievers, nor has any side volunteered to surrender. True, there had been lulls in the warfare, but no one could claim that the conflict between Muslims and nonbelievers had stopped. Ordinary canons state that Muslims may have assaulted the hostile tribes and forced them to submit. However, Muslims did not do so. When the adversary stopped fighting, Muslims did as well. They came to a halt because they thought there would be peace talks. However, when it became clear that the disbelievers were not talking about peace and were not willing to surrender, the Prophet (s.a.w) believed that the moment had come to terminate the conflict, either by a peace treaty or by one side surrendering to the other. If there was to be peace, the war had to cease. Following the Battle of the Ditch, the Prophet (s.a.w) seemed resolved to achieve one of two outcomes: peace or capitulation. It was unthinkable for Muslims to submit to nonbelievers. God had prophesied that Islam would triumph over its persecutors. During his stay in Mecca, the Prophet (s.a.w) made declarations to that effect. Could Muslims have then filed a peace suit? A peace movement might be started by either the stronger or the weaker party. When the weaker party seeks peace, it must cede a portion of its territory or income, either temporarily or permanently, or accept other terms set by the opponent. When the stronger side offers peace, it is believed that it does not want to completely destroy the weaker side, but rather to allow it to preserve entire or partial independence in exchange for specific terms. In previous confrontations between Muslims and nonbelievers, the latter had suffered loss after defeat. Their power, however, had not been shattered. They had only failed in their efforts to exterminate Muslims. Failure to destroy another does not imply failure. It just signifies that aggressiveness has not yet succeeded; unsuccessful assaults may be repeated. As a result, the Meccans had not been defeated; only their assault against Muslims had failed. Muslims were clearly the weaker party militarily. True, their defense was still maintained, but they were a pitiful minority, a minority that, although able to withstand the majority's assault, was unable to go on the offensive. As a result, Muslims had not yet achieved independence. If they had sued for peace, it would have signaled that their defense had failed and they were now willing to accept the disbelievers' demands. They would have made a horrible peace offer to Islam. It would have meant self-destruction. It would have given fresh vitality to an opponent who had been discouraged by successive losses. A increasing feeling of failure would have given way to newfound optimism and drive. Disbelievers would have assumed that, after saving Medina, Muslims were still gloomy about their final triumph over disbelievers. As a result, a proposition of peace could not have come from the Muslim side. It may have started from the Meccan side or from a third side, if one could have been discovered. However, no third side could be located. Medina was pitted against all of Arabia in the ensuing battle. It was therefore the disbelievers who might have sued the Muslims for peace, but there was no evidence of this. Thus, the conflict between Muslims and Arabs may have lasted indefinitely. The Muslims were unable and unwilling to sue for peace. As a result, civil conflict in Arabia seemed to have no end in sight, at least not for another hundred years.

If Muslims wished to put a stop to the fighting, they only had one option. They were unwilling to give up their conscience to the Arabs, that is, to relinquish their freedom to profess, practice, and teach whatever they pleased; therefore there was no peace movement among the disbelievers. Muslims had successfully repelled repeated assault. It was consequently up to them to push the Arabs to either surrender or accept peace. The Prophet (s.a.w) made the decision.

Was it battle that the Prophet (s.a.w) desired? He did not wish to bring about conflict, but rather peace. If he had not intervened at this point, Arabia would have remained in the grasp of civil strife. The move he made was the only way to find peace. Long conflicts have occurred throughout history. Some have lasted a century, while others have just lasted thirty years or so. Long conflicts have always stemmed from either side's failure to take decisive action. As previously said, decisive action can only take one of two forms: total capitulation or negotiated peace.

Could the Prophet (s.a.w) have stayed silent? Could he have withdrawn himself and his tiny band of Muslims behind Medina's walls and permitted everything else to happen on its own? This was just not feasible. The violence had begun with the disbelievers. Passivity would have meant the continuance of the conflict, not its termination. It would have meant that the infidels might have attacked Medina anytime they pleased. They could halt whenever they wanted and strike whenever they wanted. A lull in fighting did not signify the end of the conflict. It was just a calculated move.

WAR TEACHINGS IN JUDAISM AND CHRISTIANITY

But now the issue is whether it is ever ethical to fight for one's religion. Let us now proceed to this subject.

Religion is taught in several ways on the issue of war. We have mentioned the Old Testament's doctrine. Moses is given the mandate to invade Canaan by force, vanquish its inhabitants, and establish his own people there (Deut. 20: 10-18). Despite this instruction in the Book of Mosesas, and despite the practical example of the Prophets Joshuaas, Davidas, and others, Jews and Christians continue to worship their Prophets and view their writings as the writings of God.

We had Jesusas who taught towards the close of the Mosaic tradition;

But I say to you, resist not evil; but whomever smiteth thee on the right cheek, turn to him the other as well (Matthew 5: 39).

Christians have often quoted this Jesusas teaching to show that Jesusas taught against war. However, there are passages in the New Testament that seem to teach the exact opposite. For example, one text says:

Do not think that I have come to bring peace on earth: I have come to send a sword (Matthew 10: 34).

Another section states:

Then he addressed them. But now, whomever has a purse, take it, and also his scrip: and whoever has no sword, sell his garment, and buy one (Luke 22: 36).

The final two verses of the three contradict the first. Why did Jesus preach about turning the other cheek if he came to fight? It seems that we must either acknowledge a contradiction in the New Testament or explain one of the conflicting doctrines in an appropriate way. We're not interested in whether or not it's ever possible to turn the other cheek. We are just concerned with pointing out that no Christian people have ever hesitated to wage war throughout their lengthy history. When Christians first came to power in Rome, they fought both defensive and offensive battles. They are today's main nations, and they continue to engage in both defensive and offensive conflicts. Only now is the victor's side sanctified by the rest of the Christian world. Their victory is seen as the triumph of Christian culture. Christianity has come to represent whatever is dominant and successful. When two Christian powers go to war, one claims to be defending Christian beliefs. The winning power is sanctified as the real Christian force. However, from the time of Jesus to the present, Christendom has been engaged in conflict, and all signs are that it will continue to be so. As a result, the practical verdict of Christian peoples is that war is the true teaching of the New Testament, and that turning the other cheek was either an opportunist teaching dictated by the helplessness of early Christians, or it is meant to apply only to individuals, not States and peoples.

Second, even if we think that Jesus preached peace rather than conflict, this does not imply that individuals who do not follow this message are not holy and honored. For Christendom has always admired warriors like Moses, Joshua, and David. Not only that, but the Church has canonized national heroes who perished in battles. The Popes declared them saints.

THE QUEEN'S QURAN ON WAR AND PEACE

Islam's doctrine differs from both of these beliefs. It finds a happy medium between the two. Islam, unlike Moses, does not preach hostility. It also does not teach a contradiction, as modern (and likely corrupt) Christianity does. It does not expect us to turn the other cheek while also selling our garments to acquire a weapon. Islam's message corresponds to man's basic tendencies and fosters peace in the only manner feasible.

Although Islam bans violence, it encourages us to fight if failure to fight endangers peace and promotes conflict. It is our obligation to resist if failing to fight implies the extinction of free belief and the pursuit of truth. This is the doctrine upon which peace may be constructed, and it is the teaching with which the Prophet (s.a.w) formed his own policies and practices. At Mecca, the Prophet (s.a.w) suffered repeatedly and persistently, but he did not confront the hostility of which he was an innocent victim.

When he retreated to Medina, the adversary was attempting to eradicate Islam; it was therefore vital to battle the enemy in defense of truth and freedom of religion.

The sections in the Qur'an that deal with battle are quoted below.

(1) In 22: 40-42, we find:

Permission to fight is given to those against whom war is made because they have been wronged—and Allah indeed has the power to help them—Those who have been driven out of their homes unjustly only because they said, "Our Lord is Allah"—And if Allah did not repel some men by means of others, cloisters and churches and synagogues and mosques, wherein the name of Allah is frequently commemorated, would surely have been pulled down. And Allah will undoubtedly assist anybody who assists Him. Allah is certainly Mighty and Powerful.—Those who, if We establish them on earth, would observe Prayer, pay Zakat, and enjoin good and prohibit evil. And Allah is the ultimate arbiter of all matters.

The phrase seems to indicate that victims of assault are granted permission to fight. God is more than capable of assisting the victims—those who have been forced to flee their homes because of their beliefs. The permission is sensible because there would be no freedom of religion and worship in the world if God did not oppose the cruel with the support of the virtuous. God must assist people who work to promote liberty and worship. As a result, fighting is authorized when a people has long suffered from wanton aggression—when the attacker has no reason to be aggressive and attempts to interfere with his victim's religion. If and when the victim achieves power, his obligation is to create religious freedom and to preserve all faiths and sacred sites. His authority is not to be utilized for his personal glory, but for the benefit of the people, the advancement of the nation, and the general promotion of peace. This instruction is both exceptional and clear and exact. It says that early Muslims went to battle because they were forced to do so. Islam forbade aggressive warfare. Muslims are promised political authority, but they are admonished that this power must be utilized for the betterment of the poor and the advancement of peace and development, not for self-aggrandizement.

(2) In (2: 191-194), we find:

And battle in Allah's name against those who oppose you but do not transgress. Allah, without a doubt, does not love transgressors. And kill them wherever you encounter them, and drive them out of the places where they have driven you out, for persecution is worse than murdering. And do not fight them in or near the Sacred Mosque until they fight you, and then fight them: such is the requital for disbelievers. But if they repent, Allah is Most Forgiving and Merciful. And battle them until there is no persecution and faith for Allah is practiced. But if they stop, remember that no animosity is permitted except against aggressors.

Fighting is to be done for God's sake, not for our own, or out of rage or self-promotion, and even fighting is to be devoid of excesses, for excesses are displeasing to God. Fighting occurs between combatant groups. Individual assaults are prohibited. Aggression against a religion must be answered with aggressive opposition, since such aggression is worse than bloodshed. Muslims are not to battle near the Sacred Mosque until the adversary first attacks. Fighting near the Sacred Mosque violates the public's right to pilgrimage. However, if the adversary assaults, Muslims are permitted to respond, since this is the appropriate recompense for aggression. However, if the adversary ceases to exist, Muslims must cease to exist as well, and forgive and forget the past. Fighting will continue as long as religious persecution and religious freedom do not coexist. Religion exists to glorify God. It is unacceptable to employ force or coercion in religion. If the Kafirs stop doing it and make religion free, Muslims must stop battling the Kafirs. Arms must be raised against those who perpetrate excesses. When the excesses stop, the fighting must stop as well.

We may categorize the verses as teaching the following rules:

(i) War is to be fought exclusively for the cause of God, not for selfish reasons, self-aggrandizement, or the promotion of any other objectives.

(ii) We can only go to battle against the one who assaults us first.

(iii) We can only fight those who fight against us. We cannot battle people who do not participate in combat.

(iv) It is our responsibility to minimize warfare even after the adversary has launched it. Extending the conflict, either geographically or in terms of weaponry deployed, is wrong.

(v) We are only to battle a regular army sent by the adversary to fight on his side. We are not to fight those on the other side.

(vi) In times of war, all religious ceremonies and observances are immune. If the adversary spares sites where religious activities are performed, Muslims must likewise refrain from fighting in such locations.

(vii) If the adversary utilizes a place of worship as a basis for an assault, Muslims may retaliate. If they do so, they will have no responsibility. Fighting is prohibited, even in the vicinity of sacred sites. It is strictly unlawful to assault religious sites and damage or injure them in any way. A sacred site exploited as a base of operations may draw retaliation. The adversary will then have responsibility for any damage done to the site, not Muslims.

(viii) If the adversary understands the danger and error of utilizing a sacred site as a base and shifts the battleground, Muslims must adapt. The fact that the adversary launched the assault from a holy site is not a cause to strike such site.

Muslims must shift their battlefront as fast as their adversary does. (ix) Fighting will continue only as long as there is interference with religion and religious freedom. When religion becomes free and interference with it is no longer permissible, and the adversary announces and begins to behave appropriately, there will be no war, even if it is initiated by the enemy.

(3) In 8:39-41, we find:

Tell those who do not believe that if they repent, the past will be forgiven them; but if they return, the example of the previous people has already gone before them.

And battle them until there is no more persecution and religion is only for Allah's sake. But if they repent, Allah is undoubtedly watching what they do. And if they turn away, remember that Allah is your Protector. What a wonderful Protector and Helper you are.

That is to say, Muslims have been obliged to fight in conflicts. However, if the adversary ceases to exist, Muslims must cease to exist as well and forgive the past. But if the opponent does not relent and continues to assault Muslims, he should recall what happened to the adversaries of previous Prophets. Muslims must resist as long as religious persecution continues, religion is not for God, and involvement in religious issues is not prohibited. When the aggressor stops, Muslims must stop as well. They are not to continue fighting since the opponent follows a false faith. God recognizes the worth of ideas and deeds and will reward them accordingly. Muslims have no authority to interfere with another people's religion, even if it seems to them to be incorrect. If the opponent continues to wage war after an offer of peace, Muslims may be certain of victory despite their meager numbers. Because God will assist them, and who can assist better than God?

These verses were revealed at the Battle of Badr. This was the first regular conflict between Muslims and nonbelievers. Muslims were the victims of unwarranted hostility in it. The adversary had decided to disrupt Medina's and the surrounding territory's tranquility. Despite this, the Muslims were victorious, and key enemy commanders were assassinated. To respond to such unjustified attack seems natural, right, and essential. However, Muslims are instructed to quit fighting as soon as the opponent stops. All the opponent has to give up is the right to believe and worship freely.

(4) In 8:62—63, we find:

And if they lean toward peace, lean toward it as well, and put your confidence in Allah. He is, without a doubt, All-Hearing and All-Knowing. And if they aim to fool thee, Allah is definitely enough for thee. He is the one who has fortified you with His aid and the believers.

That is, if the disbelievers ever tilt towards peace during a struggle, Muslims must accept the offer immediately and make peace. Muslims must do so even if it means being mislead. They must place their faith in God. Cheating will not work against Muslims who depend on God's aid. Their successes are owed to God, not to them. God has stood with the Prophet (s.a.w) and his followers even in the darkest and most trying times. So He will stand with them in the face of deception. A peace offer must be accepted. It is not to be disregarded on the grounds that it may be a ploy used by the adversary to buy time for a new assault.

The emphasis on peace in the lines is significant. It foreshadows the peace treaty made by the Prophet (s.a.w) at Hudaibiya. The Prophet (s.a.w) is warned that the adversary will sue for peace at some point. The offer is not to be rejected because the opponent was the aggressor and had committed excesses, or because he cannot be trusted. The straight road taught by Islam demands a Muslim to accept a peace offer.

Acceptance is desirable for reasons of both piety and policy.

(5) In 4: 95, we find:

Believers, rejoice! When you go out in the cause of Allah, conduct appropriate research and do not say to anybody who welcomes you with a greeting of peace, "Thou art not a believer." You seek the riches of this world, yet there are excellent things in plenty with Allah. You were like this previously, but Allah bestowed His favor on you, therefore conduct a thorough examination. Allah is undoubtedly aware of everything you do.

That is, when Muslims go to battle, they must ensure that the unreasonableness of war has been communicated to the opponent and that he still wishes to fight. Even However, if a peace proposal is received from a person or a group, Muslims are not to reject it on the grounds that it is not honest. If Muslims reject peace initiatives, they will be battling for self-aggrandizement and earthly riches rather than God. Worldly riches and fame come from God in the same way as religion does. The goal is not to kill. Someone we want to murder today could be guided tomorrow. Could Muslims have converted to Islam if they had not been spared? Muslims must refrain from murdering since lives saved may turn out to be guided lives. God is perfectly aware of what mankind do and for what purposes and motivations they do it.

The passage indicates that even after a conflict has started, Muslims must convince themselves that the opponent is intent on aggression. It is very uncommon for no aggression to be planned, but for the opponent to begin war preparations out of excitement and terror. Muslims are not to go to battle until they are certain that the opponent has prepared an aggressive assault. If it is discovered, or if the opponent claims, that his preparations are for self-defense, Muslims must accept the assertion and refrain from fighting. They are not to claim that the enemy's preparations indicate only to aggressiveness; maybe he meant violence, but his purpose has altered. Aren't intents and motivations always shifting? Didn't Islam's foes become friends?

(6) Regarding the inviolability of treaties, the Qur'an states unequivocally:

Except for those idolaters with whom you have signed a pact and who have not since failed you in anything or assisted anybody against you. So keep the pact you signed with them until the end of their tenure. Allah, without a doubt, likes the pious (9: 4).

Pagans who make an agreement with Muslims, maintain the contract, and do not aid the enemy against Muslims will be treated equally by Muslims. Piety compels Muslims to fulfill their side of an agreement both in text and spirit.

(7) The Qur'an commands an opponent in war with Muslims who seeks to learn the Message of Islam:

V

That is, if any of those at war with Muslims take sanctuary with Muslims in order to study Islam and consider its Message, they are to do so for as long as is practically required for such a purpose.

(8) The Qur'an says regarding captives of war:

It is not incumbent for a Prophet to hold prisoners until he participates in regular combat in the region. You covet worldly possessions, but Allah desires the Hereafter for you. Allah is Mighty and Wise (8:68).

That is, a Prophet does not become a prisoner of his adversary until there is a genuine conflict with tremendous slaughter. The method of creating captives of opposing tribes without conflict and bloodshed that existed before to—and even after—the arrival of Islam is rendered illegal here. Prisoners may only be seized from fighters after a battle.

(9) Guidelines for the release of convicts are also established. As a result, we have:

Then, either as a favor or by paying a ransom, release them until the battle is over (47:5).

According to Islam, the greatest option is to release detainees without demanding a ransom. Because this is not always feasible, ransom release is also an option.

(10) There is a provision for prisoners of war who are unable to pay for their own release and have no one who can or would pay. Often, relatives are able to pay but refuse because they wish to keep their relatives imprisoned—possibly with the goal of misappropriating their possessions while they are away. The following provision is found in the Qur'an:

And those who wish a document of manumission from among those in your right hands, write it for them if you see any good in them, and give them from Allah's riches which He has bestowed upon you (24: 34).

That is, people who do not deserve to be released without ransom but do not have someone to pay ransom for them—if they still want their freedom—can gain it by signing an undertaking that if they are permitted to work and earn, they would pay their ransom. They will be permitted to do so, however, only if their ability to work and earn is practically guaranteed. If their competency is shown, Muslims should support them financially in their efforts to work and earn. Individual Muslims who can afford to pay should do so, or a public subscription could be established to help these unfortunates get back on their feet.

The chapters from the Qur'an mentioned above convey Islamic doctrine on the issue of war and peace. They inform us when, according to Islam, it is permissible to go to battle and what boundaries Muslims must obey while going to war.

WAR PRECEPTS FROM THE PROPHET

However, Muslim teaching does not depend only of Qur'anic principles. It also incorporates the Prophet (s.a.w)'s principles and example. What he did or taught in real-life circumstances is also an important aspect of Islamic teaching. We have included some of the Prophet (s.a.w)'s sayings on war and peace.

(i) Muslims are prohibited from mutilating the deceased (Muslim).

(ii) Muslims are not permitted to cheat (Muslim).

(iii) Neither children nor women (Muslim) are to be slain.

(iv) Priests, religious officials, and religious leaders must not be harmed (Tahavi).

(v) The elderly and infirm, as well as women and children, are not to be slain. The potential of peace should be kept in mind at all times (Abu Dawud).

(vi) When Muslims visit enemy land, they should not instill fear among the locals. They should not tolerate mistreatment of ordinary people (Muslims).

(vii) A Muslim army should not camp in an area that is inconvenient for the general populace. When marching, it should take care not to obstruct traffic or give annoyance to other travelers.

(viii) No facial deformity is permissible (Bukhari and Muslim).

(ix) The adversary should suffer the fewest casualties feasible (Abu Dawud).

(x) When placing prisoners of war under protection, those who are closely connected should be placed together (Abu Dawud).

(xi) Prisoners should be comfortable. Muslims should be concerned with the welfare of their captives more than their own (Tirmidhi).

(xii) Foreign emissaries and delegates should be treated with utmost courtesy. Any errors or discourtesies they make should be overlooked (Abu Dawud, Kitab al jihad).

(xiii) If a Muslim commits the sin of mistreating a prisoner of war, he must atone by releasing the prisoner without compensation.

(xiv) When a Muslim takes responsibility of a prisoner of war, he is to feed and clothe the prisoner in the same manner as the Muslim himself (Bukhari).

The Holy Prophet (s.a.w) was so adamant about these fighting army standards that he said that anybody who did not follow them would fight not for God, but for his own nasty self (Abu Dawud).

Abu Bakrra, the First Khalifah of Islam, supplemented the Prophet (s.a.w)'s commandments with some of his own. One of the instructions inserted here is also part of Muslim teaching:

(xv) Public structures and fruit-bearing trees (as well as food crops) must not be harmed (Mu'atta).

It is clear from the Prophet (s.a.w)'s sayings and the directives of the First Khalifah of Islam that Islam has adopted actions that have the effect of averting or halting a conflict or lessening its harm. As previously said, the ideas taught by Islam are more than just religious precepts; they have practical application in the example of the Prophet (s.a.w) and the early Khalifahs of Islam. As everyone knows, the Prophet (s.a.w) not only preached these concepts, but he also practiced and insisted on their adherence.

In our present day, no other teaching seems to be capable of resolving the dilemma of war and peace. Mosesas' message is diametrically opposed to our notions of justice and fairness. Today, it is also impossible to put such teaching into practice. Jesusas' doctrine is and has always been unworkable. Christians have never attempted to put this doctrine into effect throughout their history. Only the message of Islam is feasible; it has been both taught and practiced by its proponents, and its practice can generate and sustain global peace.

Mr. Gandhi evidently preached in our time that even if war is imposed on us, we should not go to war. We must not fight. However, this instruction has never been put into reality in the history of the globe. It has never been tried in the crucible. As a result, it is hard to tell what significance this instruction may have in terms of war and peace. Mr. Gandhi lived to see the Indian Congress achieve political independence. Nonetheless, the Congress government has not abolished the army or any of India's other military forces.

It is merely planning their Indianization. It also has ambitions to reinstall Indian commanders who formed the Indian National Army (and were sacked by British authorities) during the Japanese onslaught on Burma and India in the last stages of the recent World War. Mr. Gandhi has often raised his voice in support of victims of violent acts and sought the release of those responsible. This demonstrates, at the very least, that Mr. Gandhi's doctrine cannot be put into effect, and that Mr. Gandhi is aware of this as are all of his followers. At the very least, no practical example has been provided to demonstrate the world how nonviolence might be utilized when armed conflicts emerge between nations and states, or how nonviolence can be used to prevent or end a war. Preaching a way for ending conflicts but never being able to provide a practical instance of that approach suggests that the method is unworkable. As a result, it seems that human experience and knowledge lead to just one technique of averting or ending conflict, and that approach was taught and practiced by Islam's Prophet (s.a.w).

DISBELIEVERS' SPORADIC ATTACKS

The Arab confederates returned from the Battle of the Ditch defeated and sad, but they were far from comprehending that their ability to persecute Muslims was ended. Despite their setback, they understood they still had a commanding majority. Individual Muslims might be abused, beaten, and even killed. They tried to erase their sense of defeat by attacking people. They started to assault Muslims in and around Medina not long after the fight. Fazara tribal members riding on camels assaulted Muslims near Medina. They stole the camels discovered in that area, imprisoned a lady, and fled with the plunder. The lady managed to flee, but Fazara's group was successful in stealing a number of animals. A month later, a detachment of the Ghatafan tribe approached from the north, attempting to rob Muslims of their camel herds. The Prophet (s.a.w) sent Muhammad bin Maslamara and 10 mounted Companions on a reconnaissance mission and to defend the Muslim livestock. But the enemy ambushed the Muslim company and murdered them all, leaving them for dead. Muhammad bin Maslamara, on the other hand, was simply unconscious. After regaining consciousness, he gathered himself, returned to Medina, and filed a complaint. A few days later, a Prophet (s.a.w) diplomat on his route to Rome was assaulted and robbed by members from the Jurham tribe. A month later, the Banu Fazara raided a Muslim caravan and looted much. It is probable that this assault was not motivated by religious prejudice. The Banu Fazara were a marauding tribe known for theft and slaughter. The Jews of Khaibar, who were a major force in the fight of the Ditch, were likewise resolved to revenge their catastrophic loss in that fight. On the Roman boundary, they went about agitating tribal communities and officials of state.

As a result, Arab officials, unable to launch a direct assault on Medina, conspired with Jews to make life difficult for Muslims. The Prophet (s.a.w), on the other hand, had yet to commit to a determined struggle. He hoped that Arab leaders would make a peace offer, and the civil war would stop.

THE PROPHET (S.A.W) LEAVES WITH ONE THOUSAND OVER 500 COMPANIONS FOR MECCA

During this period, the Prophet (s.a.w) had a vision, which is recorded in the Qur'an as follows:

If God wills, you will enter the Sacred Mosque in safety, some with their heads shaved and others with their hair cut short, and you will not be afraid. But He knew something you didn't. He has, in fact, decreed for you a triumph that is close at hand (48: z8).

That is, God had chosen to allow Muslims to approach the Ka'ba precincts in peace, with heads shaved and hair trimmed (the visible indications of pilgrims to the Ka'ba), and without fear. But Muslims had no idea how God was going to allow this to happen. Furthermore, before Muslims could make their journey in peace, they would experience another triumph, a foreshadowing of the victory foretold in the vision.

In this vision, God predicted Muslims' final triumph, their peaceful march into Mecca, and their conquering of Mecca without the use of guns. However, the Prophet (s.a.w) interpreted it to signify that Muslims were instantly instructed by God to undertake a circuit of the Ka'ba. The Prophet (s.a.w)'s misunderstanding of the vision was to be the catalyst for the 'close at hand' triumph foretold in the vision. As a result, the Prophet (s.a.w) prepared a march towards the Ka'ba in mistake. He told Muslims about his vision and his interpretation of it, and he advised them to prepare. "You will travel solely to conduct a round of the Ka'ba," he declared, "and there will be no protests against the enemy." Late in February 628, fifteen hundred pilgrims led by the Prophet (s.a.w) began their trip to Mecca. A mounted guard of twenty went ahead of the Muslims to warn them if the enemy showed indications of attacking.

This caravan was immediately reported to the Meccans. Tradition has established the Ka'ba circuit as a universal right. It could hardly be denied to Muslims. They had said unequivocally that the only goal of their march was to complete the circle. Demonstrations of any type were prohibited by the Prophet (s.a.w). There were to be no disagreements, questions, or claims. Despite this, the Meccans began to prepare for an armed war. They erected defenses on all sides, summoned the help of the neighbouring tribes, and seemed prepared to battle. When the Prophet (s.a.w) arrived near Mecca, he learned that the Quraish were prepared to war. They were dressed in tiger skins, accompanied by their women and children, and had promised solemnly not to allow the Muslims through. The tiger skins were a symbol of ferocious fighting spirit. Soon after, the Muslims were challenged by a column of Meccans moving in the van of their army. Muslims could no longer approach until they drew the sword. The Prophet (s.a.w), on the other hand, was adamant about doing nothing of the like.

He hired a guide to lead the Muslim caravan another way across the desert. The Prophet (s.a.w) and his Companions were led by this guide to Hudaibiya, a location extremely close to Mecca.

The Prophet's (s.a.w) dromedary came to a halt and refused to continue.

"The animal is fatigued, O Prophet (s.a.w) of God; you should change your mount," a Companion said.

"No, no," the Prophet (s.a.w) responded. "The animal is not fatigued; rather, it seems like God wants us to halt here and not go any farther; hence, I offer to camp here and pray for forgiveness."

The figure is incorrect; it is more likely to be one thousand two hundred.

"I, for one, will accept any restrictions imposed by the Meccans if they would let us to do the Pilgrimage" (Halbiyya, Vol. 2, p. 13).

The Meccan army was not in Mecca at the time. It had traveled a considerable distance to meet the Muslims on the major route to Medina. If the Prophet (s.a.w) had desired, he might have marched his fifteen hundred troops into Mecca and conquered the city without opposition. But he was resolved to try just the Ka'ba circuit, and only if the Meccans let it. He would have resisted and battled the Meccans only if they had struck first. As a result, he left the main route and camped near Hudaibiya. The word quickly reached the Meccan commander, who ordered his soldiers to evacuate and station themselves near Mecca. The Meccans then sent a leader, Budail, to negotiate with the Prophet (s.a.w). The Prophet (s.a.w) clarified to Budail that he and the Muslims just intended to complete the Ka'ba circle; nevertheless, if the Meccans decided to battle, the Muslims were ready. Then 'Urwa, the Meccan commander's son-in-law, arrived at the

Prophet (s.a.w). He was quite impolite. He referred to Muslims as tramps and dregs of society, claiming that the Meccans would not allow them to enter Mecca. More Meccans arrived for negotiations, and the final thing they stated was that Muslims would not be allowed to do even the Ka'ba circuit that year. The Meccans would be embarrassed if the circuit was allowed this year. They may do so the next year.

Some Meccan allies pushed the Meccan officials to allow the Muslims to complete the round. After all, it was merely the right of way they desired. Why should they be prevented from doing so? The Meccans, on the other hand, were determined. The tribe elders then said that the Meccans did not desire peace and threatened to cut ties with them. The Meccans were convinced to attempt to strike an agreement with the Muslims out of fear. When the Prophet (s.a.w) learned of this, he sent 'Uthmanra (after the Third Khalifah of Islam) to the Meccans. 'Uthmanra had a large family in Mecca. They encircled him and promised to let him perform the circuit, but proclaimed that the Prophet (s.a.w) would not be allowed to do so until the next year. "But," 'Uthmanra responded, "I will not do the circuit unless I am accompanied by my Master." 'Uthmanra's conversations with the leaders of Mecca proved lengthy. A malicious rumor circulated that he had been killed. It reached the Prophet (s.a.w)'s ears. The Prophet (s.a.w) gathered the Companions and declared, "The life of an envoy is held sacred among all nations. I have heard that the Meccans murdered 'Uthmanra. If this is true, we must enter Mecca, whatever the consequences." The Prophet (s.a.w)'s earlier intention to enter Mecca peacefully had to be changed due to the changed circumstances. "Those who promise solemnly that if they have to go further, they will not turn back except as victors," the Prophet (s.a.w) continued, "should come forward and take the oath on my hand." The Prophet (s.a.w) had hardly finished speaking when all fifteen hundred Companions stood up and jumped over one another to hold the Prophetssa hand and take the oath. This pledge is particularly significant in the history of early Islam. It's known as the "Tree Pledge." The Prophet (s.a.w) was seated behind a tree when the oath was administered. Everyone who took the oath was proud of it till the end of his days. Not one of the fifteen hundred people in attendance held back. They all vowed that if the Muslim emissary was killed, they would not return. Either they took Mecca before dark or they all died fighting. When 'Uthmanra returned, the oath-taking was not finished. He said that the Meccans refused to allow the Muslims to perform the circuit until the next year. They had designated representatives to negotiate a solution with the Muslims. Soon after, Suhail, a Mecca leader, arrived at the Prophet (s.a.w). A resolution was reached and recorded.

HUDAIBIYA TREATY

It went like this:

In Allah's name, amen. These are the terms of peace agreed upon between Muhammad (s.a.w), son of 'Abdullah, and Suhail ibn 'Amr, Mecca's envoy. For the next 10 years, there will be no warfare. Anyone who wants to join Muhammad (s.a.w) and make an agreement with him is free to do so. Anyone who chooses to join the Quraish and form an alliance with them is free to do so. A young guy or one whose father is still living who travels to Muhammad (s.a.w) without authorization from his father or guardian will be returned to him. However, if somebody goes to the Quraish, he will not be returned. This year, Muhammad (s.a.w) will return without visiting Mecca. But next year, he and his followers will be able to enter Mecca, spend three days there, and complete the circle. The Quraish will retreat to the neighboring hills for three days. When Muhammad (s.a.w) and his companions arrive at Mecca, they will be unarmed save for the sheathed swords that all Arabian wayfarers carry (Bukhari).

During the signing of this peace treaty, two unusual things occurred. After the conditions were agreed upon, the Prophet (s.a.w) began to dictate the agreement, saying, "In the name of Allah, the Gracious, the Merciful."

Suhail protested, saying, "Allah we know and believe in, but who is this 'the Gracious and the Merciful?' This agreement is between two parties, thus both sides' religious views must be honored."

The Prophet (s.a.w) agreed immediately and told his scribe, "Only write, 'In the name of Allah,'" before going on to dictate the details of the deal. 'These are the prerequisites of peace between the people of Mecca and Muhammad (s.a.w), the Prophet (s.a.w) of God,' said the first phrase. Suhail protested again, saying, "If we felt you were a Prophet (s.a.w) of God, we would not have battled you," which the Prophet (s.a.w) accepted.

He recommended Muhammad (s.a.w) son of 'Abdullah instead of Muhammad (s.a.w), the Prophet (s.a.w) of God. The Companions were angered by the humiliation as the Prophet (s.a.w) agreed to whatever the Meccans suggested.

Their fury started to boil, and the most enraged of them all, 'Umarra, rushed to the Prophet (s.a.w) and questioned, "O Prophet (s.a.w) of God, are we not in the right?"

"Yes," the Prophet (s.a.w) said, "we are in the right." "And weren't we instructed by God that we would complete the circle of the Ka'ba?" 'Umarra inquired.

"Yes," the Prophet (s.a.w) said.

"So, what is the point of this agreement and these degrading terms?"

"True," the Prophet (s.a.w) replied, "God did foresee that we would complete the round in peace, but He did not indicate when; I judged that it would be this year."

But I may be mistaken, and does it have to be this year?" 'Umarra was hushed.

Then other Companions voiced their concerns. Some of them questioned why they had agreed to return a young Muslim to his parent or guardian without demanding the same treatment for a Muslim who turned over or went to the Meccans. The Prophet (s.a.w) clarified that there was no damage done. "Everyone who becomes a Muslim does so because he accepts the beliefs and practices instilled by Islam. He does not become a Muslim in order to join a party and adopt its customs. Such a man will propagate the Message of Islam wherever he goes, and serve as an instrument for the spread of Islam. But a man who gives up Islam is no use to us. If he no longer believes at heart what we believe, he is no longer one of us. It should now satisfy all those who believe that the penalty for apostasy in Islam is death. If this were the case, the Prophet (s.a.w) would have demanded the return and punishment of those who abandoned Islam.

After the agreement was written out and the parties' signatures were appended, a circumstance happened that put the parties' good faith to the test. The Meccan plenipotentiary, Suhail's son, stood before the Prophet (s.a.w), tied, wounded, and tired. "O Prophet (s.a.w) of God, I am a Muslim at heart, and because of my faith, I have to suffer these troubles at the hands of my father. My father was here with you, so I escaped and managed to come to you," he said. Abu Jandalra, the young man's name, appeared before the Muslims, a brother of brothers driven to desperation by his father's mistreatment. They couldn't bear the thought of having to send him back. They drew their swords, seemingly ready to kill or rescue this brother. Abu Jandalra personally pleaded with the Prophet (s.a.w) to allow him stay. Will he return him to the oppressors from whose hands he had escaped? But the Prophet (s.a.w) seemed unfazed. "Prophets do not eat their words," he told Abu Jandalra. "We have signed this agreement now. It is for you to bear with patience and put your trust in God. He will certainly provide for your freedom and the freedom of other young people like you." After the agreement was signed, the Prophet (s.a.w) returned to Medina. Soon after, another young Mecca convert, Abu Basirra, arrived in Medina. However, in accordance with the terms of the arrangement, he was also returned by the Prophet (s.a.w). On the way back, he and his guards got into a battle, during which he murdered one of the guards and managed to escape. The Meccans grumbled once again to Prophet (s.a.w). "But," the Prophet (s.a.w) explained, "we handed over your man to you; he has now escaped out of your hands; it is no longer our duty to find him and hand him over to you again." A few days later, a woman escaped to Medina, and some of her relatives went after her and demanded her return. The Prophet (s.a.w) explained that the agreement had made an exception for men, not women, and he refused to return this woman.

LETTERS OF THE PROPHET TO VARIOUS KINGS

After returning from Hudaibiya, the Prophet (s.a.w) instituted another plan for the spread of his Message. When he mentioned this to the Companions, some of them who were familiar with the customs and forms observed in kings' courts told the Prophet (s.a.w) that kings did not entertain letters that did not bear the senders' seals, so the Prophet (s.a.w) had a seal made with the words, Muhammad Rasulullahsa engraved on it.

Out of respect, Allah was placed first, followed by Rasul, and last Muhammad (s.a.w).

In Muharram 628, envoys went to different capitals, each with a letter from the Prophet (s.a.w), inviting the rulers to accept Islam. Envoys went to Heraclius, the Roman Emperor, the Kings of Iran, Egypt (the King of Egypt was then a vassal of the Kaiser) and Abyssinia. They went to other kings and rulers also. The letter addressed to the Kaiser was taken by Dihya Kalbira who was instructed to call first on the Governor of Busra. When Dihyara saw the Governor, the great Kaiser himself was in Syria on a tour of the Empire. The Governor readily passed Dihyara on to the Kaiser. When Dihyara entered the court, he was told that whoever was received in audience by the Kaiser must prostrate himself before him. Dihyara refused to do this, saying that Muslims did not bow before any human being. Dihyara, therefore, sat before the Kaiser without making the prescribed obeisances. The Kaiser had the letter read by an interpreter and asked if an Arab caravan was in the town. He said he desired to interrogate an Arab about this Arabian Prophet (s.a.w) who had sent him an invitation to accept

Islam. Abu Sufyanra happened to be in town with a commercial caravan, and the court officials took him to the Kaiser. Abu Sufyanra was ordered to stand in front of the other Arabs, who were told to correct him if he told a lie or made a wrong statement, and then Heraclius proceeded to interrogate Abu Sufyanra.

H: Do you know this individual who claims to be a Prophet (s.a.w) and has given me a letter? Can you tell me about his family?

A-S: He is related to me and hails from a noble family.

H: Have there been other Arabs who made allegations similar to his?

A-S: No.

H: Did your guys ever accuse him of lying before he made his claim?

A-S: No.

H: Were there any kings or rulers among his forefathers?

A—S: No.

H: How would you rate his overall competence and judgment capacity?

A—S: We have never noticed anything wrong with his skill or judgment.

H: Who are his followers like? Are they wealthy and powerful, or poor and humble?

A—S: Most are impoverished, modest, and youthful.

H: Do their numbers tend to rise or fall?

A—S: To expand.

H: Do his followers ever revert to their previous beliefs?

A—S: No.

H: Has he ever violated a promise before?

A—S: Not yet, but we have just engaged into a new contract with him, so we'll see what he does about it.

H: Have you fought with him yet?

A—S: Yes.

H: What was the end result?

A—S: Victory and defeat alternate between us and him like buckets on a wheel. In the Battle of Badr, for example, in which I was not present, he was able to overpower our side. In the Battle of Uhud, in which I commanded our side, we took his side to task, tore their stomachs, ears, and noses, H: But what does he teach?

A—S: That we should worship the One God and not set up equals with Him. He preaches against the idols that our forefathers worshiped, and instead wants us to worship the Only God, speak only the truth, and always abjure all vicious and corrupt practices. He exhorts us to be good to one another, to keep our covenants, and to discharge our trusts.

This fascinating discussion came to a conclusion when the Kaiser said:

I first asked you about his family and you said he belonged to a noble family. In truth, Prophets always come of noble families. I then asked you if anyone before him had made a similar claim and you said, No. I asked you this question because I thought that if in the recent past some one had made such a claim, then one could say that this Prophet (s.a.w) was imitating that claim. I then asked you whether he had ever been charged with lying before his claim had been announced and you said, No. I inferred from this that a person who does not lie about men will not lie about God. I next asked you if there had been a king among his forefathers and you said, No. From this I understood that his claim could not be a subtle plan for the recovery of the kingdom. I then asked you whether the entrants into his fold were mostly big, prosperous and powerful individuals or poor and weak. And you said in reply, that they were generally poor and weak, not proud and big, and so are the early followers of a Prophet. I then asked you whether his numbers were increasing or decreasing and you said they were increasing. At this I remembered that the followers of a Prophet go on increasing until the Prophet attains his goal. I then asked you if his followers left him out of disgust or disappointment, and you said, No. At this I remembered that the followers of Prophets are usually steadfast. They may fall away for other reasons, but not out of disgust for the faith. I then asked you if there had been fights between you and him and, if so, with what results. And you said that you and his followers were like buckets on a wheel and the Prophets are like that. In the beginning their followers suffer reverses and meet with misfortunes, but in the end they win. I then asked you about what he teaches and you said he teaches the worship of One God, truth-speaking, virtue and the importance of keeping covenants and discharging trusts. I asked you also whether he ever played false, and you said, No. And this is the way of virtuous men. It seems to me, therefore, that his claim to being a Prophet (s.a.w) is true. I was half expecting his appearance in our time, but I did not know he was going to be an Arab. If what you have told me is true, then I think his influence and his dominion will certainly spread over these lands (Bukhari).

The speech alarmed the courtiers, who began to blame the King for applauding a Teacher from another community. Protests erupted, and the court officials expelled Abu Sufyanra and his companions.

To the Chief of Rome, Heraclius, from Muhammad (s.a.w), the Servant of God and His Messenger. Whoever treads the path of divine guidance, on him be peace. After this, O King, I invite you to Islam. Become a Muslim. God will protect you from all afflictions, and reward you twice. But if you deny and refuse to accept this Message, then the sin not only of your own denial, but of the denial of your subjects, will be on your head." 'Come to a word equal between us and you that we worship none but Allah, that we associate no partner with Him, and that some of us do not accept others as lords beside Allah.' But if they turn away, then, 'Bear witness that we have surrendered to God.'" (Zurqani).

The call to Islam was an invitation to accept that God is One and Muhammad (s.a.w) is His Messenger, and that if Heraclius becomes a Muslim, he would be rewarded twice over, a reference to the fact that Islam teaches belief in both Jesusas and Muhammad (s.a.w).

When the letter was presented to the Emperor, some courtiers suggested that it be torn up and thrown away because it was an insult to the Emperor because it did not refer to him as Emperor but only as Sahibul Rum, i.e., the Chief of Rome. The Emperor, however, said that it was unwise to tear up the letter without reading it. He also said that the address, 'Chief of Rome,' was not incorrect.

When the Prophet (s.a.w) was told how Heraclius had received his letter, he seemed satisfied and pleased, and said that because of the reception which the Roman Emperor had given his letter, his Empire would be saved, and the Emperor's descendants would continue to rule over the Empire for a long time, which is exactly what happened. In later wars, a large part of the Roman Empire, in accordance with another prophecy of the Prophet (s.a.w) of Islam, passed out of the Roman Empire.

LETTER TO IRAN'S KING

The letter was sent to the King of Iran through 'Abdullah bin Hudhafara, and the wording was as follows:

In the name of Allah, the Gracious, the Merciful.. This letter is from Muhammad (s.a.w), the Messenger of God, to Chosroes, the Chief of Iran. Whoever submits to perfect guidance, and believes in Allah, and bears witness that Allah is One, and has no equal or partner, and that Muhammad (s.a.w) is His Servant and Messenger, on him be peace. O King, under God's command, I invite you to Islam.

'Abdullah bin Hudhafara claims that when he arrived at the court of Chosroes, he applied for admission to the royal presence. He handed over the letter to the Emperor, who ordered an interpreter to read it and explain its contents. On hearing the contents, the Chosroes became enraged and tore the letter to pieces. 'Abdullah bin Hudhafara reported the incident to the Prophet (s.a.w), who said:

What the Chosroes did to our letter, God will do to his Empire (i.e., tear it apart).

The fit of temper which the Chosroes showed on this occasion was the result of the pernicious propaganda carried on against Islam by Jews who had migrated from Roman territory to Iran. These Jewish refugees took a leading part in anti-Roman intrigues sponsored in Iran, and had, therefore, become favourites at the Iranian court. The Chosroes was full of rage against the Prophet (s.a.w). The reports about the Prophet (s.a.w) which the Jews had taken to Iran, it seemed to him, were confirmed by this letter. He thought the Prophet (s.a.w) was an aggressive adventurer with designs on Iran. Soon after, the Chosroes wrote to the Governor of Yemen, saying that one of the Quraish in Arabia had announced himself a Prophet (s.a.w). His claims were becoming excessive. The Governor was asked to send two men charged with the duty of arresting this Quraishite and bringing him to the court of Iran. Badhan, the Governor of Yemen under the Chosroes, sent an army chief with a mounted companion to the Prophet (s.a.w). He also gave them a letter addressed to the Prophet (s.a.w), in which he said that on receipt of the letter the Prophet (s.a.w) should at once accompany the two messengers to the court of Iran.

The two planned to go first to Mecca. When somewhere near Ta'if, they were told that the Prophet (s.a.w) lived in Medina. So they went to Medina. On arrival this army chief told the Prophet (s.a.w) that Badhan, the Governor of Yemen, had been ordered by the Chosroes to arrange for the Prophet's (s.a.w) arrest and despatch to Iran. If the Prophet (s.a.w) refused to obey, he and his people were to be destroyed and their country made desolate. Out of compassion for the Prophet (s.a.w), this delegate from Yemen insisted that the Prophet (s.a.w) should obey and agree to be led to Iran. Having listened to this, the Prophet (s.a.w) suggested that the delegates should see him again the following day. Overnight the Prophet (s.a.w) prayed to God Who informed him that the insolence of the Chosroes had cost him his life. "We have set his own son against him, and this son will murder his father on Monday the 10th Jumad al-'Ula of this year." According to some reports, the revelation said, "The son has murdered the father this very night." It is possible that that very night was the 10th Jumad al'Ula In the morning, the Prophet (s.a.w) sent for the Yemen delegates and told them of what had been revealed to him overnight. Then he prepared a letter for Badhan saying that the Chosroes was due to be murdered on a certain day of a certain month. When the Governor of Yemen received the letter he said, "If this man be a true Prophet (s.a.w), it will be even as he says. If he is not true, God help him and his country." Soon after, a boat from Iran arrived in Yemen, bringing a letter from the Emperor of Iran to the Governor of Yemen. The letter bore a new seal, which led the Governor to believe that the prophecy of the Arabian Prophet (s.a.w) had come true. A new seal meant a new king. He opened the letter.

I have murdered my father because his rule had become corrupt and unjust. He murdered the nobles and treated his subjects with cruelty. As soon as you receive this letter, gather all officers and ask them to affirm their loyalty to me. Regarding my father's orders for the arrest of an Arabian Prophet (s.a.w), you should regard those orders as cancelled (Tabari, Vol. 3, pp. 1572-1574 and Hisham p. 46).

These incidents so moved Badhan and several of his associates that they immediately announced their faith in Islam and told the Prophet (s.a.w).

AN APPEAL TO THE NEGUS

'Amr bin Umayya Damrira delivered the letter to Negus, King of Abyssinia. It went like this:

Muhammad (s.a.w), the Prophet of God, writes to Negus, King of Abyssinia, in the name of Allah, the Gracious, the Merciful. God's peace be with you, King. I honor the One and Only God before you. Nobody else is worthy of adoration. He is the King of monarchs, the source of all excellences, without flaws; He gives tranquility to all His slaves and protects His creations. I give evidence that Jesus, son of Maryas, was a God-sent Messenger who came to fulfill God's promises to Mary. Mary had given her life to God. I ask you to join me in attaching ourselves to and following the One and Only God. I ask you to join me in following me and believing in the God Who sent me. I am His representative. I encourage you and your soldiers to join the Almighty God's

Faith. I hereby release my obligation. I have brought the
Message of God to you and explained its significance to you.
I have done it sincerely, and I hope you will appreciate the
seriousness that has inspired my communication. Whoever
obeys God's counsel becomes heir to God's benefits
(Zurqani).

When this letter reached the Negus, he treated it with great consideration and reverence. He raised his eyes to it, dismounted from the throne, and ordered an ivory casket for it. Then he placed it in the box and said, "While this letter is secure, my kingdom is safe." He was correct. For a thousand years, Muslim armies were on the march to conquest. They moved in all directions and passed by Abyssinia on all sides, but they did not approach the Negus' little kingdom?; and this because of two notable deeds of the Negus: the safety he provided for early Muslim refugees and the devotion he gave to the Prophet's (s.a.w) message. The Roman Empire was shattered. The Chosroes' dominions were lost. The kingdoms of China and India vanished, but this little kingdom of the Negus survived because its monarch welcomed and sheltered the first Muslim refugees and shown respect and veneration for the Prophet's (s.a.w) message.

In this manner, Muslims repaid the Negus' magnanimity. Compare this to the treatment meted out by a Christian people in this period of civilization to the Christian kingdom of the Negus. They bombed and devastated Abyssinia's open cities from the air. The royal family was forced to seek safety abroad and leave their homeland for many years. Two distinct persons handled the same people in two different ways. Because of the magnanimity of one of its monarchs, Muslims revered and protected Abyssinia. In the name of civilisation, a Christian country conquered and ravaged it. It demonstrates how healthy and long-lasting the Prophet's (s.a.w) teaching and example are. Muslims revered a

Christian monarchy as a result of their thanks. Christian greed targeted the same kingdom, oblivious to the fact that it was Christian.

LETTER TO EGYPT'S RULER

Hatib ibn Abi Balta'ara delivered the letter to Muqauqis. The wording of this letter was identical to that sent to the Roman Emperor. According to the letter to the Roman Emperor, the sin of denying Roman subjects will befall him. According to the letter to the Muqauqis, the monarch would bear the guilt of denying the Copts. It went like this:

In the name of Allah, the Merciful and Gracious. This letter is from Muhammad (s.a.w), Allah's Messenger, to Muqauqis, the Coptic Chief. Peace be upon him who walks the road of righteousness. I ask you to embrace Islam's Message. You will be rescued if you believe, and your prize will be doubled. If you did not believe, you will bear the sin of the Coptic denial. "O People of the Book! come to a word equal between us and you that we worship none but Allah, and that we associate no partner with Him, and that some of us do not take others for lords beside Allah; but if they turn away, say, 'Bear witness that we have submitted to God."

When Hatibra arrived in Egypt, he did not discover Muqauqisin as the capital. Ilatib accompanied him to Alexandria, where he presided over a court near the shore. Hatibra traveled by boat. The court was well fortified. As a result, Hatibra displayed the letter from a distance and started speaking loudly. Hatibra was brought to him by the Muqauqis. The Muqauqis read the letter and asked, "If this man is a true Prophet (s.a.w), why does he not pray for the destruction of his enemies?" Hatibra replied, "You believe in Jesusas. He was mistreated by his people, yet he did not pray for their destruction." The King paid Hatibra a tribute and called him a wise envoy of a wise man. He had responded effectively to the queries posed to him. Hatibra then spoke again. "Before you," he said, "there was a king who was proud, arrogant, and cruel. He was the Pharaoh who persecuted Mosesas, and at the end he was overtaken by divine punishment. Show no pride, therefore. Believe in this Prophet (s.a.w) of God. By God Mosesas did not foretell about Jesusas as clearly as Jesusas foretold about Muhammad (s.a.w).

Hearing this, Muqauqis disclosed that he had heard of this Prophet (s.a.w)'s teaching and thought that he did not teach or prohibit anything beneficial. He'd also done some research and discovered that he wasn't a sorcerer or soothsayer. He'd heard of some of his forecasts coming true. Then he summoned an ivory box, put the Prophet (s.a.w)'s letter inside, sealed it, and passed it over to a servant girl for safekeeping. He also responded to the Prophet (s.a.w) with a letter. This letter's text is preserved throughout history. It goes like this:

In the name of Allah, the Merciful and Gracious. Muqauqis, Coptic King, to Muhammad (s.a.w), son of 'Abdullah. Peace be with you. Following that, I state that I have read your letter and considered its contents as well as the beliefs to which you have invited me. I am aware that the Hebrew Prophet (s.a.w) predicted the arrival of a Propheta in our day. But I expected him to emerge in Syria. I greeted your envoy and gave him a gift of one thousand dinars and five khil'ats, and I sent you two Egyptian females as a gift. My people, the Copts, hold these young ladies in high regard. Maryra is one of them, while Sirinra is the other. I'm also sending you twenty high-quality Egyptian linen outfits. I'll also send you a mule to ride. Finally, I pray once more for God's peace for you (Zurqani and Tabari).

It is obvious from this letter that, although Muqauqis handled the letter with respect, he did not adopt Islam.

LETTER TO BAHRAIN'S CHIEF

The Prophet (s.a.w) also wrote to Mundhir Taimi.

Bahrain's Prime Minister. 'Ala' ibn Hadramira carried this letter. This letter's content has been lost. When this Chief heard about it, he believed it and wrote to the Prophet (s.a.w), claiming that he and many of his friends and supporters had chosen to join Islam. Some, on the other hand, had elected to remain outdoors. He also claimed to have Jews and Magians living beneath him. What could he do about them?

The Prophet (s.a.w) responded back to this Chief, saying:

I am pleased that you have accepted Islam. Your responsibility is to obey the delegates and messengers whom I will send to you. Anyone who obeys them obeys me. The courier who delivered my letter to you commended you and convinced me of your genuineness. I have prayed to God on behalf of your people. Attempt to teach them the ways and practices of Islam. Keep their things safe. No one should have more than four wives. Past misdeeds have been forgiven. You will continue to dominate over your people as long as you are nice and moral. Jews and Magians, on the other hand, just had to pay a tax. As a result, put no additional expectations on them. In terms of the general population, individuals who do not have enough land to sustain themselves should have four dirhams and some fabric to wear (Zurqani and Khamis).

The Prophet (s.a.w) also sent letters to the King of 'Uman, the Chief of Yamama, the King of Ghassan, the Chief of Bani Nahd, a Yemeni tribe, the Chief of Hamdan, another Yemeni tribe, the Chief of Bani 'Alim, and the Chief of the Hadrami tribe. The majority of them converted to Islam.

These writings demonstrate the Prophet's (s.a.w) full confidence in God. They also demonstrate that the Prophet (s.a.w) thought from the start that he had been sent by God not to any one nation or area, but to all the peoples of the globe. True, the recipients of these letters got them in a variety of ways. Some of them immediately adopted Islam. Others considered the letters but refused to adopt Islam. Others treated them with common civility. Others displayed scorn and pride. But it is also true, and history bears testimony to this, that the receivers of these letters or their peoples were fated in line with how they handled these messages.

THE ENDING OF KHAIBAR

As previously stated, Jews and other opponents of Islam were now busily inciting tribes against Muslims. They were now confident that Arabia could not resist Islam's growing influence and that Arab tribes could not invade Medina. As a result, the Jews started to flirt with the Christian tribes who had established on the Roman Empire's southern border. At the same time, they began writing to their Iraqi co-religionists in opposition to the Prophet (s.a.w). They attempted to incite the Iranian Chosroes against Islam by false information sent through letters. As a consequence of Jewish scheming, the Chosroes turned against Islam and even sent the Governor of Yemen instructions to arrest the Prophet (s.a.w). The Prophet (s.a.w) were saved only via unique divine intervention and heavenly mercy, and the Emperor of Iran's evil intention was foiled. It should go without saying that, except for the heavenly assistance that the Prophet (s.a.w) received throughout his lifetime, the gentle movement of early Islam would have been snuffed out by the hatred and antagonism of the Emperors of Rome and Iran. When the Chosroes ordered the arrest of the Prophet (s.a.w), the Emperor was ousted and executed by his own son before the instructions could be carried out, and his orders for the arrest of the Prophet (s.a.w) were annulled by the new ruler. Because the rulers of Yemen were amazed by this miracle, Yemen quickly became a province of the Muslim Empire. The intrigues that the Jews continued to concoct against Muslims and their town of Medina necessitated their removal from Medina. If they were permitted to continue living close, their intrigues would almost certainly lead to much more killing and mayhem. After returning from Hudaibiya, the Prophet (s.a.w) waited five months before deciding to expel them from Khaibar. Khaibar was just a short distance from Medina, and the Jews found it quite simple to continue their intrigues from here. With this goal in mind, the Prophet (s.a.w) marched on Khaibar in August 628 A.D. He was accompanied by a force of 1,600 troops. As previously stated, Khaibar was a fortified town. It was bordered on all sides by cliffs perched with little fortifications. It was no simple undertaking to conquer such a region with such a tiny army. After some combat, the tiny positions on the outskirts of Khaibar fell. But when the Jews gathered in the town's major fort, all assaults on it and all sorts of tactics utilized against it appeared to fail. The Prophet (s.a.w) had a revelation one day that Khaibar would fall into the hands of 'Alira. The Prophet (s.a.w) announced this to his followers the next morning, saying, "Today, I will hand over the black flag of Islam to him who is dear to God, His Prophet (s.a.w), and all the Muslims; God has ordained that our victory at Khaibar should take place at his hands." The next day, he sent for 'Alira and handed him the flag. 'Alira was impatient. He led his troops to the center fort. Despite the fact that the Jews had gathered in force inside this fort, 'Alira and his army were able to take it before dusk. A peace treaty was concluded. All Jews, their wives, and their children were required to leave Khaibar and relocate to a location distant from Medina. Their property and things will be taken over by Muslims. The peace would not protect anybody who attempted to hide any of his property or businesses, or who made an incorrect statement. He would have to pay the penalty for breach of trust.

During the siege of Khaibar, three intriguing things occurred. One of these is a divine sign, while the other two reveal the Prophet (s.a.w)'s excellent moral character.

Kinana, a Khaibar chief's widow, married the Prophet (s.a.w). The Prophet (s.a.w) saw some marks on her face, the imprint of a hand. "What is this on your face, Safiyyara?" the Prophet (s.a.w) inquired.

"It was like this," Safiyyara said. "I saw the moon fall in my lap in a dream, and I told my husband about it, and no sooner had I told him about it, my husband gave me a hefty smack on the face and said, 'You wish to marry the King of Arabia,'" (Hisham). Arabia's national symbol was the moon. The moon on the lap indicated a close relationship with the King of Arabia. A divided moon or a sinking moon indicated discord in the Arab State or its demise.

Safiyyara's dream is a symbol of the Holy Prophet (s.a.w)'s truth. It also shows that God discloses the future to His servants via dreams. Unbelievers have less grace than believers. When Safiyyara witnessed this dream, she was a Jewess. Her spouse was assassinated at the siege of Khaibar. This siege was a retaliation for the Jews' violation of trust. Safiyyara was imprisoned and assigned to a Companion in the prisoner distribution. It was later discovered that she was the widow of a chief. It was consequently thought that living with the Prophet (s.a.w) would be more in keeping with her station. The Prophet (s.a.w), on the other hand, elected to elevate her to the position of wife, and she accepted. Her desire was realized in this manner.

There were two other instances. One story is about a shepherd who looked after a Jewish chief's livestock. This shepherd converted to Islam. After his conversion, he told the Prophet (s.a.w), "I cannot return to my people now, O Prophet of Godsa; what should I do with my former master's sheep and goats?"

"Direct the animals' faces toward Khaibar and give them a shove; God will guide them back to their lord," the Prophet (s.a.w) remarked. The shepherd obeyed, and the herd arrived to the Jewish fort. They were met by the fort's guards (Hisham, Vol 2, p.191). The episode demonstrates how seriously the Prophet (s.a.w) saw the issue of individual rights and how crucial it was in his opinion for a trustee to fulfill his obligation. During a conflict, the winners have the right to take the property and possessions of the losers. We live in a time of civilization and culture, but can we match it? Is it ever the case that a withdrawing adversary leaves behind goods that the victors return to their owners? In this occasion, the goats belonged to one of the opposing soldiers. The goats' return meant switching to enemy food, which would last them many months. The adversary could withstand the siege for a long period with it. However, the Prophet (s.a.w) had the goats returned in order to demonstrate upon a new convert the significance of keeping a promise.

The third incidence is a Jewish lady who attempted to poison Prophet (s.a.w). She inquired of the Companions what parts of an animal the Prophet (s.a.w) enjoyed as a meal. He favored lamb or goat shoulder, she was informed. On hot stones, the lady butchered a goat and prepared cutlets. Then she laced a lethal poison with them, particularly in shoulder portions, hoping the Prophet (s.a.w) would like them.

After doing the evening prayers in congregation, the Prophet (s.a.w) was returning to his tent. "Is there anything I can do for you, lady?" he inquired, seeing this woman waiting for him beside his tent.

"Yes, Abu'l Qasimsa, you may receive a gift from me," the Prophet (s.a.w) said, instructing a Companion to take whatever the lady had brought. When the Prophet (s.a.w) sat down to dine, this gift of roasted pork was also placed in front of him. The Prophet (s.a.w) nibbled on a mouthful. A morsel was also taken by Companion Bishr ibn al-Bara' ibn al-Ma'rurra. The other Companions at the table extended out their hands to consume the meat. But the Prophet (s.a.w) interrupted them, stating he suspected the meat was tainted. Bishrra responded by saying that he had the same notion. He wanted to throw the meat away, but he was concerned it might disturb the Prophet (s.a.w). "Seeing you swallow a mouthful," he added, "I too took one, but I quickly started to wish you hadn't had yours at all." Bishrra soon grew unwell and, according to some accounts, died there and then. According to some stories, he died following a period of illness. The Prophet (s.a.w) then summoned the lady and inquired as to whether she had poisoned the meal. The lady inquired as to how the Prophet (s.a.w) became aware of it. The Prophet (s.a.w) was holding a slice in his hand and stated, "My hand told me this," implying that he could discern its flavor. The lady acknowledged to her actions. "What drove you to do this?" the Prophet (s.a.w) inquired.

"My people were at war with you, and my relatives were slaughtered in this fight, so I poisoned you, knowing that if you were an imposter, you would die and we would be secure, but if you were a Prophet (s.a.w), God would rescue you."

Hearing this explanation, the Prophet (s.a.w) pardoned the lady, despite the fact that she had incurred the death punishment (Muslim). The Prophet (s.a.w) was always willing to forgive, and he only punished when it was necessary, when it was suspected that the guilty one would continue to do harm.

THE PROPHET'S VISION WAS ACCOMPLISHED

The Prophet (s.a.w) was scheduled to go to Mecca for the tour of the Ka'ba in the sixth year after the Hijra, in February 629 to be precise. The Meccan leaders had agreed to this. When it was time for the Prophet (s.a.w) to go, he gathered two thousand disciples and headed out for Mecca. When he arrived to Marrazzuhran, a rest stop near Mecca, he ordered his followers to remove their armour. These were gathered at one location. The Prophet (s.a.w) and his followers entered the Sacred Enclosure with only sheathed swords, in exact accordance with the stipulations of the agreement reached at Hudaibiya; returning to Mecca after seven years' exile, it was no ordinary occurrence for two thousand people to enter Mecca. They recalled the tortures they had through during their time in Mecca. At the same time, they realized how merciful God had been in allowing them to return and make a peaceful circle of the Ka'ba. Their rage was only equal to their delight. The residents of Mecca had come out of their homes and climbed the hills to witness the Muslims. The Muslims were filled with fire, excitement, and pride. They intended to convince the Meccans that God's promises to them had all come true. 'Abdullah bin Rawahara began singing war songs, but the Prophet (s.a.w) stopped him and said, "No war songs. Only say, There is none to be worshipped except the One God. It is God Who helped the Prophet (s.a.w) and raised the believers from depravity to dignity, and Who drove off the enemy" (Halbiyya, Vol. 3, p. 73).

The Prophet (s.a.w) and his Companions paused at Mecca for three days after circumnavigating the Ka'ba and running between the hills of Safa and Marwa. 'Abbasra had a widowed sister-in-law named Maimunara, and he offered to the Prophet (s.a.w) that they marry. The Prophet (s.a.w) concurred. On the fourth day, the Meccans insisted that the Muslims leave. The Prophet (s.a.w) ordered the retreat and instructed his people to return to Medina. He carried out the arrangement so faithfully and with such sensitivity to Meccan sensibilities that he abandoned his newlywed bride in Mecca. He arranged for her to accompany him with the caravan carrying the pilgrims' personal items. The Prophet (s.a.w) rode his camel and soon found himself beyond the holy boundaries. For the night, the Prophet (s.a.w) slept at Sarif, and Maimunara joined him in his tent.

We might have deleted this trivial element from a brief summary of the Prophet (s.a.w)'s life, but the occurrence has one crucial importance, and that is this. European authors have criticized the Prophet (s.a.w) for having several wives. They believe that having several spouses demonstrates personal laxity and a love of pleasure. The commitment and self-consuming love that the Prophet's (s.a.w) women felt for him, however, contradicts this perception of the Prophet's (s.a.w) marriages. Their commitment and love demonstrated that the Prophet's (s.a.w)'s marriage was pure, selfless, and spiritual. It was so unique in this regard that no man can claim to have treated his single wife as well as the Prophet (s.a.w) did his many. If the Prophet's (s.a.w)'s marriage had been driven by pleasure, it would very definitely have led in his women being indifferent, if not unfriendly to him. But the facts show differently. All of the Prophet's (s.a.w) wives were loyal to him because of his selfless and high-minded example. They responded to his selfless example with unwavering loyalty. Many historical occurrences demonstrate this. One is about Maimunara herself. In a tent in the desert, she first encountered the Prophet (s.a.w). If their marriage connections had been strained, if the Prophet (s.a.w) had favoured certain wives over others based on their physical attractiveness, Maimunara would not have remembered her first encounter with the Prophet (s.a.w) fondly. She would have forgotten everything about her marriage with the Prophet (s.a.w) if it had been accompanied with unpleasant or indifferent recollections. Maimunara survived for a long time after the Prophet's death. She died old, but she couldn't forget what her marriage to the Prophet (s.a.w) had meant to her. On the eve of her death at the age of eighty, when the pleasures of the flesh are forgotten and only things of lasting value and virtue move the heart, she asked to be buried one day's journey from Mecca, at the very spot where the Prophet (s.a.w) had camped on his way back to Medina, and where she had first met him after his marriage. There are countless tales of love, both real and imagined, but none are more poignant than this.

Soon after this historic tour of the Ka'ba, two prominent adversary generals converted to Islam. They became well-known Islamic generals. One was Khalid bin Walidra, whose talent and daring rocked the Roman Empire to its core and under whose generalship Muslims added nation after country to their Empire. The other was Egypt's conqueror, 'Amr bin al-'Asra.

MAUTA'S BATTLE

When the Prophet (s.a.w) returned from the Ka'ba, they started to hear news that Christian tribes on the Syrian frontier, led by Jews and pagans, were planning an attack on Medina. As a result, he sent a group of fifteen to discover the truth. They saw an army amassing near the Syrian border. Instead of returning immediately with the information, they lingered. Their enthusiasm for expounding Islam got the best of them, but the result was the polar opposite of what they had hoped for and anticipated.

Looking back on events, we can see that individuals who were prepared to assault the Prophet's (s.a.w) hometown in response to enemy provocation could be expected to act in no other manner. Instead of listening to the explanation, they drew their bows and began showering arrows on this group of fifteen. The party, on the other hand, remained unfazed.

They got arrows in response to their arguments, but they did not back down. They held fast against thousands and died fighting.

The Prophet (s.a.w) planned an expedition to punish the Syrians for their heinous brutality, but he had heard that the army concentrated on the frontier had scattered. As a result, he postponed his plans.

The Prophet (s.a.w), on the other hand, addressed a letter to the Emperor of Rome (or to the Chief of the Ghassan tribe, who controlled Busra in Rome's behalf). We might assume that the Prophet (s.a.w) protested in this letter about the preparations apparent on the Syrian border, as well as the foul and completely unfair slaughter of the fifteen Muslims he had dispatched to report on the border condition. Al-Harthra, a Companion of the Prophet (s.a.w), conveyed this letter. He made a pit break at Mauta, where he encountered Shurahbil, a Ghassan leader posing as a Roman official. "Are you a messenger of Muhammad (s.a.w)?" the chief inquired. He seized him, locked him up, and belaboured him to death after hearing "Yes." It is reasonable to conclude that this Ghassan ruler led the army that engaged and executed the fifteen Muslims who had just attempted to preach. The fact that he responded to al-Harthra, "Perhaps you are delivering a word from Muhammad (s.a.w)," demonstrates that he was concerned that the Prophet's (s.a.w) accusation that tribesmen under the Kaiser had assaulted Muslims would reach the Kaiser. He was terrified of having to answer for what had transpired. He reasoned that slaying the Prophet's (s.a.w) emissary would provide him with protection. The anticipation was not met. The Prophet (s.a.w) learned about the murder. To punish this and previous killings, he assembled a troop of three thousand men and sent it to Syria under the leadership of Zaid bin Harithara, the Prophet (s.a.w)'s liberated slave, whom we described in our description of his life in Mecca. If Zaid (ra) died, the Prophet (s.a.w) named Ja'far ibn Abi Talib as his successor, and 'Abdullah bin Rawahara as his successor if Ja'far died. If 'Abdullah bin Rawahara died, Muslims were to elect their own leader. A Jew who heard this exclaimed, "O Abu'l Qasimsa, if thou art a true Prophet (s.a.w), these three officers whom thou hast named are certain to die; for God fulfills the words of a Prophet (s.a.w)." Turning to Zaid (ra), he said, "Take it from me, if Muhammad (s.a.w) is true, you will not return alive." Zaid (ra), a true believer, replied, "I may return alive or not,"

The Muslim army began their lengthy march the next morning. The Prophet (s.a.w) and the Companions took it a step farther. A major and significant mission like this has never gone before without the Prophet (s.a.w) personally directing. He counseled and advised as the Prophet (s.a.w) moved along to say the mission goodbye. When they arrived at the point where the people of Medina traditionally said goodbye to friends and relatives departing for Syria, the Prophet (s.a.w) paused and said:

I implore you to fear God and to treat Muslims who accompany you fairly. Go to battle in the name of Allah and fight the enemy in Syria, who is also Allah's adversary. When you visit Syria, you will encounter people who place a high value on God in their places of worship. You should not argue with them or cause them any problems. Kill no women, children, the blind, or the elderly in the enemy land; do not chop down any trees or knock down any buildings (Halbiyya, Vol. 3).

After then, the Prophet (s.a.w) reappeared, and the Muslim army marched on. It was the first Muslim army to battle against the Christians. When Muslims arrived at the Syrian border, they learned that the Kaiser himself had entered the field with 100,000 of his own warriors and another 100,000 recruited from Arabia's Christian tribes. Faced with such a big enemy force, the Muslims half wanted to turn around and give message to the Prophet (s.a.w) in Medina. He may be able to reaffirm their numbers or offer new instructions. "My people, you set out from your homes to die as martyrs in the way of God, and now when martyrdom is in sight, you seem to flinch." 'Abdullah bin Rawahara stood up, full of fire, and said, "My people, you set out from your homes to die as martyrs in the way of God, and now when martyrdom is in sight, you seem to flinch. We have not fought so far because we were better equipped than the enemy in

Rawahara and was quite amazed. They all agreed that he was correct. The troops marched forward. They could see the Roman army approaching them as they marched. So the Muslims took up their positions at Mauta, and the combat started. Soon after, the Muslim commander, Zaid (ra), was assassinated, and the Prophet's cousin, Ja'far ibn Abi Talibra, was given the standard and leadership of the army. When he noticed that enemy pressure was rising and Muslims were not holding their own due to their absolute physical inferiority, he dismounted from his horse and severed its legs. The behavior indicated that he was not going to escape; he would rather die than flee.

flight.

To avoid stampedes and panic, Arabs severed the legs of their mounts. Ja'farra lost his right hand but retained control of the standard in his left. He also lost his left hand and had to hold the standard between two stumps pushed against his chest. He dropped down fighting, as he had promised. Then, as the Prophet (s.a.w) had instructed, 'Abdullah bin Rawahara seized the standard and assumed leadership. He, too, died fighting. The Prophet (s.a.w) now directed Muslims to gather in council and choose a commander. However, there was insufficient time to organize an election. The Muslims may have succumbed to the enemy's greatly overwhelming numbers. But, on the advice of a friend, Khalid bin Walidra seized the standard and continued battling till dusk. The next day, Khalidra returned to the battlefield with his damaged and fatigued army, but this time he used a stratagem. He switched the positions of his soldiers, swapping those in front with those in back, and those on the right flank with those on the left. They also chanted a few phrases. In terror, the adversary assumed Muslims had received reinforcements overnight and fled. Khalidra returned with his remains. A revelation had informed the Prophet (s.a.w) of these happenings. He gathered the Muslims in the mosque. His eyes were filled with tears as he stood to face them. He stated:

I'd want to inform you about the army that has gone towards the Syrian border. It battled and stood against the enemy. The standard was held by Zaid (ra), Ja'farra, and 'Abdullah bin Rawahara, in that order. All three fell heroically, one after the other. Please pray for them all. Khalid bin Walidra held the standard after them. He chose himself. He is a sword among God's weapons. So he returned after saving the Muslim army (Zad al-Ma'ad, Vol. 1, and Zurqani).

The Prophet's (s.a.w) description of Khalidra gained traction. Khalidra earned the moniker "God's Sword."

Khalidra, being one of the latter converts, was often mocked by other Muslims. He and 'Abdur Rahman bin 'Aufra had a disagreement once. 'Abdur Rahman bin 'Aufra brought a complaint against Khalidra to the Prophet (s.a.w). "Khalidra, you anger one who has been serving Islam since the time of Badr," the Prophet replied, "and I say to you that even if you give up gold the weight of Uhud in the service of Islam, you will not become as worthy of divine honor as "'Abdur Rahmanra."

"But they tease me," Khalidra continued, "and I have to respond."

"You must not insult Khalidra; he is a weapon among God's swords that stays drawn against disbelievers," the Prophet (s.a.w) stated to the others.

A few years later, the Prophet's (s.a.w) description came to fruition.

When Khalid'sra returned with the Muslim army, several Medinans branded the returning men as defeatist and spiritless. The widespread consensus was that they should have all perished fighting. The Prophet (s.a.w) chided the detractors. He said that Khalidra and his warriors were neither defeated or depressed. They were troops who came back to assault again and again. The words have a deeper meaning than first apparent. They predicted wars between Muslims and Syria.

THE PROPHET (S.A.W) MARCHES WITH TEN THOUSAND FOLLOWERS TO MECCA

In the eighth year of the Hijra, in the month of Ramadan (December, 629 A.D.), the Prophet (s.a.w) embarked on the last voyage that solidified Islam in Arabia.

At Hudaibiya, Muslims and disbelievers decided that Arab tribes should be able to join both the disbelievers and the

Prophet (s.a.w). It was also decided that the sides would not go to war against each other for 10 years until one party violated the treaty by assaulting the other. The Banu Bakr joined the Meccans under this pact, while the Khuza'a formed an alliance with Muslims. The Arab disbelievers had little respect for treaties, particularly those with Muslims. It just so happened that the Banu Bakr and the Khuza'a had some major disagreements. The Banu Bakr sought advice from the Meccans about settling ancient grudges with the Khuza'a. They claimed that the Hudaibiya pact had already been signed. Because of their agreement with the Prophet (s.a.w), the Khuza'a felt safe. The moment has come for them to assault the Khuza'a. The Meccans concurred. As a result, they and the Banu Bakr joined forces in a nocturnal raid on the Khuza'a, killing many of their soldiers. The Khuza'a sent forty of their men to Medina on fleet camels to report the violation of agreement to the Prophet (s.a.w). They said that it was now incumbent to Muslims to march on Mecca to revenge the atrocity. When the group saw the Prophet (s.a.w), he said unequivocally that he considered their troubles to be his own. "Like the rain drops you see there, Muslim troops will come down to your help," he added, pointing to a growing cloud in the sky. The Meccans were alarmed by the news of the Khuza'a mission to Medina. They sent Abu Sufyanra to Medina as soon as possible to prevent Muslims from attacking. Abu Sufyanra arrived in Medina and started to argue that since he was not present at Hudaibiya, Muslims would have to sign a new peace treaty. The Prophet (s.a.w) believed it was inappropriate to respond to this petition. Abu Sufyanra felt ecstatic, walked to the mosque, and declared:

"O People, I repeat our guarantee of peace to you on behalf of the Meccans" (Zurqani).

This speech was not understood by the inhabitants of Medina. As a result, they merely laughed. "Your argument is one-sided, and we cannot agree to it," the Prophet (s.a.w) told Abu Sufyanra. Meanwhile, the Prophet (s.a.w) had sent news to all the tribes. Assuring them that they were ready and on the march, he instructed the Muslims of Medina to equip and prepare. The Muslim army began their march on January 1st. Other Muslim tribes joined them at various points along the trip. When the army approached the Faran desert after just a few days' trip, its number had swelled to ten thousand, precisely as the Prophetas Solomon had predicted long ago. As this army marched towards Mecca, the surrounding quiet became more foreboding to the Meccans. They encouraged Abu Sufyanra to go and investigate the Muslim design. He was less than a day's travel from Mecca when he saw the whole bush lighting up with campfires at night. The Prophet (s.a.w) had ordered a fire to be lit in front of each camp. In the calm and darkness of the night, the impact of these roaring flames was terrifying. "What could this be?" Abu Sufyanra asked his companions, "Has an army dropped from the heavens? I know of no Arab army so large." They named some tribes, and at each name, Abu Sufyanra said, "No Arab tribe or people could have an army as large." (Hanzala was Abu's son.)

Sufyanra.)

"'Abbas, are you here?" Abu Sufyanra inquired.

"Yes, the army of the Prophet's (s.a.w) is approaching; act fast or face humiliation and defeat," 'Abbasra answered.

'Abbasra and Abu Sufyanra have known each other for a long time. 'Abbasra demanded that Abu Sufyanra go with him on the same mule to the Prophet (s.a.w). He grabbed Abu

Sufyan'sra's hand, yanked him up, and forced him to ride. They quickly arrived to the Prophet's (s.a.w) tent, spurring the mule. 'Abbasra was terrified that 'Umarra, who was protecting the Prophet's (s.a.w) tent, would attack and murder Abu Sufyanra. But the Prophet (s.a.w) had taken measures, declaring that if someone came across Abu Sufyanra, he should not try to murder him. The encounter significantly impressed Abu Sufyanra. He was caught aback by Islam's recent climb in fortunes. Here was the Prophet (s.a.w), who had been exiled from Mecca with just one companion. Seven years had passed, and he was now pounding on the doors of Mecca with ten thousand worshippers. The tables had been turned totally. The fugitive Prophet (s.a.w), who had fled Mecca seven years ago for fear of his life, had now returned, and Mecca was unable to stop him.

MECCA'S FALL

Abu Sufyanra's mind must have been racing. Hadn't there been a tremendous shift in seven years? And what was he going to do now that he was the Meccan leader? Was he going to put up a fight or give in? He seemed stupefied to outside viewers, troubled by such ideas. This enraged Meccan leader was seen by Prophet (s.a.w). He urged 'Abbasra to take him away for the night and amuse him, promising to meet him in the morning. 'Abbas spent the night with Abu Sufyanra. They summoned the Prophet (s.a.w) in the morning. It was time for prayers in the early morning. The flurry of activity that Abu Sufyanra saw at this early hour was unique in his experience. He had not known? neither had Meccan? that Muslims had become such early risers as a result of Islam's discipline. He saw that all of the Muslim campers had gathered for their morning prayers. Some traveled back and forth in search of water for ablutions, while others watched the attendees line up for the ritual. Abu Sufyanra was perplexed by seeing activity so early in the morning. He was terrified. Was there a fresh scheme in the works to overwhelm him?

"What can they all be doing?" he said, stunned.

"There's nothing to be scared about," 'Abbasra responded. "They're just getting ready for morning prayers."

Thousands of Muslims lined up behind the Prophet (s.a.w), doing the customary gestures and devotions at the Prophet (s.a.w)'s bidding? half prostrations, complete prostrations, rising up again, and so on. 'Abbasra was on watch duty, so he was free to converse with Abu Sufyanra.

"What might they be doing now?" Abu wondered.

Sufyanra. "Everything the Prophet (s.a.w) does, the rest do."

"What are you thinking about, Abu Sufyanra? It's only the Muslim prayer; Muslims will do everything for the Prophet (s.a.w), even forego food and drink."

"True," Abu Sufyanra stated, "I have seen large courts, the courts of the Chosroes and the Kaiser, but I have never seen any people as dedicated to their leader as Muslims are to their Prophet (s.a.w)" (Halbiyya, Vol. 2, p. 90).

Fearful and guilty, Abu Sufyanra asked 'Abbasra whether he would not petition the Prophet (s.a.w) to pardon his own people, the Meccans.

After concluding the morning prayers, 'Abbasra escorted Abu Sufyanra to the Prophet (s.a.w).

The Prophet (s.a.w) spoke to Abu Sufyanra. "Have you not realized that there is no one worthy of worship save Allah?"

"You have always been kind, compassionate, and sensitive to your kith and kin; I am confident today that if there were anybody else worthy of adoration, we may have had some aid against you from him."

"Has it not also occurred to you that I am a

"Who is Allah's Messenger?"

"I still have some reservations about my father and mother being a sacrifice to you."

While Abu Sufyanra was hesitant to recognize the Prophet (s.a.w) as God's Messenger, two of his friends who had marched out of Mecca with him to undertake reconnaissance for the Meccans became Muslims. Hakim bin Hizamra was one of them. Abu Sufyanra subsequently joined, although his inner conversion seems to have been postponed until after the capture of Mecca. Hakim bin Hizamra questioned the Prophet (s.a.w) whether Muslims would kill their own relatives.

"These people have been exceedingly brutal," the Prophet (s.a.w) stated, "they have committed excesses and shown themselves to be of poor faith. They have broken the truce they negotiated at Hudaibiya and assaulted the Khuza'a mercilessly. They have declared war in a land which God had placed inviolate."

"It is true, O Prophet (s.a.w) of God, our people have done precisely what you claim; but, instead of advancing on Mecca, you should have assaulted the Hawazin,"

Hakimra recommended it.

"The Hawazin have also been brutal and violent, and I pray God will provide me the ability to achieve all three goals: the conquering of Mecca, the dominance of Islam, and the destruction of the Hawazin."

"Will they enjoy peace if the Meccans do not draw the sword?" said Abu Sufyanra, who had been listening.

"Yes," the Prophet (s.a.w) responded, "everyone who remains within will enjoy tranquility."

"But, O Prophet (s.a.w)," 'Abbasra interjected, "Abu Sufyanra is very anxious about himself; he wants to know if his status and position among the Meccans would be honored."

"Very good," said the Prophet (s.a.w): "Whoever takes shelter in the house of Abu Sufyanra will have peace. Whoever enters the Sacred Mosque will have peace. Those who lay down their arms will have peace. Those who close their doors and stay in will have peace."

Having said this, he summoned Abu Ruwaihara and gave over the Islamic flag to him. Abu Ruwaihara had made a brotherhood contract with Bilal (ra), the negro slave. When the Prophet (s.a.w) handed him the standard, he stated, "Whoever stands under this standard will have peace," and he commanded Bilal (ra) to march in front of Abu Ruwaihara and declare to those concerned that there was peace beneath the standard carried by Abu Ruwaihara.

Ruwaihara.

THE PROPHET (S.A.W) ENTERY INTO MECCA

The arrangement was brilliant. When Muslims were persecuted in Mecca, one of their targets, Bilal (ra), was dragged through the streets by ropes wrapped around his legs. Bilal (ra) received no peace from Mecca, just bodily anguish, shame, and dishonor. On this day of his freedom, Bilal (ra) must have felt spiteful. Allowing him to punish the heinous cruelty inflicted on him in Mecca was important, but it had to be done within the parameters set by Islam. As a result, the Prophet (s.a.w) forbade Bilal (ra) from drawing his sword and smiting the necks of his former persecutors. That would have been against Islam. Instead, the Prophet (s.a.w) gave the standard of Islam to Bilal (ra)'s brother and tasked Bilal (ra) with the obligation of extending peace to all his former persecutors under the standard carried by his brother. This vengeance was beautiful and appealing. Imagine Bilal (ra) walking in front of his brother, appealing his adversaries to peace. His desire for vengeance could not have lasted. It had to have disintegrated as he approached, asking the Meccans to peace under the banner of a flag held aloft by his brother.

While the Muslims marched towards Mecca, the Prophet (s.a.w) directed 'Abbasra to transport Abu Sufyanra and his companions to a vantage point from where they could observe the Muslim army, its behavior and attitude. 'Abbasra did so, and Abu Sufyanra and his companions watched the Arab tribes pass by, on whose force the Meccans had banked all these years for their plans against Islam. That day, they marched not as soldiers of skepticism, but as warriors of faith. They were now raising Islamic chants rather than heathen ones. They marched in line not to terminate the Prophet's (s.a.w) life, but to give their lives to save his; not to spill his blood, but their own for his cause. Their goal that day was not to fight the Prophet's (s.a.w) Message and preserve the feigned unity of their own people. It was to convey the Message they had so far rejected to all areas of the earth. Its purpose was to develop human togetherness and solidarity. Column after column marched by till the Ashja' tribe came within site of Abu Sufyan'sra. Their passion to Islam and self-sacrifice were visible on their faces and audible in their songs and shouts.

"Who might they be?" wondered Abu Sufyanra.

"They belong to the Ashja' tribe."

"In all Arabia, no one held greater hate to Muhammad (s.a.w)," Abu Sufyanra said.

"We owe everything to God's favor; He transformed the minds of Islam's enemies as soon as He saw fit," 'Abbasra stated.

The Prophet (s.a.w) arrived last, flanked by the columns of Ansar and Muhajirin. They must have numbered in the thousands, clothed in suits of armour. The courageous 'Umarra led their march. The sight was the most spectacular of them all. The passion, drive, and fervor of these Muslims appeared to overflow. When Abu Sufyan'sra's gaze rested on them, he was absolutely defeated.

"Who could they be?" he wondered.

"They are the Ansarra and the Muhajirin who surround the Prophet (s.a.w)," 'Abbasra said.

"No authority on earth could oppose this army," Abu Sufyanra stated, addressing 'Abbas particularly, "'Abbasra, your nephew has become the world's most powerful ruler."

"You are still far from the truth, Abu Sufyanra; he is a Prophet (s.a.w), a Messenger of God," 'Abbasra responded.

"sure, sure, let it be a Prophet (s.a.w), not a king," Abu Sufyanra said.

As the Muslim army marched by Abu Sufyanra, the commander of the Ansar, Sa'd bin 'Ubadara, couldn't help but remark that God had made it legitimate for them to invade Mecca by force that day, and that the Quraish would be humiliated.

As the Prophet (s.a.w) passed, Abu Sufyanra raised his voice and addressed the Prophet (s.a.w), saying, "Have you allowed the massacre of your own kith and kin? I heard the commander of the Ansar, Sa'dra, and his companions say so. They said it was a day of slaughter. The sacredness of Mecca will not avert bloodshed, and the Quraish will be humiliated. Prophet (s.a.w) of God, you are the best, the most for

Abu Sufyan's appeal was dismissed. Those same Muslims who had been ridiculed and abused in the streets of Mecca, who had been evicted and forced from their houses, came to feel pity for their former persecutors. "Prophet (s.a.w) of God," they continued, "the reports which the Ansar have heard of the excesses and cruelties perpetrated by Meccans against us may cause them to seek vengeance, and we have no idea what they may do."

The Prophet (s.a.w) recognized this. Looking to Abu

"What Sa'dra has claimed is completely incorrect," he told Sufyanra.

It is not a day of bloodshed, but of forgiveness, and God will honor the Quraish and the Ka'ba."

Then he summoned Sa'dra and instructed him to return the Ansar flag to his son, Qaisra (Hisham, Vol. 2). The Ansar command therefore shifted from Sa'dra to Qaisra. It was a good decision. It appeased the Meccans and rescued Ansar from disappointment. The Prophet (s.a.w) truly trusted Qaisra, a devout young man.

An occurrence during his latter days exemplifies his religiosity. Qaisra welcomed his pals while lying on his deathbed. Some people showed there, while others did not. He was perplexed by this and inquired as to why some of his friends had not been to meet him. "Your generosity is tremendous," one person stated.

You have been assisting the underprivileged with your loans. There are many people in town that owe you money. Some may have been hesitant to come for fear of being asked to repay the debts."

"Then I was the one who kept my pals away." Please proclaim that no one now owes anything to Qaisra." Following this declaration, Qaisra had so many visits that the stairs to his home fell way.

When the Muslim army passed, 'Abbasra told Abu Sufyanra to hurry to Mecca and announce to the Meccans that the Prophet (s.a.w) had arrived and explain to them how they could all live in peace. When Abu Sufyanra arrived in Mecca, his wife, Hind, met him. A confirmed disbeliever, she was still a brave woman. She caught Abu Sufyanra by the beard and called on Meccans to come and kill her

But Abu Sufyanra could see Hind was acting stupidly. "That time is passed," he replied, "you should go home and sit behind closed doors." I've seen the Muslim army. Not even all of Arabia could tolerate it today."

He then explained the conditions under which the Prophet (s.a.w) had promised peace to the Meccans. Upon hearing these conditions, the people of Mecca fled for protection to the places named in the Prophetssa proclamation. From this proclamation, eleven men and four women were excepted. Their guilt was not that they had not believed or that they had participated in wars against Islam; it was that they had compelled Islam to believe in them.

The Prophet (s.a.w) had ordered Khalid bin Walidra not to allow any fighting unless they were fought against and unless the Meccans first started fighting. The Meccans posted in that part of town challenged Khalidra and invited him to fight. An encounter ensued in which twelve or thirteen men were killed (Hisham, Vol. 2, p. 217). Khalidra was a man of fiery temper.

The Prophet (s.a.w) immediately summoned Khalidra and said, "Did I not stop you from fighting?"

"You did, O Prophets of God, but these people came first and started shooting arrows at us. I did nothing for a while and told them we didn't want to fight. They, however, did not listen and did not stop. So I responded and scattered them."

This was the sole adverse occurrence that occurred on this occasion, and the conquest of Mecca was therefore accomplished with little bloodshed.

They asked the Prophet (s.a.w) where he would halt once he entered Mecca.

"Has 'Aqil left me a place to live in?"" asked the Prophet (s.a.w). 'Aqil was the Prophet's (s.a.w) cousin, a son of his uncle. During the years of the Prophet's (s.a.w) refuge at Medina, his relations had sold all his property, and there was no house left which the Prophet (s.a.w) could call his own. As a result, the Prophet (s.a.w) said, "I will stop at Hanif Bani Kinana." This was an open space. The Quraish and the Kinana once assembled there and

It has been three years.

The Prophet (s.a.w) chose a significant location for his stay because the Meccans had once gathered there and swore that unless the Prophet (s.a.w) was made over to them, they would not be at peace with his tribe. Now the Prophet (s.a.w) had returned to the same location, as if to tell the Meccans, "You wanted me here, so here I am." But not in the manner you desired. You wanted me to be your victim, entirely at your mercy. But I am in charge. Not just my own people, but all of Arabia, have joined me. You demanded that my people give me up to you. Instead, they handed you over to me." This victory day was a Monday, as was the day the Prophet (s.a.w) and Abu Bakrra left the cave of Thaur for their journey to Medina. On that day, standing on the hill of Thaur, the Prophet (s.a.w) turned to Mecca and said, 'Mecca! you are dearer to me than any other place, but your people would not let me live here.'

When the Prophet (s.a.w) rode into Mecca on his camel, Abu Bakrra walked behind him, holding a stirrup, reciting lines from the Surah, Al-Fath, in which the capture of Mecca had been predicted years previously.

KA'BA IS FREE OF IDOLS

The Prophet (s.a.w) rode his camel to the Ka'ba and made seven circuits of the holy precincts, staff in hand, around the house built by the Patriarch Abrahamas and his son Ishmaelas for the worship of the One and Only God, but which their misguided children had allowed to degenerate into a sanctuary for idols. The Prophet (s.a.w) smote one by one the three hundred and sixty idols in the house. Falsehood does indeed vanish away quickly." This verse was revealed before the Prophet (s.a.w) left Mecca for Medina and is part of the Chapter, Bani Isra'il, which foretold the Prophet (s.a.w)'s flight from Mecca and subsequent conquest of Mecca. The Chapter is a Meccan Chapter, a fact admitted even by European writers.

And say, 'O my Lord, make my coming in a good coming in, and my leaving out a good going out, and give me from Thyself a power that may aid me.' And, 'Truth has arrived, and falsehood has fled away, and deceit does indeed vanish away quickly!' (17: 81-82).

The conquest of Mecca is foretold here in the form of a prayer taught to the Prophet (s.a.w), in which the Prophet (s.a.w) is taught to pray for entering Mecca and departing from it under good auspices; and for the help of God in assuring an ultimate victory of truth over falsehood. The prophecy had literally come true. The recitation of these verses by Abu Bakrra was appropriate. It braced up the Muslims, and reminded the

With the capture of Mecca, the Ka'ba was restored to the duties for which it had been sanctified by the Patriarch Abrahamas many thousands of years earlier.

When the Prophet (s.a.w) smote it with his staff, and it fell down in fragments, Zubairra looked at Abu Sufyanra and with a half-suppressed smile reminded him of Uhud. "Do you remember the day when Muslims wounded and exhausted stood by and you wounded them further by shouting, 'Glory to Hubal, Glory to Hubal'?" Was it Hubal who helped you win that day? If that was Hubal, you can see how it ended today."

Abu Sufyanra was impressed, and agreed that if there had been a God other than Muhammad (s.a.w), they may not have suffered the humiliation and loss they did that day.

After ordering the wiping out of the pictures that had been drawn on the walls of the Ka'ba, the Prophet (s.a.w) withdrew to the open court and said another two rak'ats of prayer. The duty of wiping out the pictures had been entrusted to 'Umarra, who had all the pictures obliterated except that of Abrahamas. When the Prophet (s.a.w) returned to inspect and found this picture intact, he asked

It was an affront to the memory of Abrahamas, a prominent proponent of God's Oneness, to put his image on the walls of the Ka'ba, as if Abrahamas could be worshiped alongside God.

It was a wonderful day, filled with God's Signs.

Promises made by God to the Prophet (s.a.w) at a time when fulfillment seemed impossible had finally been fulfilled. The Prophet (s.a.w) was the center of devotion and faith. In and through his person, God had manifested Himself, and shown His face, as it were, again. The Prophet (s.a.w) sent for Zamzam water, drank some of it, and performed ablutions with the rest.

HIS ENEMIES ARE FORGIVEN BY THE PROPHET (S.A.W)

After the ceremonies and obligations were completed, the Prophet (s.a.w) addressed the Meccans and stated, "You have seen how real God's promises have been." Now tell me what punishment you should get for the atrocities you inflicted on people whose only crime was inviting you to worship the One and Only God."

"We want you to treat us as Josephas treated his erring brethren," the Meccans said.

By chance, the Meccans used the exact words that God had used in the Surah Yusuf, revealed ten years before the conquest of Mecca, in which the Prophet (s.a.w) was told that he would treat his Meccan persecutors as Josephas had treated his brothers. By asking for the treatment that Josephas had meted out to his brothers, the Meccans admitted that the Prophet (s.a.w) of Islam was the like of Josephas, and

While the Prophet (s.a.w) was engaged in expressing his gratitude to God and in carrying out other devotions at the Ka?ba, and while he was addressing the Meccans announcing his decision to forgive and forget, misgivings arose in the minds of the Ansar, the Medinite Muslims. Some of them were upset over the scenes of homecoming and of reconciliation which they witnessed on the return of Meccan Muslims to Mecca. Was the Prophet (s.a.w) parting company with them, his friends in adversity who provided the first home to Islam? Was the Prophet (s.a.w) going to settle down at Mecca, the town from which he had to flee for his life? Such fears did not seem too remote now that Mecca had been conquered and his own tribe had joined Islam. The Prophet (s.a.w) might want to settle down in it. God informed the Prophet (s.a.w) of these misgivings of the Ansar. He raised his head, looked at the Ansar and said "You seem to think Muhammad (s.a.w) is perturbed by the love of his town, and by the ties which bind him to his tribe." "It is true," said the Ansar., "we did think of this."

"Do you know who I am?" said the Prophet (s.a.w). I am God's Servant and His Messenger. How can I abandon you? You stood with me and gave your life when the Faith of God had no earthly assistance. How can I leave you and go somewhere else? This is not feasible, Ansar. I fled Mecca for the cause of God and will never return. I will live and die beside you."

The Ansar were moved by this singular expression of love and loyalty; they bemoaned their mistrust of God and His Prophet (s.a.w), wept, and begged forgiveness, explaining that they would not be able to live in peace if the Prophet (s.a.w) left their town and went elsewhere. The Prophet (s.a.w) responded that their fear was understandable, and that, after their explanation, God and His Prophet (s.a.w) were satisfied about their innocence and acknowledged their sincerity and loyalty.

How must the Meccans have felt at this time? True, they did not shed devotional tears, but their hearts must have been full of regret and remorse, because they had not cast away with their own hands the gem discovered in their own town? They had all the more reason to regret this because the Prophet (s.a.w), having returned to Mecca, had decided to leave it again for Medina.

'IKRIMAra TURNS MUSLIM'

'Ikrimara, a son of Abu Jahl, was among those forgiven on the recommendation of the Companions. 'Ikrimara'sra wife was a Muslim at heart. She requested the Prophet (s.a.w) to forgive him. The Prophet (s.a.w) forgave. At the time, 'Ikrimara was attempting to flee to Abyssinia. His wife pursued him and found him about to embark. She reproved him." she explained.

'Ikrimara was taken aback and asked whether she truly believed the Prophet (s.a.w) would forgive him. 'Ikrimara'sra wife assured him that even he would be forgiven by the Prophet (s.a.w), and that she had already received word from him. 'Ikrimara abandoned his plan to flee to Abyssinia and returned to see the Prophet (s.a.w).

"Your wife is correct. "I really forgive you," the Prophet (s.a.w) remarked.

'Ikrimara decided that a person capable of forgiving his deadliest enemies could not be false, so he declared his faith in Islam, saying, "I bear witness that God is One and has no equal, and I bear witness that you are His Servant and His Messengersa." The Prophet (s.a.w) consoled him, saying, "'Ikrimara," he said, "I have not only forgiven you, but as proof of my regard for you, I have decided to invite you to ask me for

"There is nothing more or better I can ask you for than that you pray for me to God and seek for His pardon for whatever excesses and enormities I have perpetrated against you," 'Ikrimara answered.

When the Prophet (s.a.w) heard this entreaty, he immediately pleaded to God, saying, "My God, pardon the animosity which 'Ikrimara has begotten against me." Forgive him for the insults he has said."

"Whoever comes to me, trusting in God, is one with me," the Prophet (s.a.w) remarked as he rose up and draped his cloak over 'Ikrimara. My residence is equally his and mine."

The conversion of 'Ikrimara confirmed a prophesy given by the Holy Prophet (s.a.w) many years before: "I had a vision in which I saw that I was in Paradise," the Prophet (s.a.w) once stated to his Companions. I saw a bunch of grapes there. "But now," said the Prophet (s.a.w), "I understand my vision; the bunch of grapes was meant for 'Ikrimara." Referring to this vision on the occasion of 'Ikrimara's **conversion, the Prophet (s.a.w) said he did not understand it at first because Abu Jahl, an enemy of believers, could enter Paradise and have a bunch of grapes provided for him. Only this time, instead of the son, I was shown the father, a typical occurrence in visions and dreams" (Halbiyya, Vol. 3, p. 104).**

One of those who had been ordered to be executed as exceptions to the general amnesty was Habbarra, who had been responsible for the cruel murder of Zainabra, a daughter of the Prophet (s.a.w). He had cut the girths of Zainabra'sra camel, on which Zainabra fell to the ground and, being pregnant, suffered abortion, and a little later she died. This was one of the inhumanities which he had committed and for which he Instead of resorting to people for refuge, why not go to the Prophet (s.a.w) himself, confess my errors and misdeeds, and beg for his forgiveness?"

"Habbarra, if God has put the love of Islam in your heart, how can I refuse to pardon you?" answered the Propheta. I forgive you for anything you've done before this."

The enormities these individuals had perpetrated against Islam and Muslims cannot be described in detail, yet how readily the Prophet (s.a.w) forgave them! This attitude of forgiveness turned even the most hardened opponents into worshippers of the Prophet (s.a.w).

THE HUNAIN BATTLE

The Prophet's (s.a.w) entry into Mecca was sudden. Tribes in the vicinity of Mecca, especially those in the south, remained unaware of the event until sometime later. On hearing of it, they began to assemble their forces and to prepare for a fight with the Muslims. There were two Arab tribes, the Hawazin and the Thaqif, unusually proud of their valiant traditions. They took counsel together and after some deliberation elected Malik ibn ?Auf as their leader. They then invited the tribes round about to join them. Among the tribes invited was the Banu Sa?d. The Prophet's (s.a.w) wet-nurse, Halima, belonged to this tribe and the Prophet (s.a.w) as a child had lived among them. Men of this tribe collected in force and set out towards Mecca taking with them their families and their effects. Asked why they had done so, they replied it was in order that the soldiers might be reminded that, if they turned back and fled, their wives and children would be taken prisoners and their effects looted?so strong was their determination to fight and destroy the Muslims. This force descended in the valley of Rautas most suitable base for a battle, with its natural shelters, abundance of fodder and water, and facilities for cavalry movements. When the Prophet (s.a.w) got to know of this, he sent ?Abdullah bin Abi Hadwadra to report on the situation. ?Abdullah reported that there were military concentrations in the place and there was determination to kill and be killed. The tribe was renowned for its skill in archery, and the base they had selected afforded a very great advantage to them. The Prophet (s.a.w) approached Safwanra, a prosperous chief of Mecca for the loan of suits of armour and weapons. Safwanra replied, "You seem to put pressure on me and think I will be overawed by your growing power and make over to you whatever you ask?"

"We desire to seize nothing," the Prophet (s.a.w) answered. We simply seek a loan for these items and are willing to provide an acceptable guarantee."

The Prophet (s.a.w) borrowed three thousand lances from his cousin, Naufal bin Harithra, and about thirty thousand dirhams from 'Abdullah bin Rabi'a (Mu'atta', Musnad, and Halbiyya). When the Muslim army set out towards the Hawazin, the Meccans expressed a desire to join the Muslim side. They were not Muslims, but they had agreed to live undefeated.

The Prophet (s.a.w) objected, saying, "You speak like Mosesas' disciples." When Mosesas was traveling to Canaan, his followers noticed people worshiping idols along the route and urged to Mosesas, 'O Mosesas, create for us a god like they have gods'" (Qur'an 7: 139).

"GOD'S PROPHET (S.A.W) CALL YOU"

The Prophet (s.a.w) urged Muslims to always remember that Allah was Great and to pray to Him to save them from the superstitions of earlier peoples. Before the Muslim army reached Hunain, the Hawazin and their allies had already prepared a number of ambuscades from which to attack the

Muslims, like the fox-holes and camouflaged artillery positions of modern warfare. They had built walls around them. Behind the walls were soldiers lying in wait for the Muslims. A narrow gorge was left for Muslims to pass through. Much the larger part of the army was posted to these ambuscades, while a small number was made to line up in front of their camels. Muslims thought enemy numbers to be no more than they could see. So they went forward and attacked. When they had advanced far and the hiding enemy was satisfied that they could be attacked very easily, the soldiers lined up in front of the camels and attacked the centre of the Muslim army while the hiding archers rained their arrows on the flanks. The Meccans, who had joined for a chance to display their valour, could not stand this double attack by the enemy. They ran back to Mecca. Muslims were accustomed to difficult situations, but when two thousand soldiers mounted on horses and camels pierced their way through the Muslim army, the animals of the Muslims also took fright. There was panic in the army. Pressure came from three sides, resulting in a general rout. In this, only the Prophet (s.a.w), with twelve

Not all of the companions were unaffected.

Companions had fled from the field. About a hundred of them still remained, but they were at some distance from the Prophet (s.a.w). Only twelve remained to surround the Prophet (s.a.w). One Companion reports that he and his friends did all they could to steer their animals towards the battlefield. But the animals had been put to fright by the stampede of the Meccan animals. No effort seemed to avail. They pulled at the reins but the animals refused to turn. Sometimes they would pull the heads of the animals so as almost to make them touch their tails. But when they spurred the animals towards the battlefield, they would not go. Instead, they moved back all the more. "Our hearts beat in fear?fear for the safety of the Prophet (s.a.w)," says this Companion, "but there was nothing we could do." This was how the Companions were placed. The Prophet (s.a.w) himself stood with a handful of men, exposed on three sides to volleys of arrows. There was only one narrow pass behind them through which only a few men could pass at a time. At that moment Abu Bakrra dismounted and holding the reins of the Prophet's (s.a.w) mule said, "Prophet (s.a.w) of God, let us withdraw for a while and let the Muslim army collect itself."

"Release the reins of my mule, Abu Bakrra," exclaimed the Prophet (s.a.w), spurring the animal forward into the canyon on both sides of which were enemy ambuscades from which the archers were firing. I am not a phony. "I am a son of 'Abdul Muttalib," he said at a time when his life was in danger. He was emphasizing the fact that the Prophet (s.a.w) was truly a Prophet (s.a.w), a true Messenger of God. By emphasizing this, he meant that he was not afraid of death or the failure of his cause. However, if he remained safe despite being surrounded by archers, Muslims should not attribute any divine qualities to him. Tell them, the Prophet (s.a.w) of God calls them." ?Abbasra raised his powerful voice. The message of the Prophet (s.a.w) fell like thunder, not on deaf ears but on ears agog. It had an electric effect. The very Companions who had found themselves powerless to urge their mounts towards the battlefield, began to feel they were no longer in this world but in the next, facing God on the Judgement Day. The voice of ?Abbasra did not sound like his own voice but the voice of the angel beckoning them to render an account of their deeds. There was nothing then to stop them from turning to the battlefield again. Many of them dismounted and with only sword and shield rushed to the battlefield, leaving their animals to go where they liked. Others dismounted, cut off the heads of their animals and rushed back on foot to the Prophet (s.a.w). It is said that the Ansar on that day ran towards the Prophet (s.a.w) with the speed with which a mother-camel or a mother-cow runs to her young on hearing its cries. Before long the Prophet (s.a.w) was surrounded by a large number of Companions, mostly Ansar. The enemy again suffered a defeat.

The presence of Abu Sufyanra on the side of the Prophet (s.a.w) on this day was a mighty divine Sign, a Sign of the power of God on the one hand and of the purifying example of the Prophet (s.a.w) on the other. Only a few days before, Abu Sufyanra was a bloodthirsty enemy of the Prophet (s.a.w), commander of a bloodthirsty army determined to destroy the Muslims. But here, on this day, the same Abu

He meditated on this new proof of God's might, remembering that just ten or fifteen days earlier, this guy was recruiting an army to put an end to the Islamic Movement.

'Abbasra saw the Prophet's (s.a.w)'s surprise and said, "Prophet (s.a.w) of God, this is Abu Sufyanra, son of your uncle, and thus your brother." Aren't you happy with him?"

"I am," the Prophet (s.a.w) replied, "and I hope that God may pardon him for all the wrongs he has done," before turning to Abu Sufyanra and saying, "Brother!"" Abu Sufyanra couldn't contain his feelings and bent to kiss the Prophet's (s.a.w) foot in the stirrup he was holding (Halbiyya).

After the battle of Hunain, the Prophet (s.a.w) returned the war material he had received on loan, compensating the lenders many times over. Those who had made the loan were moved by the Prophet (s.a.w)'s care and consideration in returning the material and compensating the lenders. They felt the Prophet (s.a.w) was no ordinary man, but one whose moral example stood high above others.

A CRUEL ENEMY BECOMES A DELIGHTED FOLLOWER

The battle of Hunain always reminds historians of another interesting incident that occurred while it was taking place. Shaibara, a resident of Mecca and in the service of the Ka'ba, took part in the battle on the side of the enemy and says that he had only one goal in mind in this battle?that when the two armies met, he would find an opportunity to kill the Prophet (s.a.w). He was determined that even if the entire world joined the Prophet (s.a.w) (let alone Arabia), The Prophet (s.a.w) then said, 'Shaibara, come near me.' When I went close, the Prophet (s.a.w) stroked his hand over my chest with great fondness. As he did so, he said, 'God, relieve Shaibara of all satanic thought.'" With this little touch of affection, Shaibara changed. His hostility and enmity vanished, and from that moment on, Shaibara held the Prophet (s.a.w) dearer than anything else in the world. As Shaibara changed, the Prophet (s.a.w) invited him to come forward and fight. Even if my father had approached, I would not have hesitated to put my sword into his chest" (Halbiyya).

The Prophet (s.a.w) then marched towards Ta'if, the town that had stoned him and thrown him out, and besieged it, but later abandoned the siege at the request of his comrades. The residents of Ta'if afterwards accepted Islam freely.

BOOTY IS DISTRIBUTED BY THE PROPHET (S.A.W)

After the conquest of Mecca and the victory of Hunain, the Prophet (s.a.w) was faced with the task of distributing the money and property paid as ransom or abandoned in the battlefield by the enemy. If custom had been followed, this money and property should have been distributed among the Muslim soldiers who took part in these encounters. But on this occasion, instead of distributing it among the Muslims, the Prophet (s.a.w) distributed it among the Meccans and the people who lived round about Mecca. These people had yet to show an inclination towards the Faith. Many were professed deniers. Those who had declared their faith were yet new to it. They had no idea how self-denying a people could become after they had accepted Islam. But, instead of benefiting by the example of self-denial and self-sacrifice which they saw, instead of reciprocating the good treatment they received from the Muslims, they became more avaricious and greedier than ever. Their demands began to mount. They mobbed the Prophet (s.a.w), and pushed him to a spot under a tree with his mantle having been torn from his shoulders. At last the Prophet (s.a.w) said to the crowd, "I have nothing else to give. If I had, I would have given it to you. "I am neither a miser nor a meanie" (Bukhari, Chap on Faradul Khums).

Then, approaching his dromedary and taking off a hair, he told the throng, "Of this money and property, I desire nothing at all, not even a hair." Only one more must be reserved for the State. That is the portion that Arab custom has always recognized as reasonable and proper. That fifth will not go to me. It will be used to meet your requirements. Remember that anybody who misappropriates or misuses public funds will be disgraced in God's eyes on the Day of Judgment."

Malicious critics have claimed that the Prophet (s.a.w) wished to become a king and have a kingdom, but imagine him confronted by a mean crowd while he is already a king. If he had wished to become a king and have a kingdom, would he have treated a beggarly mob as he treated this Meccan mob? Would he have agreed to be mobbed at all in the way he was?

"Muhammad (s.a.w), I am a witness to what you are doing," exclaimed one Dhu'l Khuwaisira as he approached the Prophet (s.a.w). " inquired Prophet (s.a.w).

"You are doing an injustice," he replied.

"Woe to you," the Prophet (s.a.w) replied, "if I can be unfair, no one on the face of the world can be just" (Muslim, Kitabul Zakat).

True believers were enraged, and as this individual left the meeting, several of them said, "This man deserves to die." Will you let us murder him?"

"No," the Prophet (s.a.w) said, "how can we murder him if he obeys our rules and does no evident offense?""

"But," the believers said, "if a person says and does one thing but thinks and wishes something quite different, does he not deserve to be treated accordingly?""

"I can't interact with people based on what's in their hearts." This is not something that God has burdened me with. I can handle them based on what they say and do."

The Prophet (s.a.w) went on to tell the believers that one day this man and others of his kin would stage a rebellion in Islam, and the Prophet's (s.a.w) words came true: during the reign of 'Alira, the Fourth Khalifah of Islam, this man and his friends led the rebellion against him and became the leaders of the Khawarij, a universally condemned division of Islam.

After dealing with the Hawazin, the Prophet (s.a.w) returned to Medina, and it was another great day for its people. On this great day, the Prophet (s.a.w) reentered Medina, full of joy and aware of his determination and promise to make Medina his home.

ABU 'AMIR'S MACHINATIONS

We must now turn to the activities of one Abu ?Amir Madani. He belonged to the Khazraj tribe. Through long association with Jews and Christians he had acquired the habit of silent meditation and of repeating the names of God. Because of this habit, he was generally known as Abu ?Amir, the Hermit. He was, however, not a Christian by faith. When the Prophet (s.a.w) went to Medina after the Hijra, Abu ?Amir escaped from Medina to Mecca. When at last Mecca also submitted to the growing influence of Islam, he began to hatch a new intrigue against Islam. He changed his name and his habitual mode of dress and settled down in Quba, a village near Medina. As he had been away for a long time and had altered his appearance and his dress, the people of Medina did not recognize him. Only those hypocrites recognized him with whom he had relations in secret. He took the hypocrites of Medina into his confidence and with their concurrence planned to go to Syria and excite and provoke the Christian rulers and Christian Arabs into attacking Medina. While he was engaged in his sinister mission in the north, he had planned for the spread of disaffection in Medina. His colleagues, the hypocrites, were to spread rumours that Medina was going to be attacked by Syrian forces. As a result of this dual plot ?Abu ?Amir hoped that Muslims and Syrian Christians would go to war. If his plot did not succeed, he hoped that Muslims would themselves be provoked into attacking Syria. Even thus a war might start between Muslims and Syrians and Abu ?Amir would have something to rejoice over. Completing his plans, he went to Syria. While he was away the hypocrites at Medina?according to plan?began to spread rumours that caravans had been sighted which were coming to attack Medina. When no caravan appeared, they issued some kind of explanation.

TABUK'S EXPLANATION

These rumors grew so persistent that the Prophet (s.a.w) decided it was worthwhile to personally command a Muslim army against Syria during these trying times.

Arabia was in the grip of a famine. The harvest in the previous year had been poor and both grain and fruit were in short supply. The time for the new harvest had not yet come. It was the end of September or the beginning of October when the Prophet (s.a.w) set out on this mission. The hypocrites knew that the rumours were their own inventions. They knew also that their design was to provoke Muslims into an attack on the Syrians if the Syrians did not attack Muslims. In either case, a conflict with the great Roman Empire was to result in the destruction of Muslims. The lesson of Mauta was before them. At Mauta Muslims had to face such a huge army that it was with great difficulty that they were able to effect a retreat. The hypocrites were hoping to stage a second Mauta in which the Prophet (s.a.w) himself might lose his life. While the hypocrites were busy spreading rumours about the Syrian attack on Muslims, they also made every effort to strike fear in the minds of Muslims. The Syrians could raise very large armies which Muslims could not hope to stand against. They urged Muslims not to take part in the conflict with Syria. Their plan was, on the one hand, to provoke Muslims into attacking Syria and, on the other, to discourage them from going in large numbers. They wanted Muslims to go to war against Syria and meet with certain defeat. But as soon as the Prophet (s.a.w) announced his intention of leading this new expedition, enthusiasm ran high among Muslims. They went forward with offers of sacrifice for the sake of their faith. Muslims were ill-equipped for a war on such a scale. Their treasury was empty. Only the more prosperous Muslims had means to pay for the war. Individual Muslims vied with one another in the spirit of sacrifice for the sake of their faith. It is said that when the expedition was under way and the Prophet (s.a.w) appealed for funds, ?Uthmanra gave away the greater part of his wealth. His contribution is said to have amounted to about one thousand gold dinars, equivalent to about twenty-five thousand rupees. Other Muslims also made contributions according to their capacity. The poor Muslims were also provided with riding animals, swords and lances. Enthusiasm prevailed. There was at Medina at the time a party of Muslims who had migrated from Yemen. They were very poor. Some of them went to the Prophet (s.a.w) and offered their services for this expedition. They said, "O Prophet (s.a.w) of God, take us with you. We seek nothing more than the means of transportation." The Qur'an mentions these Muslims and their proposals in the following words:

Nor against those to whom thou saidst, 'I cannot find whereon I may ride you,' when they came to thee to saddle them; they went back, their eyes brimming with tears, out of anguish that they could not find what they might spend (9: 92).

That is to say, they are not to blame for not participating in the war because they lacked means and applied to the Prophet (s.a.w) for transportation to the battlefield. The Prophet (s.a.w) was unable to provide the transportation, so they left disappointed, believing they were poor and unable to contribute to the war between Muslims and Syrians. Abu Musara was the leader of this group. When asked what they had asked for, he said, "We did not ask for transportation." We just said that we lacked shoes and would be unable to complete the lengthy trek barefoot. "If we had only had shoes, we would have gone on foot and taken part in the war alongside our Muslim brethren." As this army was heading to Syria and Muslims had not yet forgotten what they had suffered at Mauta, every Muslim was filled with concern about the Prophet (s.a.w)'s personal safety. The women of Medina played their part, busy inducing their husbands and sons to join the war."

"Are you not embarrassed?"The Prophet (s.a.w) of God should embark on risky trips, and you should be making love to your wife?" questioned the woman. Your first mission is to head to the battleground. We shall see about the rest." It is said the Companion went out of the house at once, tightened the girths of his mount and galloped after the Prophet (s.a.w). At a distance of about three days' journey he overtook the Muslim army. The disbelievers and the hypocrites had probably thought that the Prophet (s.a.w) acting upon rumours, invented and spread by them, would spring upon the Syrian armies without a thought. They forgot that the Prophet (s.a.w) was concerned to set an example to generations of followers for all time to come. When the Prophet (s.a.w) neared Syria, he stopped and sent his men in different directions to report on the state of affairs. The men returned and reported there were no Syrian concentrations anywhere. The Prophet (s.a.w) decided to return, but stayed for a few days during which he signed agreements with some of the tribes on the border. There was no war and no fighting. The journey took the Prophet (s.a.w) about two months and a half. When the hypocrites at Medina found that their scheme for inciting war between Muslims and Syrians had failed and that the Prophet (s.a.w) was returning safe and sound, they began to fear that their intrigue had been exposed. They were afraid of the punishment which was now their due. But they did not halt their sinister plans. They equipped a party and posted it on the two sides of a narrow pass some distance from Medina. The pass was so narrow that only a single file could go through it. When the Prophet (s.a.w) and the Muslim army approached the spot, he had a warning by revelation that the enemy was in ambush on both sides of the narrow pass. The

When the Prophet (s.a.w)'s Companions arrived at the location, they found individuals in concealment with the clear purpose to attack, but these men withdrew as soon as they noticed the reconnoitring team, and the Prophet (s.a.w) chose not to follow them.

When the Prophet (s.a.w) arrived in Medina, the hypocrites who had avoided the battle began to make lame excuses, but the Prophet (s.a.w) accepted them while feeling that the time had come to expose their hypocrisy. He had a command from God that the mosque at Quba, which the hypocrites had built in order to hold their meetings in secret, be demolished, and the hypocrites were compelled to pray with other Muslims.

When the Prophet (s.a.w) returned from Tabuk, they saw that the people of Ta'if had also surrendered, and the other tribes of Arabia petitioned for admission to Islam, and in a short time, the whole Arabia was under the banner of Islam.

Islam.

THE FINAL PILGRIMAGE

The Prophet (s.a.w) made a journey to Mecca in the ninth year of the Hijra. On the day of the pilgrimage, he got revelation bearing the famous Qur'anic verse:

This day i have finalized your religion for you today and fulfilled My favor upon you, and I have selected Islam as your religion (5:4).

This sentence effectively said that the Message that the Holy Prophet (s.a.w) had delivered from God and that he had been expounding by speech and action for all these years had been accomplished. This Message was a gift in every way. The full Message included the richest gifts that man could get.

God provides. The word 'al-Islam,' which implies submission, embodies the Message. The religion of submission was supposed to be

Muslims are the world's religion. This passage was read by the Holy Prophet (s.a.w) in the valley of Muzdalifa, where pilgrims had gathered. The Prophet (s.a.w) halted in Mina on their way back from Muzdalifa. The eleventh day of the month of Dhu'l-Hijja had arrived. The Prophet (s.a.w) stepped in front of a huge crowd of Muslims and made a speech that became known as the Prophet (s.a.w)'s farewell address. During his speech, he stated the following:

Please lend me your ears, gentlemen. For I don't know whether I'll ever stand before you again in this valley and address you as I do now. God has made your lives and belongings immune to assault from one another until the Day of Judgment. God has allotted a portion of the inheritance to everyone of us. No 'will' that is harmful to the interests of a lawful heir may now be acknowledged. A kid born in any home is considered the child of that house's father. Whoever challenges the paternity of this kid will face penalty under Islamic law. Anyone who traces his birth to someone else's father or fraudulently claims to be his master will be cursed by God, His angels, and all of humanity.

O men, you have certain rights against your women, but they have some rights against you as well. Your right against them is that they live chaste lives and do not do anything that may cause dishonor to the husband in the eyes of his people. If your women fail to meet this standard, you have the power to penalize them. After a competent authority has conducted a thorough investigation and proved your right to punish, you may punish them. Even so, the penalty in such a circumstance should not be harsh. But if your women do not do this, and their behavior does not bring dishonor on their husbands, your obligation is to provide them with food, clothing, and shelter in accordance with your own standard of life. Always remember to treat your wife nicely. God has given you the responsibility of watching after them. Woman is unable to preserve her own rights. God designated you as trustees of those rights when you married. Under God's Law, you took your wives into your dwellings. As a result, you must not belittle the trust that God has put in your hands.

O men, you still have some prisoners of war in your custody. As a result, I recommend that you feed and dress them in the same manner and style that you eat and clothe yourself. If they do something bad that you can't forgive, give them to someone else. They are a part of the creation of God. Giving them grief or hardship is never appropriate.

What I say to you, guys, you must hear and remember. All Muslims are brothers and sisters to one another. You are all equal. All men are equal, regardless of country or tribe they belong to or their position in life.

While stating this, the Prophet (s.a.w) lifted his hands and connected the fingers of one hand with the fingers of the other, saying:

Human beings are equal to one another in the same way as the fingers on both hands are equal. No one has any right or supremacy over another. You're like brothers.

Following that, the Prophet (s.a.w) stated:

Do you have any idea what month it is? What country are we in? What day of the year is it?

In response, Muslims said that they were aware that it was the holy month, the hallowed country, and the day of the Hajj. The Prophet (s.a.w) then said:

Even as this month is sacred, this country is untouchable, and this day is holy, God has made every man's life, property, and honor precious. Taking a man's life or property, or attacking his honor, is as unfair and immoral as violating the holiness of this day, month, and region. What I order you now isn't only for today. It is intended to last forever. You are supposed to remember it and act on it until you depart this world to meet your Maker in the next.

Finally, he stated:

You should transmit what I have told to you to the ends of the world. Perhaps those who haven't heard me will profit more than those who have (Sihah Sitta, Tabari, Hisham, and Khamis).

The Prophet's (s.a.w) discourse exemplifies Islam's complete message and essence. It demonstrates the Prophet's great care for the wellbeing of man and the peace of the world, as well as his concern for the rights of women and other helpless animals. The Prophet (s.a.w) sensed his demise was approaching. God had given him indications about his demise. Among the worries and fears he expressed were his concern and worry over the abuse of women at the hands of males. He took care not to leave this earth without ensuring that women have the position that was rightfully theirs. Woman has been viewed as man's slave and handmaid from his birth. This was the Prophet's only concern. He also looked after prisoners of war. They were unjustly seen and treated as slaves, and they were exposed to a variety of cruelties and excesses. The Prophet (s.a.w) felt compelled to depart this earth without notifying captives of war of their God-given rights. Inequality between men afflicted the Prophet (s.a.w) as well. Occasionally, disagreements were overemphasized to the point that they could no longer be tolerated. Some folks were elevated to the heavens, while others were demoted to the depths. The circumstances that led to this inequity were factors that led to animosity and conflict between nations and countries. These issues were likewise considered by the Prophet (s.a.w). Unless the spirit of inequality was killed and conditions that induced one people to usurp the rights of another and attack their lives and possessions were removed—conditions that become rampant during times of moral decay—the world's peace and progress could not be restored. He preached that human life and belongings were holy in the same way as sacred days, sacred months, and sacred locations were. No one has ever shown as much concern and care for the welfare of women, the rights of the vulnerable, and international peace as the Prophet (s.a.w) of Islam. No one has ever done more to promote human equality than the Prophet (s.a.w). No one yearned as much for man's betterment as he did. No surprise, Islam has long maintained women's rights to own and inherit property. This right was not recognized by European countries until about one thousand three hundred years after the arrival of Islam. No matter how low the society from which he comes, everyone who converts to Islam becomes equal to everyone else. Islam's contributions to global culture are characterized by freedom and equality. Other faiths' concepts of freedom and equality lag far behind those proclaimed and practiced by Islam. A monarch, a religious leader, and a simple man all share the same rank in a Muslim mosque; there is no distinction. These distinctions continue to exist in the places of worship of other faiths and countries, despite the fact that those religions and nations claim to have done more for freedom and equality than Islam.

THE PROPHET SAYS ABOUT HIS DEATH

On the journey back, the Prophet (s.a.w) reminded his Companions of his impending demise once again. "O men, I am but one like you; I may receive the Call any day and have to go. My Kind and Vigilant Master has informed me that a Prophet (s.a.w) lives up to half the years of the Prophet (s.a.w) before him. I believe I shall soon receive the Call and depart. O my Companions, I shall have to answer God, and you will have to answer as well. What will you then say?"

"We will say that you conveyed properly the Message of Islam and committed all your life to the service of the Faith; you had the most perfect desire for the welfare of man: We will say: Allah, grant him the finest of rewards," the Companions responded.

The Prophet (s.a.w) then asked, "Do you bear witness that God is One, that Muhammad (s.a.w) is His Servant and Prophet (s.a.w), that Heaven and Hell are true, that death is certain, that there is life after death, that the Judgement Day must come, and that all the dead will one day be raised from their graves, restored to life, and that all the dead will one day be raised from their graves, restored to life, and that all the dead will one day be raised from their graves, restored to life

assembled?"

"Yes," the Companions agreed. "All of these realities are seen by us."

"Be Thou also a witness to this—that I have presented Islam to them," the Prophet (s.a.w) said, turning to God.

Following the Pilgrimage, the Prophet (s.a.w) was extremely busy educating and instructing his disciples, attempting to elevate their moral standards and reform and polish their behavior. His own death became a recurring motif in his writings, and he prepared Muslims for it.

When he stood to address the Faithful one day, he stated, "Today I have got the revelation:

When Allah's assistance and triumph arrive, and thou seest persons flocking into Allah's religion in battalions, exalt the majesty of thy Lord, with His praise, and beg pardon from Him, for He is Oft-Returning with compassion." (110: 2-4).

That is to say, a moment was approaching when, with God's aid, a large number of people would convert to Islam. It was therefore the Prophet (s.a.w)—and his followers—duty to glorify God and plead to Him to remove all barriers to the establishment of the Faith.

On this occasion, the Prophet (s.a.w) used a parable: God said to a man, 'If it pleases you, you may return to Me, or you may labor a little longer at changing the world.' The man responded he preferred to return to his Lord.

The crowd included Abu Bakrra. He had been listening to the Prophet (s.a.w)'s last talk with fervour and worry, the passion of a great believer and the anxiety of a friend and follower who saw portents of the Prophetssa's death in this address. Abu Bakrra could no longer restrain himself after hearing the tale. He burst into tears. The other Companions, who had just been listening on the surface, were taken aback when Abu Bakrra fell into tears. What is the situation with Abu Bakrra? They inquired. The Propheta was sobbing when describing Islam's upcoming victory. 'Umarra, in particular, was irritated by Abu Bakrra. Even though the Prophet (s.a.w) was bringing good news, this elderly guy was grieving. Only the Prophet (s.a.w) realized what was going on. Only Abu Bakrra, he believed, understood him. Only he saw that the scriptures that promised triumphs also foreshadowed the Prophet's (s.a.w)'s impending death.

"If it were permissible to love anyone more than others, I would have so loved Abu Bakrra," the Prophet (s.a.w) continued, "but that degree of love is only for God. O my people, all the doors that open to the mosque should be closed from today except the door of Abu Bakrra."

There was no doubt that this last command conveyed a prophesy that Abu Bakrra would be the First Khalifah after the Prophet (s.a.w). To lead the Faithful in prayer, he would have to come to the mosque five times a day and keep the door of his residence open into the mosque. Years later, when 'Umarra was Khalifah, he questioned some of those there what the line "When the assistance of God and victory arrive" meant. Clearly, he recalled the circumstances in which the Prophet (s.a.w) told Muslims this, as well as the passages that followed. He must also recall that at the time, only Abu Bakrra knew the significance of these lines. 'Umarra was attempting to assess Muslims' comprehension of these scriptures. They had failed to comprehend them at the time of their revelation; do they now realize what they meant? Ibni 'Abbasra, who had to have been ten or eleven at the time of their revelation and was now seventeen or eighteen, offered to respond. "Leader of the Faithful, these verses contained a prophecy about the death of the Holy Prophet (s.a.w). When a Prophet's (s.a.w) work is done, he wishes no longer to live in the world," he said. "The verses spoke of the imminent victory of Islam. This victory had a sad side, and that was the impending departure of the Prophet (s.a.w) from this world."

THE PROPHETS' LAST DAYA

Finally, the day arrived that every human being must confront. The Prophet's sa task was completed. All that God had for him to disclose for the sake of mankind has been revealed. Muhammad (s.a.w)'s spirit has given his people fresh life. A new country, a new way of life, and new institutions had emerged; in short, a new heaven and a new earth. The groundwork for a new world order had been built. The ground had been ploughed and irrigated, and seed had been distributed in preparation for a fresh crop. And now the harvest was beginning to appear. It was not, however, his responsibility to harvest it. It was just up to him to plough, sow, and water. He arrived as a laborer, stayed as a laborer, and was about to leave as a laborer. He found his reward in the pleasure and approval of his God, his Maker and Master, rather than in the goods of this world. When it was time to reap the crop, he chose to go to Him, leaving others to reap.

The Holy Prophet (s.a.w) became sick. He continued to attend the mosque and lead the prayers for a few days. He eventually got too feeble to do so. The Companions ra had become so used to his everyday companionship that they couldn't think he would die. But he had been telling them about his death over and again. "If a man makes a mistake, it is better for him to make amends for it in this very world so that he has no regrets in the next," he said one day, "so I say, if I have done any wrong to any of you, it may be only unwittingly, let him come forward and ask me to make amends. If I have injured any of you, let him come forward and take his revenge. I do not wish to be put to shame when I face my God

The Prophet's (s.a.w) offer was welcomed solemnly by all the Companions, save one, who spoke up and said, "O Prophet (s.a.w) of God, I once sustained an injury from you." We were queuing up for fight as you went by, and you buried your elbow into my side. Everything was done unintentionally, but you stated we could revenge even unintended wrongs. The Companions, who had received the Prophet's (s.a.w) offer in solemn silence, were enraged at the insolence and stupidity of this man, who had failed completely to understand the spirit of the Prophet's (s.a.w) offer and the solemnity of the occasion. But the Companion seemed adamant—determined to take the Prophet (s.a.w) at his word.

"You are welcome to exact your vengeance," the Prophet (s.a.w) responded.

"Come and strike me like I struck you," he replied, turning his back on him.

"But," this Companion pointed out, "when you struck me, my side was naked since I was wearing no shirt at the time."

"Raise my shirt," said the Prophet (s.a.w), "and let him strike my side with his elbow," which they did, but instead of striking the Prophet (s.a.w)'s exposed side, this Companion leaned forward with bedewed eyes and kissed the Prophet (s.a.w).

Prophet's (s.a.w) is naked.

"What exactly is this?"" inquired Prophet (s.a.w).

"Didn't you mention your time with us was coming to an end?" How many more chances will we get to touch you in the flesh and show our love and admiration for you? True, you struck me with your elbow, but who could conceive of retaliating? I had this thought just now. You promised to let us exact our vengeance. "Let me kiss you under cover of vengeance," I told myself.

The wrathful Companions started to wish the notion had come to them.

THE PROPHET (S.A.W) HAS DIED

But the Prophet (s.a.w) was ill, and the illness seemed to worsen. Death seemed to draw nearer and nearer, and depression and gloom descended on the hearts of the Companions. The sun shone over Medina as brightly as ever, but to the Companions it seemed paler and paler. The day dawned as before, but it seemed to bring darkness, not light. "I can't breathe properly," 'A'ishara murmured, sitting up and holding his head. The death-pangs were obvious. The Prophet (s.a.w), disturbed, gazed now to this side and now to that, saying again, "Woe to the Jews and the Christians." They fostered the worship of their Prophets' tombs." This may be considered his deathbed message to his followers. As he lay dying, he appeared to declare to his followers, "You will learn to regard me above all other Prophet (s.a.w)s, and more successful than any of them." But be careful not to make my tomb an object of devotion. Let my grave stay just that: a grave. Others may revere their Prophet (s.a.w)s' graves and convert them into pilgrimage sites, locations where they may mend and do austerities, make sacrifices, and give gratitude. Others may do it, but you will not. You must remember your one and only goal, which is to serve the One and Only God."

After warning Muslims about the importance of defending the hard-won concept of One God and the distinction between God and Man, his eyelids drooped and his eyes closed, and all he said was, "To my Friend the Highest of the High—to my Friend the Highest of the High—to my Friend the Highest of the High," and he passed away.

The news reached the mosque. There many Companionsra had assembled, having given up their private tasks. They were expecting to hear better news but instead heard of the Prophet's (s.a.w) death. It came like a bolt from the blue. Abu Bakrra was out. 'Umarra was in the mosque, but he was utterly stupefied with grief. It angered him if he heard anyone say the Prophet (s.a.w) was dead. He even drew his sword and threatened to kill those who should say the Prophet (s.a.w) had died. There was much the Prophet (s.a.w) had yet to do, so the Prophet (s.a.w) could not die. True, his soul had departed from his body, but it had gone only to meet its Maker. Just as Mosesas had gone for a time to meet his Maker only to return, the Prophet (s.a.w) must return to do what had been left undone. There were the hypocrites, for instance, with whom they had yet to deal. 'Umarra walked about sword in hand almost as a mad man. As he walked he said: "Whosoever says the Prophet (s.a.w) has died will himself die at 'Umarra's hands." The Companions felt braced and they halfbelieved what 'Umarra said. The Prophet (s.a.w) could not die. There must have been a mistake. In the meantime some

Companions rushed in search of Abu Bakrra, located him, and informed him what had transpired. Abu Bakrra hurried immediately to Medina's mosque, entered 'A'isha'sra's apartment, and asked her, "Has the Prophet (s.a.w) died?""

"Yes," 'A'ishara answered, then walked directly to the Prophet's (s.a.w) corpse, uncovered the face, bowed down, and kissed the forehead, tears of love and anguish falling from his eyes, and he murmured, "God is our witness." Death will not strike you again."

It was a sentence full of meaning. It was Abu Bakrra's reply to what 'Umarra had been saying out of his mad grief. The Prophet (s.a.w) had died once. That was his physical death— the death everyone must die. But he was not to have a second death. There was to be no spiritual death—no death to the beliefs which he had established in his followers and for the establishment of which he had taken such pains. One of those beliefs—one of the more important beliefs—he had taught was that even Prophet (s.a.w)s were human and even they must die. Muslims were not going to forget this so soon after the Prophet (s.a.w)'s own death. Having said this great sentence over the dead body of the Prophet (s.a.w), Abu Bakrra came out and, piercing through the lines of the Faithful, advanced silently to the pulpit. As he stood, 'Umarra stood by him, his sword drawn as before, determined that if Abu Bakrra said the Prophet (s.a.w) had died Abu Bakrra must lose his head. As Abu Bakrra started to speak, 'Umarra pulled at his shirt, wanting to stop him from speaking but Abu Bakrra snatched back his shirt and refused to stop.

He then recited the following passage from the Qur'an:

And Muhammad (s.a.w) is simply a Messenger; indeed, all Messengers have died before him; would you therefore turn back on your heels if he dies or is slain? (3: 145).

That is to say, Muhammad (s.a.w) was a man with a Message from God, and all of the previous men with Messages from God had perished.

Would they turn back on everything they had been taught and learnt if Muhammad (s.a.w) died? This verse was revealed at the time of Uhud. Rumour had spread that the Prophet (s.a.w) had been killed by the enemy. Many Muslims lost heart and withdrew from the battle. The verse came from heaven to brace them. It had the same effect on this occasion. But those among you who worshiped Muhammad (s.a.w), let them know from me that Muhammad (s.a.w) is dead." The Companions regained their balance after hearing this timely speech. 'Umarra himself was changed when he heard Abu Bakrra recite the verse quoted above. He began to return to his senses and recover his lost judgement. By the time Abu Bakrra finished the recitation of the verse, 'Umar'sra spiritual eye was fully opened.

Many expressed the grief that overtook Muslims upon the death of the Prophet (s.a.w), but the pithy and profound expression given to it in his couplet by Hassanra, the poet of early Islam, remains to this day the best and most enduring. He said: 'Thou wast the pupil of my eye. Now that thou hast died, my eye hath become blind. I care not who dies now. For I feared only thy death.'

This couplet expressed the sentiments of every Muslim, and for months men, women, and children walked the streets of Medina repeating Hassan bin Thabitra's couplet.

PERSONALITY AND CHARACTER OF THE PROPHET

HAVING briefly described the outstanding events in the life of the Holy Prophet (s.a.w) we would now attempt a short sketch of his character. In this connection we have available the collective testimony of his own people which they bore to his character before he claimed to be a Prophet (s.a.w). At that stage he was known among his people as "The Trusty" and "The True" (Hisham). There are living at all times large numbers of people against whom no charge of dishonesty is preferred. There are also large numbers who are never exposed to a severe trial or temptation and in the ordinary affairs and concerns of life they behave with honesty and integrity, yet they are not regarded as worthy of any special distinction on that account. Special distinctions are conferred only when the life of a person illustrates in a conspicuous degree some high moral quality. Every soldier that goes into battle puts his life in jeopardy but not every such British soldier has been regarded as worthy of the award of the Victoria Cross, nor every such German soldier of the Iron Cross. There are hundreds of thousands of people in France who occupy themselves with intellectual pursuits but not every one of them is decorated with the Legion of Honour. The mere fact, therefore, that a man is trustworthy and true does not indicate that he possesses eminence in these respects, but when a whole people combines to confer upon an individual the titles of "The Trusty" and "The True", that is evidence of the possession of exceptional qualities. Had it been the practice of the people of Mecca to confer such a distinction upon some individual in each generation, even then the recipient would have been looked upon as occupying a high position. But the history of Mecca and of Arabia furnishes no indication that it was customary for the Arabs to confer these or similar titles upon eminent individuals in each generation. On the contrary, through centuries of Arab history we find that it was only in the case of the Holy Prophet (s.a.w) of Islam that his people conferred the titles of "The Trusty" and "The True". This is proof of the fact that the Holy Prophet (s.a.w) possessed these qualities in so eminent a degree that within the knowledge and the memory of his people no other individual could be regarded as his equal in these respects. The Arabs were well known for their keenness of mind and what they chose to regard as rare must in truth have been rare and unique.

When the Holy Prophet (s.a.w) was summoned by God to assume the burden and responsibilities of prophethood, his wife, KHADIJA(ra), testified to his high moral qualities—an incident that has been related in the biographical portion of this General Introduction. We will now proceed to illustrate some of his high moral qualities so that the reader can appreciate even those aspects of his character that are not widely known.

THE PROPHET'S (S.A.W) MINDFULNESS AND CLEANLINESS OF BODY

It is said of the Holy Prophet (s.a.w) that his speech was always pure and that he was not given to the use of oaths (Tirmidhi), which was unusual for an Arab. This is not to say that Arabs at the time of the Holy Prophet (s.a.w) used foul language on a regular basis, but there is no doubt that they were in the habit of punctuating their speech with a generous measure of oaths, a habit that persists among them even today.

He was very particular, even punctilious, about physical cleanliness; he used to brush his teeth several times a day and was so fond of the practice that he once said that if he weren't afraid that the ordinance would be onerous, he would make it obligatory for every Muslim to brush his teeth before each of the five daily prayers; he always washed his hands before and after each meal; and, after eating anything cooked, he always rinsed his mouth.

In the Islamic polity, a mosque is the only prescribed place of gathering for Muslims, so the Holy Prophet (s.a.w) placed special emphasis on the cleanliness of mosques, especially on occasions when people were expected to gather in them, and directed that on such occasions, incense should be burned in the mosques to purify the air (Abu Dawud). He also directed that nobody should go to a mosque on the occasion of a congregation or gathering after eating.

He insisted on streets being kept clean and clear of twigs, stones, and all articles or matter that were likely to obstruct or prove offensive. Whenever he found such matter or article lying in a street, he would remove it, and he used to say that a person who helps to keep streets and roads clean and clear earns spiritual merit in the eyes of God.

THE SIMPLE LIFE OF THE PROPHET

When it came to food and drink, the Prophet (s.a.w) was extremely simple. He never expressed displeasure with illprepared or ill-cooked food; if he could eat it, he would do so to save the person who had prepared it from disappointment. If a dish was unpalatable, he simply refrained from partaking of it and never expressed his disapproval of it.

On one occasion while he was passing along a road he noticed some people gathered round a roast kid ready to enjoy the feast. When they saw the Holy Prophet (s.a.w) they invited him to join them, but he declined. This was not due to his not having a liking for roast meat but to the fact that he did not approve of people indulging in a feast in the open where they could be observed by poor people who had themselves not enough to eat. It is related of him that on other occasions he did partake of roast meat. 'A'ishara has related that the Holy Prophet (s.a.w) did not, till the day of his death, on any occasion, eat his fill on three consecutive days. He was very particular that a person should not go to a meal in another person's house uninvited. On one occasion somebody invited him to a meal and requested that he might bring four other persons with him. When he arrived at the house of his host he found that a sixth person had also joined his party. The host came to the door to receive him and his party and the Holy Prophet (s.a.w) drew his attention to the fact that there were now six of them and that it was for the host to decide whether he would permit the sixth person to join them in the meal or whether the latter should depart. The host, of course, readily invited the sixth person also (Bukhari, Kitab alAt'ima).

When the Holy Prophet (s.a.w) sat down to eat, he always began by invoking Allah's name and blessings, and when he finished, he said, "All praise is due to Allah, Who has given us to eat: Praise, abundant and sincere and ever-increasing: Praise, which does not leave an impression on one's mind that one has rendered enough praise but which creates in one's mind the feeling that enough has not been said and Oh my God! do Thou infuse our souls with these feelings." At times, he said, "All thanks is due to God, Who has supplied our hunger and need." May our hearts ever yearn for His praise and never be ungrateful to Him." He always admonished his Companions to stop eating before they were full and used to say that one man's food should always suffice for two. Whenever any special food was prepared in his house, he used to suggest that a portion of it be sent as a present to his neighbours; and presents of food and other articles were constantly sent from his house to his neighbours' houses (Muslim).

He always tried to ascertain from the faces of those who were in his company whether any of them was in need of sustenance. Abu Hurairara relates the following incident: On one occasion he had been without food for over three days. He stood at the entrance to the mosque and observed Abu Bakrra passing near. He asked Abu Bakrra the meaning of a verse of the Qur'an which enjoins the feeding of the poor. Abu Bakrra explained its meaning and passed on. Abu Hurairara when relating this incident used to say with indignation that he too understood the Qur'an as well as Abu Bakrra did. His object in asking the latter to explain the meaning of the verse had been that Abu Bakrra might guess that he was hungry and might arrange to get food for him. Shortly after, 'Umarra passed by and Abu Hurairara asked him also to explain the meaning of the verse. 'Umarra also explained its meaning and passed on. Abu Hurairara, like all Companions of the Holy Prophet (s.a.w), was loath to make a direct request and when he perceived that his indirect attempts to draw attention to his condition had failed, he began to feel very faint. Thereupon he heard his name being called in a very soft and tender voice. Looking to the side from which the voice came he saw that the Holy Prophet (s.a.w) was looking out from the window of his house and was smiling. He inquired of Abu Hurairara: "Are you hungry?"Abu Hurairara responded, "Verily, O Messenger of Allahsa! "I'm hungry."

"There is no food in our home either, but someone has just given us a cup of milk," the Holy Prophet (s.a.w) stated. "Go to the mosque and see if there are any other people there who are hungry like you," Abu Hurairara continues. "I thought to myself, I am hungry enough to consume the entire amount of milk in the cup, but the Prophet (s.a.w) has asked me to invite any other people who may be in a similar situation, which means that I will only get a small portion of the milk." But I had to follow out the Prophet's (s.a.w)'s commands, so I entered the mosque and discovered six people seated inside, whom I took to the Prophet's (s.a.w)'s door. He placed the cup of milk in one of their hands and instructed him to drink. When he had finished and removed the cup from his lips, the Prophet (s.a.w) insisted on his swallowing it again and again till he had gotten his full. Similarly, he insisted on each of the six drinking his full of milk. I was frightened that if he invited anybody to drink, there would be nothing left for me. After the six had finished their milk, the Prophet (s.a.w) handed me the cup, and I noticed that there was still plenty of milk in it. In my case, he insisted that I drink my fill and made me drink a second and third time, and at the end he drank what was left in the cup himself and thanked God and shut the door" (Bukhari, Kitabul Riqaq). The Holy Prophet's (s.a.w) object in offering the milk to Abu Hurairara last of all may have been to indicate to him that he should have continued to endure the pangs of hunger, trusting in God, and

He always ate and drank with his right hand and always stopped three times to take breath in the middle of a drink. One reason for this may be that if a person who is thirsty drinks water at one stretch he is apt to drink too much and thus upset his digestion. In the matter of eating the rule that he followed was that he partook of all things that are pure and permissible but not in a manner which would savour of indulgence or would deprive other people of their due share. As has been stated, his normal food was always very simple but if anybody presented him with something specially prepared he did not decline it. He did not, however, hanker after good food, though he had a particular liking for honey and for dates. As regards dates, he used to say that there was a special relationship between a Muslim and the date tree whose leaves and bark and fruit, both ripe and unripe, and even the stones of whose fruit could all be put to some use or the other and no part of which was without its proper use. The same was the case with a true Muslim. No act of his was without its beneficence and all that he did promoted the welfare of mankind (Bukhari and Muslim).

The Holy Prophet (s.a.w) preferred simplicity in dress. His own dress normally consisted of a shirt and an izar or a shirt and a pair of trousers. He always wore his izar or his trousers so that the garment covered his body up to a point above his ankles. He did not approve of the knee or any portion of the body above the knee being exposed without extreme necessity. He did not approve of the use, whether as part of dress or in the way of curtains, etc., of cloth which had figures embroidered or painted on it, especially if the figures were large and might be interpreted as representing gods or goddesses or other objects of worship. On one occasion he found a curtain hanging in his house bearing large figures and he directed it to be removed. He, however, saw no harm in the use of cloth bearing small figures which could not be so interpreted. He never wore silk himself and did not consider it permissible for Muslim men to wear it. For the purpose of authenticating the letters that he wrote to certain sovereigns inviting them to accept Islam he caused to be prepared a signet-ring, but directed that it should be made of silver and not of gold, for he said that the wearing of gold had been prohibited to Muslim men (Bukhari and Muslim). Muslim women are permitted to wear silk and gold but in their case also the Holy Prophet's (s.a.w) direction was that excess should be avoided. On one occasion he called for subscriptions for the relief of the poor and a lady took off one of her bracelets and placed it before him as her contribution. Addressing her, he said: "Does not your other hand deserve to be saved from the Fire?" The lady then removed her bracelet from the other hand and offered it for the purpose that he had in mind. None of his wives possessed ornaments of any significant value, and other Muslim women also very rarely possessed any ornaments. He deprecated the hoarding of money or bullion, as he held that it was harmful to the interests of the poorer sections of the community and resulted in upsetting the economy of a country.

On one occasion, 'Umarra suggested to the Holy Prophet (s.a.w) that because he had to receive Embassies from great monarchs, he should have a rich cloak prepared for himself to wear on such ceremonial occasions. The Prophet (s.a.w) rejected the suggestion, saying, "It would not be pleasing to God for me to adopt ways like this." "I shall meet everyone in the clothes that I normally wear." On one occasion, silk garments were presented to him, and he sent one to 'Umarra, who said, "How can I wear it when you have disapproved of wearing silk garments?" The Holy Prophet (s.a.w) observed, "Every present is not meant for personal use." His meaning was that because the garment was silk, 'Umarra should have presented it to his wife or daughter, or should have given it to some charity.

"When the Holy Prophet (s.a.w) used to get up at night for prayers, I used to lie on one side of the bedding and stretched out my legs while he was in the standing posture and folded them back when he had to prostrate himself (Muslim, Tirmidhi)."

He maintained the same level of simplicity in his living surroundings. His dwelling usually had one room and a tiny patio. A rope was stretched half way across the room so that when he entertained company, a piece of fabric could be draped from the rope to divide a section of the room from the area inhabited by his wife. His existence was so basic that 'A'ishara said that throughout the Prophet (s.a.w)'s lifetime, they often had to survive on dates and water, and that on the day of his death, there was no food in the home save a few dates (Bukhari).

MUHAMMAD'S sa RELATIONSHIP WITH GOD

The Holy Prophet's (s.a.w) life seems to have been controlled and colored by his love for and devotion to God.

Despite the tremendous obligations that had been placed on his shoulders, the majority of his time throughout the day and night was spent in worship and adoration of God. He'd get out of bed at midnight and commit himself to God's worship until it was time to travel to the mosque for morning prayers. He would occasionally stand so long in prayer late at night that his feet would swell, and anybody who saw him in that state were always moved. 'A'ishara once said to him, "God has honoured you with His love and nearness; why then do you subject yourself to so much discomfort and inconvenience?" He replied, "If God has conferred His love and nearness upon me by His Grace and Mercy, is it not my duty in return to be always rendering thanks to Him? Gratitude should increase in proportion to the favors received" (Bukhari, Kitabul Kusuf).

He never embarked on a project without divine direction or approval. It has already been stated in the biographical section that, despite the harsh persecution he faced from the people of Mecca, he did not leave the city until he got the divine instruction to do so. When the persecution grew unbearable and he granted his Companions permission to move to Abyssinia, several of them voiced a wish for him to follow them. He refused to do so because he had not obtained divine authorization to do so. Thus, at a time of hardship and persecution when people want to keep their friends and relatives near to them, he led his Companions to seek safety in Abyssinia while remaining in Mecca since God had not yet commanded him to depart.

Whenever he heard the word of God spoken, he was overtaken with emotion, and tears would well up in his eyes, particularly if the words underlined his personal obligations. According to 'Abdullah bin Mas'udra, the Holy Prophet (s.a.w) once ordered him to recite several lines of the Qur'an to him. "O Messenger of Allahsa! The Qur'an has been revealed to you (i.e., you know it best of all), how should I repeat it to you?" the Holy Prophet (s.a.w) said.

'Abdullah bin Mas'udra then proceeded to recite Surah Al-Nisa'. When he recounted the verse, "And how will it fare with them when We bring a witness from every nation, and bring thee as a witness against them?" (4: 42), the Holy Prophet (s.a.w) cried, "Enough!" Enough!" 'Abdullah bin Mas'udra glanced up and saw tears gushing from the Holy of Holies.

Eyes of the Prophet (Bukhari, Kitab Fada'ilul Qur'an).

He was so particular about joining the congregational prayers that, even during severe illness when it is permissible not only to say one's prayers in one's room but also to say them lying in bed, he would go to the mosque to lead the prayers himself. On one occasion when he was unable to proceed to the mosque, he directed that Abu Bakrra should lead the prayers.

It is a common practice to give expression to one's pleasure or to draw attention to any particular matter by the clapping of hands and the Arabs used to follow the same practice. The Holy Prophet (s.a.w), however, so loved the remembrance of God that for these purposes also he substituted the praise and remembrance of God in place of the clapping of hands. On one occasion while he was occupied with some important matter, the time of the next service drew near and he directed that Abu Bakrra should lead the prayers. Shortly thereafter he was able to conclude the business upon which he was engaged and proceeded at once to the mosque. Abu Bakrra was leading the prayers but when the congregation perceived that the Holy Prophet (s.a.w) had arrived, they began to clap their hands for the purpose both of giving expression to their joy at his arrival and also to draw Abu Bakrra's attention to the fact that the Prophet (s.a.w) himself had arrived. Thereupon Abu Bakrra stepped back and made room for the Holy Prophet (s.a.w) to lead the prayers. When the prayers were over, the Prophet (s.a.w) addressed Abu Bakrra and said: "Why did you step back after I had directed you to lead the prayers?" Abu Bakrra said, "O Allah's Messenger! How could the son of Abu Quhafara lead the prayers in the presence of Allahsa's Messenger?" The Prophet (s.a.w) then addressed the crowd, saying, "Why did you clap your hands? It is inappropriate for you to clap your hands while remembering God. If, during the course of your prayers, your attention is called to anything, instead of clapping your hands, speak the name of God loudly. This would call attention to whatever needed to be noted" (Bukhari).

The Prophet (s.a.w) did not approve of prayers or worship being performed as a penance or imposition. On one occasion, he returned home and noticed a rope dangling between two pillars. He inquired as to its purpose, and was told that his wife Zainabra was in the habit of supporting herself with the rope when she became tired during her prayers. He ordered the rope to be removed, and said that prayers should be performed only as long as one felt easy and comfortable.

When his end was near and he was in the grip of death agony, he turned from side to side exclaiming: "May the curse of God descend upon those Jews and Christians who have converted the graves of their Prophets into places of worship" (Bukhari). He had in mind those Jews and Christians who prostrated themselves at the graves of their Prophets and saints and addressed their prayers to them.

His extreme sense of jealousy for the honour of God has already been referred to in the biographical portion. The people of Mecca sought to place all sorts of temptations in his way to persuade him to give up his opposition to idol-worship (Tabari). His uncle Abu Talib also tried to dissuade him and expressed his fear that if he persisted in his denunciation of idol-worship, Abu Talib would have to choose between ceasing to give him his protection and the bitter opposition of his people. The only reply that the Prophet (s.a.w) made to his uncle on that occasion was: "If these people were to place the sun on my right hand and the moon on my left, I would not desist from proclaiming and preaching the Unity of God" (Zurqani). Again, during the Battle of Uhud when a remnant of wounded Muslims were grouped round him at the foot of a hill and their enemies were giving vent to their feeling of jubilation at having broken the Muslim ranks in shouts of victory and their leader Abu Sufyanra called out: "May Hubal (one of the idols worshipped by the Meccans) be exalted! May the name of Hubal be glorified!" Despite aware that his personal safety and the protection of the little band of Muslims assembled around him lay in remaining quiet, the Holy Propheta could no longer resist himself and commanded his Companions to exclaim in response, "To Allah alone belongs victory and glory! Victory and honor belong only to Allah!"Bukhari" (Arabic).

It was a common misconception among the followers of different religions before the advent of Islam that heavenly and terrestrial manifestations took place to mark occasions of joy and sorrow for Prophets, saints and other great men and that even the movements of the heavenly bodies could be controlled by them. For instance, it is related of some of them that they caused the sun to become stationary in its course or stopped the progress of the moon or caused running water to become still. Islam taught that such notions were baseless and that references to phenomena of this kind in religious Scriptures were only by way of metaphor which, instead of being interpreted in accordance with its correct significance, had given rise to superstitions. Nevertheless, some among Muslims were prone to attribute these phenomena to events in the lives of the great Prophet (s.a.w)s. In the closing years of the Holy Prophet's (s.a.w) life his son Ibrahim died at the age of two and a half years. An eclipse of the sun occurred on the same day. Some Muslims in Medina gave currency to the idea that the sun had been darkened on the occasion of the death of the Prophet's (s.a.w) son as a mark of divine condolence. When this was mentioned to the Holy Prophet (s.a.w) he expressed great displeasure and severely condemned the notion. He explained that the sun and the moon and other heavenly bodies were all governed by divine laws and that their movements and the phenomena connected with them had no relation to the life or death of any person (Bukhari).

Rain is always welcome and eagerly awaited in Arabia, which is a very dry country, and the Arabs used to imagine that the coming of rain was controlled by the movements of stars. Whenever anyone expressed that idea, the Holy Prophet (s.a.w) used to be very upset and admonished his people not to attribute favors bestowed upon them by Providence to other sources. He explained that rain and other natural phenomena were all governed by divine laws and that they were not constrained by them.

He had complete faith in God, which no bad condition could shake. On one occasion, an adversary of his, finding him sleeping and defenseless, stood over his head with a drawn sword and threatened to dispatch him immediately, before asking, "Who can save you from this predicament?""The Holy Prophet (s.a.w) calmly replied: "Allah." He uttered this word with such perfect assurance that even his disbelieving enemy was forced to acknowledge the loftiness of his faith and trust in God, and the sword fell from his hand, and he, who a moment before was bent on his destruction, stood before him like a convicted criminal awaiting sentence (Muslim, Kitabul Fada'il and Bukhari, Kitabul Jihad).

On the opposite end of the spectrum was his complete humility in the face of the Divine, as Abu Hurairara describes: "One day I heard the Holy Prophet (s.a.w) remark that no one would earn redemption via his own good actions." 'O Messenger of Allahsa!' I exclaimed. 'Surely you will enter Paradise via your own good works,' he said, 'but I, too, cannot join Paradise through my own good works unless that God's Grace and Mercy encompass me' (Bukhari, Kitabur Riqaq).

He always exhorted people to choose and follow the right path and to be diligent in their search for means whereby they could attain nearness to God. He taught that no man should desire death for himself, for if he is good he will, by living longer, be able to achieve greater good; and if he is evil, he may, if given time, be able to repent of his evil ways and start on a good way. His love for, and devotion to, God found expression in many ways. For instance, whenever after a dry season the first rain-drops began to descend, he would put out his tongue to catch a rain-drop and would exclaim: "Here is the latest favour from my Lord." He was constantly occupied in praying for God's forgiveness and beneficence, more particularly when he was sitting among people so that those who were in his company or were connected with him and Muslims generally should save themselves from divine wrath and should become deserving of divine forgiveness. The consciousness that he was always in the presence of God never deserted him. When he used to lie down to sleep, he would say: "O Allah! "Let me die (sleep) with Thy name on my lips, and let me wake with Thy name on my lips," he would say when he awoke. "All praise is due to God who has brought me to life after death (sleep), and one day we will all be gathered unto Him" (Bukhari).

He desired for God's presence all the time, and one of his favorite prayers was "O Allah! Fill my heart with Thy light, and my eyes with Thy light, and my ears with Thy light, and put Thy light on my right, and Thy light on my left, and Thy light above me, and Thy light below me, and Thy light in front of me, and Thy light behind me, and convert the whole of me into light, O Allah" (Bukhari).

According to Ibn 'Abbasra, "shortly before the Holy Prophet's (s.a.w) death, Musailima (the false prophet) came to Medina and said that if Muhammad (s.a.w) appointed him as his successor, he would accept him." Musailima was followed by a vast entourage, and the tribe with which he was associated was the biggest of Arabia's tribes. When the Holy Prophet (s.a.w) learned of his arrival, he hastened to see him with Thabit bin Qais bin Shamsra. He had a dry palm twig in his hand. He walked up to Musailima's camp and stood in front of him. Meanwhile, more of his Companions had arrived and formed a circle about him. "It has been conveyed to me that you have said that if I were to appoint you my successor you would be ready to follow me," he said to Musailima, "but I am not willing to bestow even this dried palm twig upon you contrary to God's commands. Your end will be as God has appointed. If you turn your back on me God will bring you to naught. I perceive very clearly that God will deal out to you what He has revealed to me." Abu Hurairara was also present. Someone asked the Prophet (s.a.w) what he meant when he said that God would give Musailima what had been revealed to him. "I saw in a dream two bracelets round my wrists which I disliked. While still in my dream, I was directed by God to blow upon the bracelets. When I blew upon them, both of them disappeared, which I interpreted to mean that two false claimants (to prophethood) would appear after me," the Holy Prophet (s.a.w) replied (Bukhari, Kitabul Maghazi). This happened at the conclusion of the Holy Prophet's (s.a.w) life. The final and greatest of the Arab tribes that had not yet embraced him was ready to submit, and its only condition was that the Holy Prophet (s.a.w) pick its ruler as his successor. Nothing could have stopped the Prophet (s.a.w) from guaranteeing the unity of Arabia by offering his succession to the leader of the biggest tribe in Arabia if he had been motivated by personal interests. The Holy Prophet (s.a.w) having no son of his own, and no dynastic desire could have prevented such an arrangement, but he never considered even the tiniest item to be his and at his complete discretion. As a result, he could not cope with Muslim leadership as if it were his gift. He saw it as a holy heavenly trust and believed that God would bestow it on whoever He saw suitable. As a result, he scorned Musailima's offer and informed him that, much alone Muslim leadership, he was unwilling to put even a dry palm twig on him.

When he spoke or spoke about God, it looked to spectators that his whole existence was gripped by a fervor of love for and devotion to God.

He was constantly adamant about the need of simplicity in divine worship. The mosque he erected at Medina, where he constantly lead prayers, had just a clay floor devoid of any covering or matting, and the roof, formed of dried palm branches and leaves, leaked whenever it rained. On such occasions, the Holy Prophet[a] and the congregation would be drenched with rain and mud, but he would continue with the prayers until the end, and he never indicated that he would postpone the service or relocate to a more weather-tight shelter (Bukhari, Kitabus Saum).

He was very cautious about his companions. 'Abdullah bin 'Umar[ra] was a man of great piety and moral purity. The Holy Prophet (s.a.w) once observed of him, "'Abdullah bin 'Umar[ra] would be an even finer man if he were more regular with respect to his Tahajjud prayers." When this was relayed to 'Abdullah bin 'Umar[ra], he never missed these prayers after that. It is said that the Holy Prophet (s.a.w), when visiting his daughter Fatima[ra], questioned of her and his son-in-law, 'Ali[ra], if they were regular in their Tahajjud prayers. "O Messenger of Allah[sa]! We try to get up for Tahajjud prayers, but on occasion when God so wills that we are unable to wake up in time, we miss them," 'Ali[ra] replied. He returned and, on the way, repeated several times a Qur'anic verse that means that a man is often reluctant to admit his fault and tries to cover it up with excuses (Bukhari, Kitabul Kusuf). 'Ali[ra] should not have ascribed his default to God by declaring that when God willed that they should not wake up, they were unable to wake up in time,' the Prophet (s.a.w) meant, but rather have confessed his own inadequacy in the issue.

OPPOSITION TO PENANCE

The Holy Prophet (s.a.w), on the other hand, firmly opposed formality in worship and rejected the imposition of any penance as a form of devotion. He argued that real devotion consisted in the benevolent application of God's gifted talents. With God having given man eyes to look with, it would be impertinence to keep them closed or have them removed. It is not the right use of the capacity of sight that is wicked; it is the wrong use of the faculty that is immoral. It would be ingratitude on a man's side to deprive himself of the power of hearing, while it would be wicked for him to utilize that faculty to listen to slander and backbiting. Abstention from food (except when prescribed or otherwise desirable) may amount to suicide and thus constitute an unforgivable sin, but it would also be sinful for a man to devote himself entirely to food and drink or to engage in the eating or drinking of forbidden or undesirable articles. This is a golden ideal taught and underlined by the Holy Prophet (s.a.w) of Islam and not instilled by any earlier Prophet.

The proper use of natural capacities forms high moral traits; their frustration or stultification is foolishness. It is their incorrect application that is harmful or immoral. Their correct application is real virtue. This is the core of the moral lessons instilled by Islam's Holy Prophet (s.a.w). In a nutshell, this was a portrait of his own life and acts. "Whenever the Holy Prophet (s.a.w) had a choice of two courses of action, he always chose the easier of the two, provided it was free from all suspicion of error or sin, and where a course of action was open to such suspicion, the Holy Prophet (s.a.w) of all men gave it the widest berth," 'A'ishara says (Muslim, Kitabul Fada'il). This is, certainly, the finest and most ideal path available to man. Many folks actively seek agony and privations, not to achieve God's pleasure, for God's pleasure is not won by inflicting pointless pain and privations on oneself, but to deceive people. Such individuals have little natural character and seek to conceal their flaws and gain favor in the eyes of others by adopting artificial qualities. However, the goal of Islam's Holy Prophet (s.a.w) was to achieve true morality and gain God's favor. As a result, he was absolutely devoid of pretense and make-believe. It made no difference to him whether the rest of the world thought of him negatively or positively. All that mattered to him was his current situation and how God would judge him. He was grateful if, in addition to his conscience's testimony and God's approbation, he also received the truthful testimony of humanity, but if folks looked at him with jaundiced eyes, he felt sad for them and placed no significance on their opinion.

HIS ATTITUDE TOWARDS HIS WIFE

He was incredibly kind and fair to his wives. If one of them failed to behave herself with regard to him, he just smiled and passed the issue over. He told 'A'ishara one day, "'A'ishara, whenever you are upset with me, I always get to know it." 'A'ishara inquired, "How is that?" He replied, "I have noticed that when you are pleased with me and in the course of conversation you have to refer to God, you refer to Him as the Lord of Muhammad (s.a.w), but when you are not pleased with me, you refer to Him as the Lord of Ibrahimas." KHADIJA(ra) was his first wife, and she had made significant sacrifices for him. She was significantly older than the Prophet (s.a.w). After her died, he married younger ladies, yet he never let KHADIJA(ra)'s memories fade. Whenever one of KHADIJA(ra)'s friends came to see him, he would up to greet her (Muslim). He was often overtaken with emotion whenever he came across an item that belonged to or was associated with KHADIJA(ra). A son-in-law of the Prophet (s.a.w) was among the captives seized by the Muslims at the Battle of Badr. He didn't have anything to give as a ransom. His wife Zainabra (the Prophet's (s.a.w) daughter) sent to Medina a necklace that had belonged to her mother (KHADIJA(ra)) as a ransom for her husband. The Prophet (s.a.w) recognized the jewellery and was deeply moved when he saw it. "I have no authority to give any direction in this matter, but I know that this necklace is cherished by Zainabra as a last memento of her deceased mother, and, provided it commends itself to you, I would suggest that she should not be deprived of it and that it may be returned to her," he said to his Companions. They indicated that nothing would give them greater pleasure and readily accepted his suggestion (Halbiyya, Vol. 2). He often extolled KHADIJA(ra) to his other wives, emphasizing her merits and the sacrifices she had made for Islam. On one such occasion, 'A'ishara became irritated and said, "O Messenger of Allah, why go on talking about the old lady? God has bestowed better, younger, and more attractive wives upon you." Hearing this, the Holy Prophet (s.a.w) was overcome with emotion and protested, "O no, 'A'ishara! You have no idea how good KHADIJA(ra) was to me."

(Bukhari).

HIGH ETHICAL QUALITIES

He was always patient in the face of hardship. He was never disheartened by adversity, nor did he allow any personal desire to take hold of him. His father died before his birth, and his mother died when he was a little kid, as previously stated. He was raised by his grandpa till the age of eight, and when his grandfather died, he was raised by his uncle, Abu Talib. Abu Talib constantly looked after his nephew with care and indulgence, both out of natural love and because his father had specifically advised him to do so, but his wife was not impacted to the same extent. It was common for her to share stuff among her own children while leaving out their tiny cousin. If Abu Talib happened to go into the home on such a day, he'd see his young nephew sitting aside, a picture of dignity with no hint of sulkiness or resentment on his face. The uncle, recognizing his responsibility and yielding to the claims of affection, would run to the nephew, clasp him to his bosom, and cry out: "Do pay attention to this child of mine also! Do pay attention to this child of mine also!" Such incidents were not uncommon, and those who witnessed them were unanimous in their testimony that the young Muhammad (s.a.w) never gave any indication that he was affected by them or that he was jealous of his nephew. Later in life, when he was in a position to do so, he took on the burden of caring for and raising two of his uncle's kids, 'Alira and Ja'farra, and he did it admirably.

Throughout his life, the Holy Prophet (s.a.w) had to endure a series of painful events. He was born an orphan, his mother died while he was a youngster, and he lost his grandpa when he was eight years old. He had to face the loss of multiple children one after the other after marriage, and eventually his loving and dedicated wife KHADIJA(ra) died. Some of the ladies he married following Khadija's(ra) died during his lifetime, and he had to endure the loss of his son Ibrahim at the end of his life. He took all of these losses and disasters pleasantly, and none of them had any effect on his steely determination or the urbanity of his demeanor. His private emotions were never expressed in public, and he always greeted everyone with a kind smile and treated everyone equally well. On one occasion, he saw a widow who had lost a kid crying aloud over her child's grave. He urged her to be patient and to recognize God's will as paramount. "If you had ever suffered the loss of a child as I have, you would have realized how difficult it is to be patient under such an affliction," the woman replied, unaware that she was being addressed by the Holy Prophet (s.a.w). Except when referring to his own losses or sorrows in this indirect manner, he never bothered to linger on them, nor did he allow them to interfere in any way with his unending devotion to people and joyous sharing of their burdens.

HIS CONTROL OVER HIMSELF

He was always in perfect control of himself. Even after becoming a Sovereign, he always listened to everyone patiently, and if someone treated him impertinently, he bore with him and never tried revenge. In the East, one method to show respect for a person is to avoid using his real name while addressing him. Muslims addressed the Holy Prophet (s.a.w) as "O Messenger of Allahsa," whereas non-Muslims addressed him as "Abu'l Qasimsa" (Qasim's father; Qasim is the name of one of his sons). In Medina, a Jew approached him and had a conversation with him. Throughout the conversation, he addressed him as "O Muhammad (s.a.w), O Muhammad (s.a.w)." The Prophet (s.a.w) took no notice to his manner of approach and continued patiently expounding on the subject at hand to him. His Companionsra, on the other hand, were becoming upset by his interlocutor's impolite manner of speech, until one of them, unable to stop himself any longer, warned the Jew not to address the Prophet (s.a.w) by his own name, but rather as Abu'l Qasimsa. The Jew said that he would only address him by the name given to him by his parents. "He is correct," the Prophet (s.a.w) responded to his Companions, "I was called Muhammad (s.a.w) at the time of my birth, and there is no cause to be disturbed by his calling me by that name."

People would sometimes stop him in their tracks and engage him in conversation, explaining their requirements and preferring their demands to him. He always stood calmly and waited for everyone to finish before proceeding. People shaking hands with him on sometimes maintained hold of his hand for considerable time, which he found awkward and caused a waste of valuable time, but he was never the first to withdraw his hand. People came to him freely, laying their problems and concerns before him and asking for his assistance. He never turned down an opportunity to assist. He was sometimes bombarded with demands, and they were unreasonable, yet he continued to comply with them to the best of his ability. On occasion, after fulfilling a request, he would advise the individual in question to have more faith in God and to avoid seeking help from others. On one occasion, a devout Muslim begged him for money multiple times, and each time he obliged, but in the end he replied, "It is ideal for a man to put his confidence in God and to avoid making requests." The individual in question was a serious guy. He did not offer to return what he had already gotten out of respect for the Prophet (s.a.w)'s sentiments, but he did proclaim that in the future he would never make a request to anybody under any conditions. Years later, he was riding on a horse in a fight, and in the midst of it, when the clamor and turmoil and clash of armaments were at their height, and he was besieged by his adversaries, his whip dropped from his grasp. Perceiving his predicament, a Muslim soldier on foot bent down to pick up the whip for him, but the mounted man begged him to stop and jumped from his horse, picking up the whip himself, explaining to the soldier that he had long since promised the Holy Prophet (s.a.w) that he would never make any request to anyone, and that allowing the soldier to pick up the whip for him would have amounted to him making an indirect request and thus being punished.

JUSTICE AND ETHICAL DEALING

Arabs were prone to favoritism and applied various standards to different people. Even in today's so-called civilized societies, there is a reluctance to hold notable people or those in high positions or offices accountable for their actions, even while the law is strictly enforced against the regular citizen. The Holy Prophet (s.a.w), on the other hand, were exceptional in maintaining consistent principles of justice and fair dealing. On one occasion, he heard a case in which a young lady from a well-known family was found to have committed stealing. This prompted widespread concern because if the young lady received the standard sentence, a prominent family would be humiliated and discredited. Many others wanted to intervene with the Prophet (s.a.w) on the offender's behalf but were frightened to do so. Usamara was eventually persuaded to take up the task. Usamara went to the Holy Prophet (s.a.w) but the moment the latter perceived the trend of his submission he was much upset and said: "You had better desist. Nations have come to a bad end for showing favours to highly placed persons while pressing hard on the common people. Islam does not permit this and I will certainly not do it. Verily, if my own daughter, Fatimara, were to commit an offence I would not hesitate to impose the appropriate penalty" (Bukhari, Kitabul Hudud).

It has previously been mentioned that when the Prophet's uncle 'Abbasra became a prisoner at the Battle of Badr, he was tied up with a rope like the other captives to prevent his escape. He moaned in anguish throughout the night because the rope was so firmly wrapped around him. The Prophet (s.a.w) couldn't sleep because he heard his moans. When the Companions of the Prophet (s.a.w) saw this, they untied the rope that restrained 'Abbasra. When the Prophet (s.a.w) learned of this, he ordered that all inmates be treated equally, claiming that there was no need to favor his own kin. He urged that they either relax the ties of all the inmates or tighten 'Abbasra's chains like the others. Because the Companions of the Prophet (s.a.w) did not want him to feel uneasy because of his uncle, they agreed to closely watch the captives and release their shackles (Zurqani, Vol. 3, p. 279).

Even in times of conflict, he was meticulous about adhering to all acknowledged laws and traditions. On one occasion, he sent a reconnaissance group of his Companions. On the final day of the Sacred Month, Rajab, they came upon some hostile soldiers. Because they thought it would be risky to let them escape and bring the news of the scouting team to Mecca, they assaulted them, and one of them was killed during the battle. Following the return of the scouting team to Medina, the Meccans started to complain that the Muslim scouts had slain one of their men during the Sacred Month. The Meccans had frequently violated the sanctity of the Sacred Months in relation to the Muslims whenever it suited them, and it would have been a suitable response to their protest to say that because the Meccans had themselves set aside the Sacred Months convention, they were not entitled to insist on their observance by Muslims. However, the Prophet (s.a.w) did not respond in this manner. He harshly scolded the party members, refused to take the plunder, and, according to some stories, even paid the blood-money for the individual slain, until the revelation of 2: 218 clarified the whole situation (Tabari and Halbiyya).

those are normally cautious not to harm the sentiments of their friends and relatives, but the Holy Prophet (s.a.w) was particularly concerned in this area, especially when it came to those who opposed him. On one occasion, a Jew approached him and expressed his displeasure because Abu Bakrra had offended him by declaring that God had elevated Muhammad (s.a.w) above Mosesas. The Prophet (s.a.w) called Abu Bakrra and inquired as to what had occurred. Abu Bakrra recounted that the Jew began by claiming that he swore by Mosesas, whom God had elevated beyond all people, and that he (Abu Bakrra) then countered by swearing by Muhammad (s.a.w), whom God had raised over Mosesas. "You should not have stated this because the sentiments of other people should be respected; nobody should raise me over Mosesas," the Prophet (s.a.w) remarked (Bukhari, Kitabut Tauhid). This was not to say that the Holy Prophet (s.a.w) did not have a greater rank than Mosesa, but that an assertion like this directed at a Jew was likely to offend him and should have been avoided.

RESPECT FOR THE POOR

The Holy Prophet (s.a.w) was always concerned with improving the lot of the poorest members of the community and elevating their social standing. A wealthy guy happened to walk by when he was seated with his Companionsra on one occasion. The Prophet (s.a.w) asked one of his Companionsra what he thought of him. "He is a well-to-do and well-connected man. If he were to ask for the hand of a girl in marriage, the request would be favorably considered, and if he were to intercede on behalf of anyone, the intercession would be accepted," he replied. The Prophet (s.a.w) questioned about the same Companionra's opinion of him. "O Messenger of Allahsa! He is a poor man. If he were to request the hand of a girl in marriage, the request would not be favourably received, if he were to intercede on behalf of any person, the intercession would be rejected, and if he were to seek to engage anybody in conversation, no attention would be paid to him," he replied.

In Medina, a poor Muslim lady used to scrub the Holy Prophet's (s.a.w) mosque. When the Prophet (s.a.w) did not see her at the mosque for a few days and inquired about her, he was informed that she had died. "Why was I not informed when she died? I would have wished to join her funeral prayers," he said, adding, "Perhaps you did not consider her worthy of consideration because she was poor. This was not right. Direct me to her grave." He used to say that there were people with tangled hair whose bodies were covered in dust and who were not welcomed by those who were well-off, but who were so highly valued by God that if they swore in His name, trusting in God's beneficence, that a certain matter would take a certain turn, He would support them." (Muslim, Kitabul Birr Was Sila). I'm afraid you may have offended these God's servants. If such is the case, God will be angry with you." Abu Bakrra immediately returned to those individuals and enquired, "Brothers of mine! Were you offended by what I said?" They said, "We took no offense at what you stated. Please accept God's forgiveness!Kitabul Fada'l (Muslim).

While, however, the Prophet (s.a.w) insisted that poor people should be respected and their feelings should not be injured and strove to fulfil their needs, he also sought to instil the sentiment of self-respect into them and taught them not to beg for favours. He used to say that it behoved a poor man not to seek to be content with a date or two or with a mouthful or two of food but to restrain himself from making a request, however severely he might be tried (Bukhari, Kitabul Kusuf). On the other hand he used to say that no entertainment would be blessed unless some poor people were also invited to it. 'A'ishara relates that a poor woman came to visit her on one occasion accompanied by her two little daughters. 'A'ishara had nothing with her at the time except one date which she gave to the woman. The woman divided it between her little daughters and then they all departed. When the Prophet (s.a.w) came home 'A'ishara related this to him and he said: "If a poor man has daughters and he treats them with consideration, God will save him from the torments of Hell," and added: "God will bestow Paradise upon this woman on account of the consideration she showed towards her daughters" (Muslim). On one occasion he was told that one of his Companions, Sa'dra, who was a well-to-do person, was boasting of his enterprise to others. When the Prophet (s.a.w) heard this, he said: "Let no man imagine that his wealth or standing or power is the result merely of his own efforts or enterprise. That is not the case. "Your power, status, and fortune are all won via the poor," he said in one of his prayers. Keep me modest while I am living and when I die, and may my resurrection on the Day of Judgement be among the humble" (Tirmidhi, Abwabul Zuhad).

On one occasion during the hot weather when he was passing through a street, he observed a very poor Muslim carrying heavy loads from one place to another. He was very plain of features which were rendered still more unattractive by a heavy coating of perspiration and dust. He bore a melancholy look. The Holy Prophet (s.a.w) approached him stealthily from the back and, as children sometimes do in fun, he put forward his hands and covered the labourer's eyes with them, expecting him to guess who he was. The man put back his own hands and feeling over the body of the Prophet (s.a.w) realized that it was the Holy Prophet (s.a.w) himself. He probably guessed also that nobody else would show such intimate affection for a man in his condition. Being pleased and encouraged, he pressed against the Holy Prophet's (s.a.w) body and clasped him to himself from the back rubbing his dust and sweat-covered body against the clothes of the Prophet (s.a.w), desiring perhaps to ascertain how far the Prophet (s.a.w) would be willing to indulge him. The Prophet (s.a.w) went on smiling and did not ask him to desist. When the man had been put in a thoroughly happy mood the Prophet (s.a.w) said to him: "I possess a slave; do you think anybody will be willing to buy him?" The guy recognized that, excluding the Holy Prophet (s.a.w), no one in the whole world would be willing to find any merit in him, and with a mournful sigh, he replied: "O Messenger of Allahsa! Nobody in the world would be willing to buy me." The Prophet (s.a.w) said, "No! No! That is not acceptable. "You are valuable in God's sight" (Sharhussunna).

Not only was he concerned about the welfare of the poor, but he constantly exhorted others to do the same. According to

Abu Musa Ash'arira, if a needy person approached the Holy Prophet (s.a.w) and made a request, he would say to those around him, "You should also support his request so that you may acquire merit by becoming sharers in promoting a good deed" (Bukhari and Muslim), his goal being to create on the one hand in the minds

PROTECTING THE INTERESTS OF THE POOR

When Islam became widely accepted throughout Arabia, the Holy Prophet (s.a.w) frequently received large amounts of goods and money, which he immediately distributed to those in need. On one occasion, his daughter Fatimara came to him and, showing him her calloused hands from the labor involved in crushing grain with stones, requested that a slave be assigned to her to lighten her labor. The Prophet (s.a.w) replied, "I shall tell you." When you go to bed at night, you should worship God thirty-three times, confirm His perfection thirty-four times, and His magnificence thirty-three times. This will benefit you much more than the custody of a slave."

(Bukhari).

While distributing money on one occasion a coin fell from his hands and rolled out of sight. Having finished with the distribution he went to the mosque and led the prayers. It was his practice to remain sitting for a short while after the conclusion of the prayers, occupied in the remembrance of God and thereafter to let people approach him and put questions to him or proffer requests. On this occasion, as soon as the prayers were concluded, he got up and proceeded quickly to his house. He looked for the missing coin and, having recovered it, came back and bestowed it upon a needy person, explaining that the coin had fallen from his hands during the distribution of money and the matter had gone out of his mind but he suddenly recollected it while-leading the prayers and he was made uneasy by the thought that if he were to die before he could recover the coin and give it away to some person in need, he would be held responsible for it before God; that was the reason why he had left the mosque in such a hurry to recover the coin (Bukhari, Kitabul Kusuf).

In order to fully protect the interests of the poor and needy, he went so far as to stipulate that no charity should ever be bestowed upon his descendants, fearing that Muslims, out of their love for and devotion to himself, would eventually make his descendants the primary objects of their charity, depriving the poor and needy of their due share. On one occasion, someone brought to him a quantity of dates and offered them as charity. This belongs to God's wretched creatures" (Bukhari, Kitabul Kusuf).

SLAVERY TREATMENT

He constantly exhorted those who owned slaves to treat them kindly and well. He had laid down that if the owner of a slave beat his slave or abused him, the only reparation that he could make was to set the slave free (Muslim, Kitabul Iman). He devised means for, and encouraged, the freeing of slaves on every pretext. He said: "If a person owning a slave sets him free, God will in recompense save every part of his body corresponding to every part of the slave's body from the torment of Hell." Again, he laid down that a slave should be asked to perform only such tasks as he could easily accomplish and that when he was set to do a task, his master should help him in performing it so that the slave should experience no feeling of humiliation or degradation (Muslim). If a master went on a journey accompanied by a slave, it was his duty to share his mount with the slave either by both riding together or each riding in turn. Abu Hurairara, who used to spend the whole of his time after becoming a Muslim in the company of the Prophet (s.a.w) and who had repeatedly heard the Prophet's (s.a.w) injunctions regarding the treatment of slaves, has said: "I call God to witness in Whose hands is my life that were it not for the opportunities that I get of joining in holy war and of performing the Pilgrimage and were it not that I have opportunities of serving my old mother, I would have desired to die a slave, for the Holy Prophet (s.a.w) constantly insisted upon slaves being well and kindly treated" (Muslim). Ma'rur bin Suwaidra relates: "I saw Abu Dharr Ghaffarira (a Companionra of the Holy Prophet (s.a.w)) wearing clothes exactly similar to those worn by his slave. I asked him why, and he responded, "During the lifetime of the Holy Prophet (s.a.w), I once mocked a guy whose mother was a slave." "You still seem to entertain pre-Islamic notions. What are slaves? They are your brethren and the source of your power. God in

His wisdom confers temporary authority upon you over them. He who has such authority over his brother should feed him with the kind of food he himself eats; clothe him with the kind of clothes he himself wears; and should not set him a task beyond his strength and should himself help him in whatevereve

WOMEN'S TREATMENT

The Holy Prophet (s.a.w) was highly concerned with elevating the status of women in society and ensuring their dignity and fair and equal treatment. Islam was the first faith to provide women the ability to inherit. The Qur'an makes females, like boys, heirs to their parents' estates. A mother is made an heir to her son's or daughter's property in the same way as a wife is declared an heir to her husband's property. When a brother inherits his dead brother's property, his sister inherits it as well. Prior to Islam, no religion had so clearly and firmly defined a woman's right to inheritance and property ownership. In Islam, a woman is the ultimate owner of her own property, and her husband cannot gain authority over it just because they are married. A woman is free to do anything she wants with her property.

The Holy Prophet (s.a.w) was so concerned with the treatment of women that those around him who had not previously been accustomed to viewing women as helpmates and partners found it difficult to adjust to the standards that the Prophet (s.a.w) was eager to see established and maintained. 'Umarra relates: "My wife occasionally sought to intervene in my affairs with her counsel and I would rebuke her, saying that the Arabs had never permitted their women to intervene in their affairs. She would retort: 'That is all past. The Holy Prophet (s.a.w) lets his wives counsel him in his affairs and he does not stop them. Why don't you follow his example?' My reply used to be: As for 'A'ishara the Prophet (s.a.w) is particularly fond of her but as regards your daughter (Hafsara), if she does this she will one day have to suffer the consequences of her impertinence.' It so happened that thereafter on one occasion the Holy Prophet (s.a.w), being upset over something, decided to spend a period of time apart from his wives. When I learnt of this I said to my wife, What I had feared had come to pass. Then I went to the house of my daughter Hafsara and found her crying. I inquired of her what the matter was and whether the Prophet (s.a.w) had divorced her. She said: 'I don't know about divorce, but the Prophet (s.a.w) has decided to remain away from us for some time.' I said to her: 'Did I not often tell you not to take the same liberties with him as 'A'ishara does, for the Holy Prophet (s.a.w) is particularly fond of 'A'ishara, but you seem to have brought upon yourself what I had feared.' I then went to the Holy Prophet (s.a.w) and found him lying down on a rough matting. He was at that time wearing no shirt and his body bore the marks of the pattern of the matting. I sat down near him and said: 'O Messenger of Allah! the Kaiser and the Chosroes do not deserve any of God's favours and yet they pass their lives in great comfort and you who are His Messenger pass your days in such discomfort.' The Prophet (s.a.w) replied: 'That is not so. The Messengers of Allah are not expected to spend their time in comfort. That kind of life befits only secular monarchs.' I then related to the Prophet (s.a.w) all that had passed between me and my wife and daughter. Hearing me, the Prophet (s.a.w) laughed and said: 'It is not true that I have divorced my wives. I have merely thought it advisable to spend a little time away from them' " (Bukhari, Kitabun Nikah).

He was so sensitive to women's feelings that when he was leading the prayers, he heard the cry of a child and quickly concluded the service, explaining afterwards that he had heard the child's cry and imagined that the child's mother would be distressed by its cry, so he had concluded the service quickly so that the mother could go to the child and look after it.

When ladies were present in his caravans on any of his excursions, he always directed that the caravan proceed slowly and in phases. On one such occasion, when the men were anxious to press on, he exclaimed, "Take care of glass! Take care of glass!" implying that ladies were there and that if camels and horses were pushed to the speed, they would suffer from the animals' joltings (Bukhari, Kitabul Adab). During a combat, there was chaos amid the ranks of the mounted warriors, and the animals went uncontrollable. The Holy Prophet (s.a.w) was thrown off his horse, as were several of the ladies. One of his Companionsra, who was riding a camel directly behind the Prophet (s.a.w), leapt off and hurried towards him, shouting, "May I be your sacrifice, O Messenger of Allahsa," while the Prophet's (s.a.w) foot remained in the stirrup. He quickly released it and told his companion, "Don't worry about me, go and assist the ladies." Just before his death, one of the injunctions he addressed to Muslims and emphasized was that they should always treat women with care and consideration. It was a frequently repeated adage of his that if a man had daughters and prepared for their education and upbringing, God would rescue him from the anguish of Hell (Tirmidhi).

It was standard practice among Arabs to punish women physically for minor transgressions. The Holy Prophet (s.a.w) preached that women were equal to males as God's creations, and that they should not be beaten. When women learned of this, they went to the other extreme and started to resist males in everything, causing domestic tranquility to be constantly disrupted in many houses. 'Umarra protested to the Holy Prophet (s.a.w) about this, saying that unless women could be disciplined on occasion, they would become rebellious and there would be no way to keep them in control. Because precise Islamic teachings on the treatment of women had not yet been disclosed, the Prophet (s.a.w) said that if a woman committed a significant transgression, she may be reprimanded. This, in turn, led to many men returning to the traditional Arab practice. It was now the women's time to complain, and they brought their problems to the Prophet's (s.a.w) wives. The Prophet (s.a.w) then scolded males, telling them that anyone who treated women cruelly would never receive God's favor. Following that, women's rights were established, and for the first time, women were considered as free persons in their own right (Abu Dawud, Kitabun Nikah).

According to Mu'awiya al-Qushairira, "I inquired of the Holy Prophet (s.a.w) what claim my wife had upon me," and he replied, "Feed her with that which God bestows upon you in the way of food, and clothe her with that which God bestows upon you in the way of clothes, and do not chastise her, abuse her, or put her out of your house." He was so conscious of women's feelings and sentiments that He always went home during the day when he returned from a trip. If darkness fell towards the conclusion of his trek, he would sleep outside Medina for the night and return the following morning. He also warned his Companions that when they returned from a trip, they should not return home unexpectedly (Bukhari and Muslim). He was thinking about the reality that sex interactions are mostly influenced by feeling when he gave this instruction. In the absence of the husband, a woman may frequently neglect the care of her body and her attire, and if the husband returns home suddenly, the wife's or the husband's finer sensibilities may be offended. By directing that when a man returns from a voyage, he should come home during the day and after informing the members of his family of his homecoming, he assured that the members of his family would be ready to meet the returning member in a suitable way.

ATTITUDE TO THE DEATH

He advised everyone to prepare a will on the administration of his affairs after his death, so that people associated with him would experience the least amount of trouble after his death.

He stipulated that no one should speak ill of a deceased person, but that whatever good he had possessed should be emphasized, because no one would benefit from mentioning the deceased's weaknesses or vices, but by emphasizing his virtues, people would be inclined to pray for him (Bukhari). He insisted on paying a dead person's debts before burying him. He frequently satisfied a deceased person's liabilities himself, but if he was unable to do so, he exhorted the deceased's heirs and relatives or other persons to discharge his liabilities and would not say the funeral prayers over a deceased person until his liabilities had been discharged.

THE CARE OF NEIGHBORS

He was always very courteous and kind to his neighbors. He used to explain that the angel Gabriel had stressed neighborly regard so often that he started to suspect that a neighbor would be among the required heirs. According to Abu Dharrra, the Holy Prophet (s.a.w) said to him, "Abu Dharrra, while broth is being cooked for your family, add a little more water to it so that your neighbor may also share in it." This does not mean that the neighbor should not be invited to share in other things, but because the Arabs were mostly a migratory people and their favorite dish was broth, the Holy Prophet (s.a.w) referred to this dish as a typical one and taught that

Abu Hurairara relates: "On one occasion the Holy Prophet (s.a.w) exclaimed: 'I call God to witness that he is not a believer! I call God to witness that he is not a believer! I call God to witness that he is not a believer!' The Companions inquired: 'Who is not a believer, O Messenger of Allahsa?' and he replied: 'He whose neighbour is not secure against injury and ill-treatment at his hands.' On one occasion when he was addressing women, he said: 'If anybody finds only the foot of a goat to cook, that person should share it with his or her neighbour.' He asked people not to object to their neighbours driving pegs into their walls or putting them to any other use which occasioned no injury." Abu Hurairara relates: "The Prophet (s.a.w) said: 'He who believes in God and in the Day of Judgement should occasion no inconvenience to his neighbour: he who believes in God and in the Day of Judgement should occasion no inconvenience to his guest, and he who believes in God and in the Day of Judgement should utter only words of virtue or should keep quiet' " (Muslim).

RELATIVE TREATMENT

Most individuals suffer from the flaw that when they married and have a family, they ignore their parents. As a result, the Holy Prophet (s.a.w) placed a high value on serving one's parents and treating them with compassion and care. According to Abu Hurairara, "a man came to the Holy Prophet (s.a.w) and asked to be told who was most deserving of kind treatment at his hands. The Prophet (s.a.w) replied: 'Your mother.' The man asked, 'And next to her?' The Prophet (s.a.w) repeated, 'Again thy mother.' The man asked, 'And after my mother?' The Prophet (s.a.w) replied, 'Again thy mother.' However, the parents of several of his brides were still living, and he always treated them with respect and attention. When the Holy Prophet (s.a.w) reached Mecca as a triumphant commander after the capitulation, Abu Bakrra brought his father to see him. "Why did you bother your father to come to me? I would have happily gone to him myself," he remarked to Abu Bakrra (Halbiyya, Vol. 3, p. 99). One of his sayings was, "Unlucky is the man whose parents live to old age and he fails to earn Paradise even then," which means that serving one's parents, especially when they reach old age, attracts God's grace and favor, and thus a person who is afforded the opportunity to serve his aged parents and who fully utilizes the opportunity is bound to become confirmed in righteous ways and a recipient of God's grace.

A man once complained to the Holy Prophet (s.a.w) that the more benevolence he showed to his relatives, the more hostile they became towards him; that the more he treated them with kindness, the more they persecuted him; and that the more he showed affection towards them, the more they frowned upon him. "If what you say is true, you are exceedingly fortunate, because you will always be the receiver of God's succour," the Prophet (s.a.w) stated (Muslim, Kitabul Birr Was Sila). When the Holy Prophet (s.a.w) was exhorting people to donate alms and charity on one occasion, one of his Companions, Abu Talha Ansarira, approached him and volunteered to devote an orchard for charitable purposes. "What a wonderful charity! What an excellent charity! What a great charity!" shouted the Prophet (s.a.w), adding, "Having devoted this orchard to the service of the needy, I now want you to share it among your destitute relatives" (Bukhari, Kitabut Tafsir). On one occasion, a man approached him and said, "O Messenger of Allahsa! I am prepared to make a covenant of Hijrat and a covenant to take part in the holy war, for I am anxious to win the pleasure of God." The Holy Prophet (s.a.w) inquired whether either of his parents was alive, and the man replied, "Both are alive." He then asked, "Are you indeed anxious to win God's pleasure?" When the man replied in the affirmative, the Prophet (s.a.w) said, "Then go back to your parents and serve them, and serve them well." He emphasized that one's non-Muslim relations, like one's Muslim relations, were equally entitled to be treated kindly and with consideration. One of Abu Bakr'sra wives, a non-Muslim, paid a visit to her daughter Asma'ra and asked the Holy Prophet (s.a.w) whether she might serve her and offer gifts to her, to which the Holy Prophet (s.a.w) answered, "Certainly, because she is thy mother" (Bukhari, Kitabul Adab).

He was considerate to not just his close family, but also to distant relatives and anybody linked with them. Whenever he sacrificed an animal, he would send a piece of the meat to KHADIJA(ra)'s (his dead wife's) acquaintances and warned his women not to forget them on such occasions. When Khadija's(ra) was seated with some of his Companions several years after his death, Khadija's(ra)'s sister, Halahra, came to visit him and begged permission to enter. Her voice sounded very much like KHADIJA(ra)'s in the Prophet's (s.a.w) ears, and when he heard it, he exclaimed, "Oh Lord! This is Halahra, Khadija's(ra) sister!" Indeed, true affection always manifests itself in such a way that one becomes fond of and considerate towards all those who may be connected with a person whom one loves or holds in high regard.

Anas bin Malikra recalls being in the company of Jarir bin 'Abdullahra on a voyage and seeing how the latter busied himself in caring after him like a servant looks after his master. Jarir bin 'Abdullahra was older than Anasra, who was ashamed and objected to Jarirra putting himself out on his behalf. "I used to observe how devotedly the Ansar served the Holy Prophet (s.a.w), and being impressed with their devotion to and love for the Holy Prophet (s.a.w), I had resolved in my mind that if I ever happened to be in the company of an Ansari, I would serve him like a servant; thus, I am only carrying out my resolve, and you should not seek to dissuade me," Jarirra replied (Muslim). This story demonstrates that when one person genuinely loves another, his love spreads to others who honestly serve the object of his passion. Similarly, individuals who sincerely honor their parents are always respectful and courteous to others who are related to their parents via emotion or connection. On one occasion, the Holy Prophet (s.a.w) emphasized that it is the utmost virtue for a man to honor his father's friends. 'Abdullah bin 'Umarra was among those addressed. Many years later, while on pilgrimage, he encountered a Bedouin and gave him his own horse, as well as his turban. One of his buddies pointed out that he had been too generous, since a Bedouin would be content with very little. "This guy's father was a friend of my father's," 'Abdullah bin 'Umarra replied, "and I have heard the Holy Prophet (s.a.w) state that it is one of the finest qualities for a man to respect his father's friends."

MAINTAINING GOOD COMPANY

He always chose to associate with the righteous, and if he saw any flaw in any of his Companionsra, he gently and privately rebuked him. According to Abu Musa Ash'arira, "the Holy Prophet (s.a.w) illustrated the benefit to be derived from good friends and virtuous companions and the injury to be incurred from evil friends and vicious companions by saying: 'A man who keeps company with virtuous people is like a person who carries about musk with him. If he partakes of it, he derives benefit from it, if he sells it, he profits from it, and if

PROTECTING PEOPLE'S FAITH

The Holy Prophet (s.a.w) took great care to avoid any such misconceptions. His wife Safiyyara came to meet him at the mosque on one occasion. When it came time for her to return home, it was becoming dark, so the Prophet (s.a.w) decided to accompany her. On the way, he passed by two men and, in order to avoid any speculation on their part as to his companion, he stopped them and said, lifting the veil from his wife's face, "See, this is Safiyyara my wife." They objected, saying, "O Messenger of Allahsa! why did you imagine that we should fall into any misconception regarding you?" The Prophet (s.a.w) replied, "Satan (i.e., evil thoughts) often courses through a man'

OVERLOOKING OTHERS' FAULTS

He never publicized the flaws and failings of others and advised others not to publicize their own flaws. He used to say, "If a person covers up the faults of another, God will cover up his faults on the Day of Judgement." He also said, "Everyone of my followers can escape the consequences of his errors (i.e., by true repentance and reform) except those who continue proclaiming their wrongdoing," and illustrated this by saying, "A man commits a sin at night and God covers it up; in the morning he meets his friends and boasts before them:.

Some individuals mistakenly believe that confessing wrongdoing leads to repentance; in reality, it just encourages immodesty. Sin is an evil, and whomever falls into it and becomes a victim of humiliation and regret has an opportunity to return to the path of purity and holiness via repentance. His situation is similar to that of someone who has been tempted by evil but is pursued by goodness, and as soon as an opportunity presents itself, the evil is overcome and the sinner is reclaimed by virtue. Those who declare their faults and take pride in them, on the other hand, lose all feeling of good and evil and become incapable of repentance.

On one occasion, a man approached the Holy Prophet (s.a.w) and said, "I have been guilty of adultery," which, when proven by adequate proof, is a serious offense in Islamic Law. When the Holy Prophet (s.a.w) heard the man's confession, he turned away and got preoccupied with something else. He was implying that the correct cure in such a circumstance was repentance rather than public confession. However, the guy was unaware of this and, supposing that the Prophet (s.a.w) had not heard him, went and stood in front of him, addressing him and repeating his confession. The Holy Prophet (s.a.w) moved away once again, but the guy returned and stood in front of him, repeating his confession. "I had desired that this guy should not have revealed his fault until God had signaled His decision with respect to him, but since he has repeated his confession four times, I am bound to take action," remarked the Prophet (s.a.w) (Tirmidhi). 'He then added, "This man has himself confessed and has not been charged by the woman concerning whom he makes the confession; the woman should be questioned and, if she denies her guilt, she should not be molested; and only this man should be punished in accordance with his confession; but, if she confesses, she should also be punished." The individual attempted to flee while the punishment was being carried out, but the people chased him and carried out the penalty. When the Prophet (s.a.w) learned of this, he was outraged. He said that the defendant was condemned based on his own confession. His effort to flee constituted a retraction of his confession, and he should not have been sentenced to a punishment imposed purely on the basis of his confession.

The Prophet (s.a.w) said that the Law was exclusively concerned with overt actions. During a conflict, a group of Muslims came upon a non-Muslim who liked to lay in wait in lonely locations, and anytime he came across a lone Muslim, he would assault and murder him. Usama bin Zaid (ra) chased him on this time and, having overtaken and captured him, pulled his sword to slay him. When the guy realized there was no way out, he uttered the first part of the Muslim confession of faith, "There is no entity worthy of worship but Allah," signifying that he had adopted Islam. Usamara ignored this and murdered him. When these and other events from the campaign were linked to the Holy Prophet (s.a.w), he summoned Usamara and questioned him. When Usamara confirmed the account of the incident, the Prophet (s.a.w) said, "How will it be with you on the Day of Judgement when his confession of faith will bear witness in his favour?" Usamara replied, "O Messenger of Allahsa! that man was a murderer of Muslims and his declaring himself to be a Muslim was merely a ruse to escape just retribution." But the Prophet (s.a.w) continued, "Usamara, how will it be with you when Usamara objected, claiming that the man's recitation of the confession of faith was motivated by his dread of death and not by repentance. The Holy Prophet (s.a.w) then said:

"Did you peer into his heart to see whether he was telling the truth or not?" Usamara asks, "How will you answer on the Day of Judgement when his confession of faith will be cited in evidence against you?"

The Holy Prophet (s.a.w) was always willing to forgive people's mistakes and offenses. One of those involved in the defamation of his wife, 'A'ishara, was reliant on the generosity of Abu Bakrra ('A'ishara's father) for his survival. When it became evident that the charge against 'A'ishara was untrue, Abu Bakrra withdrew his support for him. This, too, demonstrates Abu Bakr'sra's remarkable moderation and control. An ordinary person would have gone to great lengths to punish a dependant who had defamed his daughter. When the Prophet (s.a.w) learned of what Abu Bakrra had done, he confronted him, stating that although the man was at fault, it did not behoove a person like Abu Bakrra to deprive him of his means of livelihood because of his transgression. Abu Bakrra then renewed his support for the guy (Bukhari, Kitabut Tafsir).

PERSERVANCE IN ADVERSITY

"For a Muslim, life is all full of good and nobody but a true believer finds himself in that position; for, if he meets with success, he is grateful to God and becomes the recipient of greater favours from Him; on the other hand, if he suffers pain or tribulation, he endures it with patience and thus again makes himself deserving of God's favors," the Holy Prophet (s.a.w) used to say. "Have patience! Your father will experience no agony after this day," he remarked, implying that all his woes were restricted to this world and that once he was liberated from this life and entered the presence of his Maker, he would be free of all sorrow. During the course of an epidemic, he would not approve of people traveling from one stricken community to another, since this tends to spread the plague. He used to claim that during an epidemic, if a person remained in his own town and avoided spreading virus to unaffected places, he would be considered a martyr (Bukhari, Kitabut Tibb).

MUTUAL COOPERATION

He used to preach that one of the finest Islamic traits was that a man should not meddle in topics about which he was unconcerned, and that individuals should refrain from criticizing others and intervening in matters about which they were unconcerned. This is a notion that, if widely endorsed and implemented, would go a long way toward ensuring global peace and order. A substantial portion of our problems stem from the majority of people's proclivity for excessive involvement and withholding assistance when it is required in giving aid for those in need.

The Holy Prophet (s.a.w) placed a high value on mutual collaboration. He had established it a law that if anybody was summoned to pay a sum of money as a punishment and was unable to do so, his neighbors, fellow citizens, or tribesmen should make up the difference by raising a subscription. People would come and live near the Prophet (s.a.w), giving their time to the service of Islam in different ways. He constantly advised their families to take on the burden of caring for their minimal needs. According to

Anasra, two brothers adopted Islam during the time of the Holy Prophet (s.a.w), with one remaining with the Holy Prophet (s.a.w) and the other continuing with his customary vocation. Later, the latter protested to the Holy See.

Prophet (s.a.w) discovered that his brother was wasting his time. "God provides for you too on behalf of your brother," the Holy Prophet (s.a.w) remarked, "and it behoves you consequently to provide provision for him and allow him free to serve the Faith" (Tirmidhi).

When the Prophet's (s.a.w) company arrived at their camping location during the course of a trip, his Companions promptly began their individual chores in setting up camp for the night. "You have assigned no task to me. I shall go and collect fuel for cooking," the Holy Prophet (s.a.w) said. His Companions objected, saying, "O Messenger of Allahsa! why should you occupy yourself in that way when all of us are here to do whatever may be necessary?" He replied, "No, No. It is my duty to do my share of whatever may be necessary," and he collected fire-wood from the jungle to cook the food (Zurqani, Vol. 4, p.

TRUTHFULNESS

According to legend, the Holy Prophet (s.a.w) was so strict about honesty that he was called among his people as "The Trusty" and "The True." He was as concerned that Muslims adhere to the same truth standards that he did. He saw truth as the foundation of all morality, righteousness, and correct behavior. He taught that a true person is one who is so convinced of the truth that God counts him as such.

On one occasion, a prisoner who had been convicted of the murder of several Muslims was transported to the Holy Prophet (s.a.w). 'Umarra, who was also there, thought that the guy merited the death punishment and kept looking at the Prophet (s.a.w), anticipating the Prophet (s.a.w) to announce that the man should be executed at any time. Following the dismissal of the man by the Holy Prophet (s.a.w), 'Umarra contended that he should have been executed as the only suitable sentence. The Prophet (s.a.w) replied: "If that is so, why did you not kill him?" 'Umarra replied: "O Messenger of Allahsa! if you had but given me an indication even by a flicker of your eyelids, I would have done so." To this the Prophet (s.a.w) rejoined: "A Prophet (s.a.w) does not act equivocally. How could I have employed my eye to indicate the imposition of a death penalty upon the man while my tongue was employed in talking amicably to him?" (Hisham, Vol. 2, p. 217).

A man once came to the Holy Prophet (s.a.w) and said, "O Messengersa of Allah! I suffer from three evils: falsehood, indulgence in strong drinks, and fornication. I have tried my utmost to get rid of them but have not succeeded. Will you tell me what to do?" The Prophet (s.a.w) replied, "If you make a firm promise to me to give up one of them, I guarantee that you will be rid of the other two." "Give up lying," the Prophet (s.a.w) urged. A little time later, the guy returned and informed the Holy Prophet (s.a.w) that he had followed his counsel and was now free of all three vices. The Prophet (s.a.w) asked him for the details of his struggle and the man said: "One day I wanted to indulge in liquor and was about to do so when I bethought myself of my promise to you and realized that if any of my friends asked me whether I had taken liquor, I would have to admit it as I could no longer utter a falsehood. This would mean that I would acquire an evil reputation among my friends and they would in future avoid me. Thinking thus, I persuaded myself to postpone drinking to some later occasion and was able to withstand the temptation at the time. In the same way when I found myself inclined towards fornication I argued with myself that indulgence in the vice would expose me to the loss of the esteem of my friends as I would either have to tell a falsehood if questioned by them, thus breaking my promise to you, or I would have to admit my sin. In this way I continued to struggle between my resolve to fulfil my promise to you and my desire to indulge in liquor and in adultery. When some time had passed I began to lose the inclination to indulge in these vices and the resolve to keep away from falsehood has now saved me from the other two also."

INQUISITIVENESS

The Holy Prophet (s.a.w) consistently warned against inquisitiveness and encouraged people to think favorably of one another. "The Prophet (s.a.w) said: 'Save yourselves from thinking ill of others, for this is the greatest falsehood, and do not be inquisitive or apply epithets to each other out of contempt, nor be envious of each other, nor entertain ill feelings towards each other; let each of you regard himself as the servant of God and treat others as his brothers, as God has commanded," Abu Hurairara says.

DEALING WITH FRANK AND STRAIGHTFORWARD

He was concerned about protecting Muslims from any type of injustice in their dealings. On one occasion, while walking through the market, he saw a lot of maize being auctioned off. He pushed his arm into the stack and discovered that, although the surface layer of corn was dry, the corn within was moist. He asked the owner what was causing this. The guy stated that an unexpected downpour had soaked some of the maize. The Prophet (s.a.w) said that in such scenario, he should have left the damp coating of corn on the exterior so that potential buyers could assess its true condition. "He who behaves unjustly with others will never become a valuable member of society," he remarked (Muslim). He insisted on trade and commerce being completely devoid of any allegation of unethical behavior. He urged buyers to constantly scrutinize the items and articles they intended to buy, and he barred anybody from starting discussions for a transaction while another person was doing so. He also prohibited commodity hoarding in anticipation of a market increase and insisted on the market being supplied on a regular basis.

PESSIMISM

He was a pessimist's worst nightmare. He used to argue that whomever was responsible for propagating pessimism among the people was responsible for their collapse, since gloomy views discourage people and halt development

(Muslim, Part II, Vol. 2). He cautioned his people against arrogance and boastfulness on the one hand, and pessimism on the other. He urged them to choose the medium road between these two extremes. Muslims must strive hard in the hope that God would reward their efforts with the finest possible outcomes. Everyone should endeavor to go ahead and support the welfare and growth of the community, but everyone should be devoid of any sense of pride or boastfulness.

ANIMAL CRUNCHAGE

He advised people against animal abuse and urged them to treat animals with kindness. He used to tell about a Jewish lady who was chastised by God for starving her pet to death. He also liked to tell the tale of a lady who discovered a thirsty dog by a deep well. She removed her shoe and dropped it into the well, drawing up some water. She gave the thirsty dog some water to drink. This excellent gesture gained her forgiveness from God for all of her prior misdeeds.

According to 'Abdullah bin Mas'udra, "while we were on a journey with the Holy Prophet (s.a.w), we saw two young doves in a nest and caught them. They were still very small. When their mother returned to the nest, not finding her little ones in it, she began to fly wildly round and round. When the Holy Prophet (s.a.w) arrived at the spot, he observed the dove and said, 'If any of you has caught its young 'Abdullah bin Mas'udra also claims that once they saw an ant-hill and set fire to it by piling straw on top of it, only to be reprimanded by the Holy Prophet (s.a.w). On one occasion, the Prophet (s.a.w) saw a donkey's face being branded. He questioned as to the rationale for this and was informed that the Romans used this procedure to distinguish high-bred animals. The Prophet (s.a.w) said that since the face is a particularly sensitive area of the body, an animal should not be branded on the face and that if it must be branded, it should be done on the haunches (Abu Dawud and Tirmidhi). Since then, Muslims have always branded animals on their haunches, and Europeans have followed suit.

IN RELIGIOUS MATTER TOLERANCE

The Holy Prophet (s.a.w) not only underlined the need of religious tolerance, but they also established a very high standard in this regard. A delegation from a Christian tribe in Najran paid him a visit in Medina to discuss religious issues. Several Church authorities were present. The discussion took place in the mosque and lasted many hours. At one point, the deputation's leader requested permission to leave the mosque and perform their religious ceremony elsewhere. The Holy Prophet (s.a.w) said that there was no need for them to leave the mosque, which was itself a location dedicated to God's worship, and that they may do their duty there (Zurqani).

BRAVERY

The biography section contains many examples of his bravery and heroism. It is sufficient to provide one example here. Medina was once filled with rumors that the Romans were assembling a big army for an attack. At the period, Muslims were often on the move at night. The desert was filled with tumult one night. Muslims rushed out of their houses, and some congregated in the mosque, waiting for the Holy Prophet (s.a.w) to come and give them advice for dealing with the emergency. They then saw the Holy Prophet (s.a.w) riding a horse and returning from the direction of the noises. They learned that the Prophet (s.a.w) had mounted a horse and gone in the direction from where the noises had originated to see whether there was any need for worry, rather than waiting for others to gather so that he might ride in company. When he returned, he informed his Companions that there was no need for concern and that they might go back to their houses and sleep (Bukhari, chapter on Shuja'at f il Harb).

THINKING ABOUT THE UNCULTURED

He was especially sensitive to individuals who did not know how to act due to a lack of cultural training. On one occasion, a desert dweller who had just lately adopted Islam and was sitting in the presence of the Holy Prophet (s.a.w) in the mosque stood up and walked away a few feet before settling down in a mosque corner to pass water. Some of the Prophets' Companionsa stood up to prevent him from doing so. The Prophet (s.a.w) halted them, telling out that any meddling with the guy would be inconvenient for him and may even bring him harm. He instructed his companions to leave the guy alone and to clean up the mess later.

THE KEEPING OF PROMISES

The Holy Prophet (s.a.w) was quite strict about covenant fulfillment. On one occasion, an emissary came to him on a particular assignment, and after a few days, he was persuaded of the reality of Islam and urged that he announce his commitment to it. The Prophet (s.a.w) reminded him that this was not suitable since he was there as a delegate and that he needed to return to the headquarters of his Government without establishing a new allegiance. If, after returning home, he was still persuaded of Islam's reality, he may return as a free person and profess his acceptance of it (Abu Dawud, chapter on Wafa bil 'Ahd).

RESPECT FOR HUMANITY'S SERVANTS

He gave great honor to individuals who committed their time and resources to serving humanity. The Arab tribe, the Banu Ta'i, began hostilities against the Prophet (s.a.w), and their soldiers were crushed in the next conflict, with several taken prisoner. One of them was Hatim Ta'i's daughter, whose kindness had become an Arab proverb. When Hatim's daughter told the Holy Prophet (s.a.w) of her ancestry, he regarded her with great respect and, as a consequence of her intercession, he absolved all the punishments imposed on her people for their hostility.

(Vol. 3, p. 227).

The nature of the Holy Prophet (s.a.w) is so multifaceted that it cannot be completely addressed in a few paragraphs.

THE PROPHETS' LIFE AS AN OPEN BOOK

The life of the Holy Founder of Islamsa is like an open book, and one may flip to any page and find intriguing facts. No other Teacher or Prophet's life is as well-documented and available to study as the lives of the Holy Prophet (s.a.w). True, the availability of documented truth has provided nasty detractors with an opportunity. However, after the critiques have been evaluated and dismissed, the faith and devotion that arise cannot be inspired by any other life. Obscure lifestyles are immune to criticism, but they fail to inspire conviction and trust in their followers. Some disappointments and struggles are unavoidable. However, a life as detailed as the Prophet's (s.a.w)'s stimulates thought and, eventually, conviction. When all criticism and incorrect assumptions are gone, such a life is destined to endear itself to us entirely and forever.

However, it should be obvious that the tale of a life so open and rich cannot be recounted in such a quick manner. It is only possible to try a sliver of it. But even a fleeting look is worthwhile. A religious text, as we say, has limited attraction unless it is reinforced with knowledge of its Teacher. Many faiths have missed the purpose. The Hindu faith, for example, preserves the Vedas, but it can tell us nothing about the Rishis who received the Vedas from God. The necessity to augment a message with an account of the messenger does not seem to have struck Hindu adherents. Jewish and Christian academics, on the other hand, have no qualms in condemning their own Prophets. They forget that a revelation that has failed to regain its intended audience is of little service to others. If the receiver is difficult to deal with, the question of why God chose him emerges. Should He have done so? Neither hypothesis seems plausible. To believe that revelation fails to recover certain people is as absurd as believing that God has no choice but to chose inept recipients for some of His revelations. However, concepts of this kind have made their way into several faiths, maybe due to the distance that now exists between them and their Founders, or because human mind, before to the introduction of Islam, was incapable of seeing the fallacy of these notions. The importance of keeping a book and its Teacher together was recognized very early in Islam. The youthful 'A'ishara was one of the Prophet's (s.a.w) holy consorts. She married the Prophet (s.a.w) when she was thirteen to fourteen years old. She was married to him for almost eight years. She was around twenty-two years old when the Prophet (s.a.w) died. She was young and ignorant, but she understood that an instruction cannot exist apart from its instructor. When asked to explain the Prophet's (s.a.w) persona, she immediately replied that it was the Qur'an (Abu Dawud). What he did was exactly what the Qur'an taught, and what the Qur'an taught was nothing but what he did. It is to the Prophet (s.a.w)'s credit that an uneducated young lady was able to understand a truth that had eluded Hindu, Jewish, and Christian experts.

In a single remark, 'A'ishara stated a major and fundamental truth: it is impossible for a good and honest teacher to teach one thing but practice another, or to practice one thing but teach another. The Prophet (s.a.w) was a trustworthy teacher. This is clearly what 'A'ishara intended to express. He did what he preached and preached what he did. Knowing him is knowing the Qur'an, and knowing the Qur'an is knowing him.

Conclusion: The Legacy of Prophet Muhammad - A Timeless Journey of Inspiration

As we draw the final curtain on the pages of the "History of Prophet Muhammad," we find ourselves standing at the crossroads of time, enriched by a journey through the life and teachings of a remarkable individual whose legacy continues to resonate across the ages. This book has been more than a chronological account—it has been an immersive voyage into the heart and essence of a visionary leader, a beloved messenger, and a guiding light for humanity.

Through the annals of history, we have traversed the desert landscapes of Arabia, where a child named Muhammad was born into a world on the brink of transformation. We've witnessed his early years, marked by integrity and wisdom beyond his age. As the tapestry of his life unfolded, we explored his unwavering commitment to justice, compassion, and the well-being of all living beings.

From the inception of his prophethood, we have journeyed alongside Muhammad as he embarked on a mission of enlightenment, courageously facing adversity, and defying the norms of his time. We've marveled at his unshakable faith, his capacity for forgiveness, and his role as a unifying force that transcended cultural boundaries.

This book has not only chronicled historical events—it has illuminated the timeless principles and ethics that Prophet Muhammad championed. We've delved into his teachings on social justice, the dignity of women, the importance of knowledge, and the sanctity of human life. We've seen how his actions underscored the interconnectedness of spirituality and daily life, leaving an indelible mark on the hearts of believers for generations to come.

As we reflect upon the life of Prophet Muhammad, we recognize that his legacy is not confined to a specific era—it is a legacy that continues to inspire and guide individuals from all walks of life. His teachings have fostered compassion, encouraged introspection, and promoted the pursuit of truth and goodness. His character has set a standard for leadership that embodies humility, integrity, and service to others.

In closing, the "History of Prophet Muhammad" is not merely a recounting of events—it is a tribute to a timeless figure whose influence extends beyond the boundaries of time and geography. May his example continue to illuminate our paths, serving as a source of inspiration, wisdom, and a beacon of hope in an ever-changing world.

With gratitude for the opportunity to journey through history's pages,

[Ahmad Al-mannar]

Printed in Great Britain
by Amazon

e14fee83-3f5a-447f-bf0f-58c1eb6f5e93R01